CHARLES II'S PORTUGUESE QUEEN

For my husband Richard

CHARLES II'S PORTUGUESE QUEEN

The Legacy of Catherine of Braganza

Susan Abernethy

PEN & SWORD HISTORY
AN IMPRINT OF PEN & SWORD BOOKS LTD.
YORKSHIRE – PHILADELPHIA

First published in Great Britain in 2025 by
PEN AND SWORD HISTORY
An imprint of
Pen & Sword Books Ltd
Yorkshire – Philadelphia

ISBN 978 1 03612 164 8

A CIP catalogue record for this book is available from the British Library.

Typeset in Times New Roman 10/13 by
SJmagic DESIGN SERVICES, India.
Printed and bound in the UK by CPI Group (UK) Ltd.

The Publisher's authorised representative in the EU for product safety is Authorised Rep Compliance Ltd., Ground Floor, 71 Lower Baggot Street, Dublin D02 P593, Ireland.
www.arccompliance.com

For a complete list of Pen & Sword titles please contact
PEN & SWORD BOOKS LIMITED
George House, Units 12 & 13, Beevor Street, Off Pontefract Road,
Barnsley, South Yorkshire, S71 1HN, England
E-mail: enquiries@pen-and-sword.co.uk
Website: www.pen-and-sword.co.uk

or

PEN AND SWORD BOOKS
1950 Lawrence Rd, Havertown, PA 19083, USA
E-mail: uspen-and-sword@casematepublishers.com
Website: www.penandswordbooks.com

MIX
Paper | Supporting responsible forestry
FSC® C013604

Contents

Introduction

Historians regularly refer to Catherine of Braganza as the 'forgotten queen'. There is much truth in this statement. She died in 1705 and a full, detailed biography remained unwritten about her until 1915. Another biography in English was published in 1937 and one in Portuguese in 1941, which to this day has never been translated into English. Historians can readily find biographies and studies of Charles II's mistresses, but curiously little on his wife. These older biographies are written in effusive Edwardian prose and perpetuate many of the myths about Catherine which sometimes put her in a poor light. Contemporary chroniclers tended to write disapprovingly of Catherine because of her Catholicism.

Another shortcoming of these biographies is the lack of detailed information on her life in Portugal, from birth until age 23 when she sailed to England for her marriage, and from the age of 54 when she departed England to return to her beloved Portugal. In all these cases, the narrative regarding these years is limited to a few paragraphs.

Since the last detailed biography of England's Portuguese queen, there has been a great deal of new scholarship on the ritual and practice of medieval and early modern queenship. Some duties highlighted by scholars for queens include the bearing of an heir for the continuation of the dynasty they married into, intercession for appropriate causes, and cultural, artistic and religious patronage. There is a need for integrating this new scholarship into Catherine's story.

They have never forgotten Catherine in Portugal. In fact, she considered herself Portuguese through and through, and during her stay in England she never forgot her motherland. In her own words, she considered her marriage as a personal sacrifice to what was best for Portugal. We can witness the people's reverence of Catherine in the ceremony of her funeral. It is imperative to put Catherine in the context of the history of Portugal and their seaborne empire. Also, Portugal and England had strong political and commercial ties dating back to the mid-fourteenth century, which played a key role in the culmination of the marriage treaty of 1661.

It is my hope to rectify some of these issues with a new biography integrating the history of Portugal and their seaborne empire and Catherine's place in it, adding new information on her religious, cultural and artistic patronage of Catholic Baroque culture in Protestant England and providing previous unknown details of her life in Portugal. This book will highlight Catherine's life as much as possible with only minimal details of her husband's mistresses. Because we do not have much documentation in Catherine's own words, included in this biography are quotes from those who saw and interacted with her, giving us a glimpse of the real Catherine of Braganza.

Also highlighted is the legacy of her marriage, especially for England. Because of their long-standing political and commercial alliance and Catherine's dowry, Portugal's impressive territories would be annexed by England, allowing them to become Europe's new seaborne empire. And English society would absorb many of the items and social rituals Catherine brought with her. In the words of Portuguese historian Malyn Newitt, she was the most successful member of the Braganza dynasty.

My intention is to present a well-researched, scholarly historical perspective of Catherine of Braganza's life for those who are familiar with her, and in an enjoyable and readable form, for readers who do not know the subject.

For readability, all contemporary quotes have been edited for spelling, grammar and punctuation.

Susan Abernethy
Denver, CO
©2024

Chapter One

Sunny Portugal

Early Origins of the Anglo-Portuguese Alliance

Catherine mentions 'sunny Portugal' in many of her letters to her brother when she was negotiating her return to her beloved home after the death of her husband. Portugal is a comparatively small country in Europe with limited resources and a sparse population. Taking this into account, how did Portugal become the founder of a global seaborne empire? How did Catherine of Braganza, who wasn't even the daughter of a king when she was born, become the first and only Portuguese queen consort of England, Scotland and Ireland? And how did Catherine's marriage to the Stuart king, Charles II, become the catalyst for England to develop into the empire upon which the sun never set?

Early on, England and Portugal had unwritten, implicit friendly ties. Anglo-Portuguese relations and cooperation originate during the time of the Second Crusade. English knights, sailing for the Holy Land, stopped in Porto where the local bishop requested their help with the Portuguese King Afonso Henriques' conquest of Lisbon during the Reconquista of the Iberian Peninsula. They eventually assisted in the siege, and many remained afterwards, choosing to fight the Muslims in Portugal rather than continuing to Jerusalem.[1]

Born out of political necessity, there came a time in the fourteenth century when both countries wanted to strengthen and recognise these ties with a written treaty. The ratification of the Treaty of Windsor on 9 May 1386 united the governments of King Richard II of England and King John I of Portugal. The terms of the treaty provided a guarantee for the reciprocal security of both nations and reinforced commercial ties.[2]

Portugal entered an epic struggle to keep its independence, which lasted for hundreds of years, narrowly warding off annexation by its next-door neighbour, Castile. England and France had engaged in intermittent hostilities since the beginning of the Hundred Years War in 1337. In 1369, the English became alarmed when an alliance formed between France and Castile, allowing France to use Castilian naval resources against the English. To counter this threat, England sought an alliance with Portugal.

In 1384, King Richard II of England sent troops to Portugal to aid in responding to threats from Castile, both real and imagined, in return for which Portuguese war-galleys and their crews joined the English in their fight against France.[3]

The Battle of Aljubarrota and the Aviz Dynasty

From 1383 until 1385, Portugal found itself amid a period known as the Portuguese Interregnum, during which there was no reigning legitimate monarch following the death of King Fernando I who had reigned since 1367. There were several factors leading up to this crisis. After a series of unsuccessful conflicts with the Kingdom of Castile, Fernando married his daughter and heir, Beatriz, to King Juan I of Castile. This agreement called for the oldest child of this match to inherit the Portuguese crown, with Fernando's wife, Leonor Teles, acting as regent.[4]

The marriage of Beatriz to the Castilian king caused alarm among the nobility of Portugal as it brought the spectre of Castilian rule, a prospect they did not find appealing. When Fernando died, Beatriz was 11 years old and had no children. Her mother acted as regent with the support of most of the landed aristocracy.[5] The growing popularity among the middle and lower ranks of the bourgeoisie of King Fernando's illegitimate half-brother John, Master of Aviz, undermined Leonor's effectiveness. John of Aviz actively sought to take the throne and Leonor's popularity dwindled, eventually leading to a revolt led by John. In December 1383 he drove Leonor from Lisbon into Castile. Assured of the support of the people of Lisbon, Aviz assumed the title of defender of the realm.[6]

King Juan I of Castile came to the aid of his mother-in-law and claimed the Portuguese throne by right of his wife Beatriz. He invaded Portugal with his forces, starting an anti-Castilian reaction and civil war broke out between the Portuguese rebels and the crown of Castile. In the beginning, King Juan's campaign of 1384 went well as he kept the forces of Aviz on the defensive.

Nuno Álvares Pereira, one of the greatest Portuguese military leaders, later known as the 'Holy Constable', successfully led the Aviz campaign in the south. In the course of the struggle, plague broke out in the Castilian camp. King Juan, reluctant to retreat, eventually relented when Queen Beatriz fell ill and many of his commanders died, forcing him to withdraw his weakened forces. In early 1385, the Cortes at Coimbra proclaimed John of Aviz King John I of Portugal. To strengthen his position and gain allies as king, John sent emissaries to England to seek an alliance, recruits to fight in his army, loans to pay his troops, and to urge John of Gaunt, Duke of Lancaster and uncle of Richard II, to renew his claim to the Castilian throne through his wife, Constanza.[7]

This would be the foundation for the Treaty of Windsor.[8] John elevated Nuno Álvares Pereira to the position of constable, and the two men went to work. King

Juan I of Castile returned to Portugal with a reconstituted army of nearly 20,000 men and attacked from the north. His army included Portuguese legitimists who opposed King John and a contingent of men-at-arms supplied by King Charles VI of France. King Juan's plan was to crush the rebels by sheer force.

Nuno Álvares Pereira had a series of victories against the superior army of King Juan, and in May routed the Castilians. The Constable convinced King John to attack the Castilian army rather than endure another siege of Lisbon, despite being overwhelmingly outnumbered. In August, the Portuguese army numbered about seven to ten thousand strong,[9] supplemented with Anglo-Welsh archers and knights recruited by and serving John of Gaunt, the English Duke of Lancaster.

The Portuguese positioned themselves at Aljubarrota, north of Lisbon near Alcobaça, a place specifically chosen for the battle. On the morning of 14 August 1385, the army of Nuno Álvares Pereira and King John, from their superior strategic position, overwhelmingly defeated the numerically larger forces of King Juan. There were lingering border clashes after this resounding Portuguese victory, but King John was now clearly in control.

The battle both validated and solidified John's status as king of Portugal and the House of Aviz as a new dynasty. King John's emissaries completed the Treaty of Windsor in May 1386. To guarantee the alliance, King John married John of Gaunt's daughter, Philippa of Lancaster, in February 1387, and the Portuguese confirmed the treaty at Coimbra on 12 August 1387.[10] The children of John and Philippa, the only English queen consort of Portugal, were known as the 'Illustrious Generation' and included Henry the Navigator and their daughter Isabel, who became the formidable Duchess of Burgundy, along with King Duarte and Pedro, who served as regent of Portugal and a saintly younger son, Fernando. We will hear more about these children later.

The English alliance cemented by the Treaty of Windsor became an even more valued asset for the kings of Portugal.[11] Queen Philippa would go to great lengths to maintain cordial relations with England and England became increasingly influential in Portuguese affairs.[12] Portugal remained independent of Castile for two centuries and both countries would enjoy the commercial benefits of the Treaty of Windsor. The Anglo-Portuguese alliance is still a valid agreement endorsed by both countries to this day.[13]

Origins and Expansion of the Portuguese Seaborne Empire

A comprehensive history of the origins and expansion of the Portuguese seaborne empire is beyond the current topic. In recounting the subject, emphasis will be on aspects of the empire as they relate to Catherine of Braganza and the terms of her marriage treaty with England. The dowry she brought to reinforce the Anglo-

Portuguese alliance included, among other considerations, two ports developed by Portuguese explorers, trading privileges with Brazil and an enormous amount of cold hard cash. These concessions were the principal attraction for King Charles II when considering Catherine as a bride. Also emphasised in this section will be the family of King John I, founder of the House of Aviz and the House of Braganza, and their role in the Portuguese exploration of West Africa and the trading route to the Indies.

Lisbon's strategic location on the Atlantic and on the banks of the Tagus River made the city ideally suited as an administrative and commercial centre.[14] Following the capture of Lisbon by crusaders in 1147, the city steadily grew in importance because of the expansion of trade between the Mediterranean and northern Europe. Many merchants and traders gathered in Lisbon and Italians established a community there as early as the thirteenth century. These traders actively sought concessions from the Portuguese Crown, enabling the Crown to sustain a permanent fleet and thus began the great naval tradition of Portugal.

During the reign of King Fernando I, the Portuguese Crown developed into a significant merchant and shipowner, allowing for growth in royal revenue through taxation and by directly taking part in and encouraging trade.[15] As Lisbon flourished in medieval times, Portuguese merchants and shipowners turned up in the Netherlands, England, and the Hanseatic League towns, and attended fairs in France. Conversely, northern Europeans frequented the Atlantic ports of the Iberian Peninsula.[16]

The Kingdom of Portugal enjoyed a period of relative peace during the fifteenth century. Throughout the reign of King John I, the Portuguese Crown would supervise the beginning of extensive Portuguese expansion. The Crown took a vigorous interest in the growth of commerce by owning ships, appointing royal *feitors*, or factors, to monitor Crown commercial interests and promoting maritime activity in diverse ways. The *feitoria*, or factories, (meaning trading depots or group of merchants living abroad), would receive instructions from the king and in return, he would receive detailed accounts from the factors and receipts for any profits.[17]

Eventually, an entire command structure developed with a fleet of royal galleys maintained for offensive, defensive and trading purposes. In the years between 1385 and 1389, King John I provided a fleet of six galleys armed with artillery to his ally from the Treaty of Windsor, King Richard II, to aid in the defence of the English coast.[18]

The Portuguese overseas expansion of the fifteenth century would be remarkable. The native sailors were tough and skilful and highly motivated by trade, religious zeal and authentic scientific curiosity.[19] Beginning with expeditions to the Atlantic islands, the Portuguese made their way to East Africa, India, China, Japan and South America. The consequences of this expansion have dominated Portugal's development even to this day.

These voyages of discovery were not just the isolated proceedings of individual merchants or adventurers. What made this exploration exceptional was a deliberate policy by the State, carried out over many generations. Initially, these strategies were under the sponsorship of the Infantes [Princes] Henry, known as 'the Navigator', and his brother Pedro, and later under the direct control of the Crown during the reign of King John II. This royal policy made the Portuguese strategies so far-reaching they launched a new era in world history.[20]

The 'Age of Discovery' came about due to a mixture of religious, economic, strategic and political factors and profit.[21] Charles Boxer enumerates the motives which inspired exploration as being (1) crusading zeal against the Muslims; (2) the desire for Guinea gold; (3) the quest for Prester John; and (4) the search for Oriental spices.[22] The early crusading zeal was initially directed only toward the Muslims of Morocco, but as the exploration of the world continued, this would expand to include all non-Christians. Prester John, a mythical and legendary Christian figure, supposedly existed in 'the Indies', a not very well defined and shifting location. The search for Prester John mingled with the quest for Guinea gold on the African continent.[23]

The Portuguese Crown sent requests to the Pope for papal bulls to reinforce the incentives for exploration and the resulting documents reflected the language of these appeals. Altogether, these papal bulls signify the initiative taken by the Crown of Portugal, and by Prince Henry and the other princes of the House of Aviz, in the supervision and organization of the work of exploration, conquest, colonisation and exploitation.[24]

The growth of the royal navy made possible Portugal's role in early exploration. But it also allowed for the development of an increase in the capacity to move substantial military forces by sea.[25] Prince Henry had been lobbying his father for a long time to go on a crusade in North Africa and King John eventually agreed to carry out his son's mission. Subsequently, the opening salvo of the Portuguese overseas expansion played out in the attack on Ceuta on the North African coast in the Strait of Gibraltar in 1415.

The Portuguese army, as made up for this invasion, was remarkably large considering the size of the kingdom and the financial condition of the Crown. Transportation for the men was in a fleet of about 100 requisitioned and chartered merchant ships acquired from Portugal, Castile, Flanders, Germany, Brittany and England. Several Portuguese merchant ships and galleys were fitted out and assembled in Oporto under the management of Prince Henry.[26]

Ceuta was a port of great strategic importance, being one of the northern terminals of the trans-Saharan caravan trade and also a harbour taking in European silver and other North African goods and artefacts, along with horses, which were transported by caravan to the Muslim kingdoms of the Sahel. These caravans would return with gold, slaves, ivory, and other luxury goods. It was also the primary port through which gold from the mines of Africa, extremely crucial to Europe, reached the Christian world and beyond.

The attack was a well-kept secret and the Portuguese army conquered Ceuta on 21 August 1415, in about thirteen hours.[27] Following the obligatory looting, they triumphantly annexed the port to the Portuguese Crown. But it swiftly became a tremendous drain on Crown resources. In addition to being cut off from the Moroccan hinterland, it was difficult to provide supplies by sea because of the vagaries of wind and weather.

Prince Henry formed the Casa de Ceuta, a type of corporation, to handle the transportation of goods. It would exercise total control over all the shipping to and from the North African port. Corporations would be the foundation of the various agencies through which the Crown monopoly over all Portuguese trade in the African Atlantic and the Indian Ocean would operate after Prince Henry's death.[28] Besides these agencies, Prince Henry allowed the establishment of a military post and permanent trading factory at Arguin in Mauritania, thus inaugurating a key feature of Portuguese Imperial policy from now on. Arguin was the first site of the overseas fortified factories in the African Atlantic, in the Indian Ocean, and in Brazil.

From this point on, they based Portuguese expansion on defending strong points set on strategically situated islands or peninsulas throughout the world. Robust Portuguese naval power and these tactical assets allowed Portugal to secure a string of ports along the Atlantic coast of Morocco well into the sixteenth century.[29] After the death of Prince Henry, these factories would be under the control, whether directly or indirectly, of the Portuguese Crown.[30]

Upon the death of King John I in 1433, his eldest son, Duarte, became king. In 1437, Duarte reluctantly approved Prince Henry's expedition to conquer Tangier. Following a siege of the city, a large Moroccan army starved the Portuguese into submission. They compelled Prince Henry to leave his younger brother, Fernando, as a hostage until Portugal surrendered Ceuta to the Moroccans. The Portuguese Cortes refused to give up the city and never brokered Fernando's release. Consequently, he would die in captivity.

King Duarte died of the plague in 1438. His young son became King Afonso V and his mother, Queen Eleonor, along with his uncle, Prince Pedro, acted as regents. King John I had an illegitimate son, also named Afonso, with his mistress, Inês Peres; he was therefore a half-brother of Prince Henry and Pedro. During Prince Pedro's regency, his illegitimate half-brother received the title Duke of Braganza and the Braganza family would do their best to assert influence over the young king. Once King Afonso assumed power in his own right, instability and civil war resulted between the supporters of Prince Pedro and those of the Duke of Braganza. The infighting would cause the death of Pedro on 20 May 1449, during the Battle of Alfarrobeira.

Following Prince Pedro's death, the Braganza faction established its supremacy at the centre of the Portuguese monarchy. Prince Henry refused to intervene.

He was eager to keep his titles, jurisdictions and commercial monopolies, not to mention his governorship of the Order of Christ, an important source of funds for his expeditions. Because of his neutrality, the young king rewarded Prince Henry with a positive confirmation of all his titles and privileges.

During the last eleven years of Prince Henry's life, he concentrated his efforts on diplomacy at the papal court, to secure further rights for the Order of Christ and to organise a new Moroccan expedition which eventually sailed in 1458.[31] This left trade open to others. Henry did not exclude foreign navigators or merchants from the exploration of the African coast. He even encouraged it by issuing licenses to those of any nationality except Castilians.[32]

In the early 1460s, the Portuguese had reached the Gulf of Guinea and the prospect of rounding the cape of Africa and reaching India seemed just within reach. Prince Henry 'the Navigator' died on 13 November 1460. For the duration of the 1460s and into the 1470s, overseas expansion declined, and the Crown turned its attention to expansion in North Africa, along with enforcing a claim to the Castilian throne. The Crown handed trade over to private enterprise with the proviso they pay a ten to twenty per cent duty on all imported merchandise.[33]

In November 1468, the Crown rented the monopoly of the trade with the African coast to the Lisbon merchant, Fernão Gomes, for five years. Under his direction, many explorers sailed down the coast, leaving traces of their discoveries in the names of capes, rivers, bays and mountains.[34] Gomes and his explorers reached what is now Ghana, known to the Portuguese as the Mina Coast and to the British as the Gold Coast. They had found the long sought-for gold. Another explorer, Pedro de Sintra, sailed from Lagos and explored more of the African Atlantic coast nearly to Liberia.[35] Sintra reached the Costa de Malagueta or the Grain Coast. About a decade later, the Portuguese discovered large quantities of malagueta pepper, also called the 'grains of paradise'.[36]

The interests of the Crown turned to expanding into Morocco rather than exploring any further along the coast of Africa. Afonso V and his brother Fernando, along with other leading nobles, indulged in their dominant interest in military expeditions to Morocco. King Afonso V continued the hopes and dreams of his uncle, Prince Henry. He attacked North Africa and gained victories, boosting his own pride and enhancing his international prestige. For King Afonso, the primary target would always be Tangier because he wanted to avenge the defeat of Prince Henry's army in 1437 and the death of the hostage, his uncle, Prince Fernando. Afonso's expedition of 1471 was successful in the attack and fall of Asilah. With the surrender of Asilah, the population of the city of Tangier deserted, allowing the port to be captured by the Portuguese.[37]

The Portuguese had gained control of virtually the whole southern shore of the Straits of Gibraltar, and their power and influence flourished in Morocco.

From 1477 until his death in 1481, Afonso V and his son, John [King John II] were essentially co-rulers.[38] Afonso gave the responsibility of Portuguese military activity in North Africa to John, who was ambitious, capable and far-sighted and had complete control of overseas strategies and policies. He would turn his focus and attention to the ports and the development and growth of Portuguese trade in Guinea.[39] Exploration of the African interior and the building of fortresses begun.

The House of Braganza Loses Influence

In 1474, with Prince John in sole charge of overseas expansion, he instigated the creation of a comprehensive plan of discovery with funding and goals. Looking for Prester John was no longer a primary reason for exploration. John's plan encompassed reaching Asia (specifically present-day India) by sea.[40] The undertaking of this plan outranked every other endeavour. Castile worked to challenge this policy, by limiting the efforts of military and economic consolidation of Portuguese control in West Africa,[41] triggering a first in maritime colonial war.

In the meantime, the Duke of Braganza and his supporters were now clearly in the ascendancy during the rest of the reign of Afonso V, and they were not interested in West Africa or the concerns of the commercial towns.[42] After the acquisition of Tangier, they negotiated a twenty-year peace with the former governor. Thereafter, they abandoned all ideas of the Reconquista of the Iberian Peninsula and replaced it with plans for the proposed union of the crowns of Castile and Portugal. Queen Isabel of Castile used the war between Portugal and Castile to claim suzerainty over the African seas and challenge the Portuguese monopoly.

The ensuing war went badly for the Portuguese. Afonso continued the fight, trying to enlist the help of France and Burgundy. The Portuguese nobility remained preoccupied with Castilian affairs until the Treaty of Alcaçovas in 1479. It took two years of negotiation by Prince John to settle the colonial differences and end the war with Castile.[43] To uphold their exclusive rights and concessions in Africa, Portugal had to give up its traditional claim to the Canary Islands and Prince John renounced all rights to the crown of Castile.[44]

Afonso V died in 1481 and John II ascended the throne. He sent his first expedition of discovery to Africa in 1482.[45] A fortress constructed at Mina included an established royal factory. The influx of gold from the area proved invaluable to the Crown.[46] On the political front, King John sought to take back as much of the Crown's patrimony in Portugal as he could from the nobility. He had the Duke of Braganza arrested for conspiring against the Crown. Found guilty and executed, the rest of his family went into exile and the Crown confiscated their properties.

The Search for a Passage to India

At this point in his reign, King John handled nearly 2000 retainers who required pensions, offices, commands, and military employment. Overseas expansion provided the king with a major source of income, allowing him to dispense the incumbent royal patronage.[47] In 1487, King John dispatched Bartolomeu Dias with instructions to discover the seaway to India, the primary aim being the trade in the coveted spices produced there.

Dias went south until he concluded he had reached the end of Africa and the seaway to India was open in 1488. He wanted to continue east, but his weary crew rebelled and they turned to go home. On the way back, they surveyed the coastline and discovered two capes. The most impressive and southernmost one he named the Cape of Good Hope in the belief it would lead to an open seaway to India. They returned to Lisbon to report their discovery to the king.[48]

King John maintained a keen interest in finding a practical route to India, but he put this mission on hold pending other reasons for the ensuing ten years.[49] His next diplomatic success came in 1494 with the Treaty of Tordesillas when he convinced the Pope to divide the non-Christian world into two hemispheres, one for Portugal and one for Castile.[50] By the time King John II died in 1495, he had set in motion everything required for Vasco da Gama to make his way to India.

King John II's successor was his wife's brother, Manuel. King Manuel I's primary focus concentrated on North Africa and peace with Castile. Manuel intended to bring all of Morocco's coastal lowlands under Portuguese control, creating an 'Algarve beyond the sea',[51] further delaying the exploration of India.[52] However, Manuel found enough money to fund a voyage which sailed for India from Lisbon in July 1497. Vasco da Gama commanded the expedition, which included three main ships plus one supply ship.

Da Gama rounded the Cape of Good Hope and sailed up the east African coast, finally completing the crossing to Malabar in southwestern India.[53] He glimpsed the coast of India on 19 May 1498, and landed four days later. They stayed for three months, sailing home loaded with spices and other sought-after merchandise. Following a troublesome voyage, da Gama and his crew, minus one ship, arrived in Lisbon in the summer of 1499. It had taken two years, but da Gama had proven it was possible and profitable to sail directly from Europe to India.[54]

A larger, more robust expedition, made up of thirteen ships, left Lisbon in March 1500 under the command of Pedro Álvares Cabral. They intended to follow da Gama's route, but the ships somehow ended up drifting further south-westward than da Gama had, resulting in the discovery of South America (Brazil) on 22 April 1500. They explored the coastline for a short time, then one ship sailed back to Portugal with the news. The Portuguese Crown had annexed a new country. The rest of the fleet proceeded to India, arriving in August 1500 and returning to Portugal about eleven months later. This voyage was shorter than da Gama's and the items Cabral brought back yielded an even higher profit than expected.[55]

Until the early seventeenth century, the Indian Ocean was, for all intents and purposes, a Portuguese sea. In the beginning, the sailors made various settlements along the western and eastern coasts of India and on the Arabian Peninsula, the Strait of Hormuz and the Persian Gulf.[56] The Portuguese knew they would never conquer India or any other region in Asia. They opted for colonization on the Indian subcontinent, strengthening and making permanent the foundations of the Portuguese trade monopoly. The Crown's representatives, the governors and the viceroys in India, continued the royal policy of putting strongholds in strategic places in all areas of the Indian Ocean, supporting them with permanent fleets to control trade and protect the factories.[57]

In 1504, the Crown formed a corporation in Lisbon called the Casa da India, with the sole mission of administering the royal monopolies for trade. This resulted in state control on any commerce with the East. All merchandise had to be reported to the Casa da India, which would sell it at a fixed price and give back to each proprietor the corresponding amount of money.

Eventually, this proved to be insufficient and in 1506, King Manuel declared an official state monopoly on all imports and sales of spices, silk and shellac (a yellowish resin secreted by the lac insect, which is made into a commercial preparation used in varnishes and polishes); on exports of gold, silver, copper, and coral; and on the trade between the Indian port of Goa and the other main factories. The Crown alone could equip and send ships to the Indian Ocean. This state of affairs would last until 1570.[58]

In 1505, King Manuel and his advisors resolved to send a viceroy to the East and to establish the Estado da India or State of India. Based in India, they considered the Estado a separate Portuguese estate in the Indian Ocean and, in reality, a network of trade routes.[59] This momentous resolution was an attempt to create a whole new dedicated Portuguese government in the Indian Ocean with its own armed force and social institutions.[60] The king appointed Francisco de Almeida first governor in India, with the rank of viceroy. Afonso de Albuquerque replaced Almeida in November 1510.

The first territory gained by Albuquerque was the island of Goa on the western coast of India, just south of Bombay. Goa was the largest port and given the most attention and resources in India. Albuquerque intended to turn Goa and its surrounding countryside and large population into Portuguese sovereign territory. In 1534, the Sultan of Gujarat ceded Bassein and its territories to Portugal and they would start a settlement in Bombay. This gave the Portuguese possession of the coastal islands and the mainland from Bombay northwards to Damão.[61] These territories, known as the Província do Norte, contained hundreds of square miles of territory with villages, small towns, seaports and fortified frontier posts.[62] By 1538, the Portuguese controlled most of the western coast of India from Bombay to Diu.[63]

In the 1550s, the settlement of Bombay flourished. In the Província do Norte, Portugal had established an unofficial supremacy with a substantial land based Imperial presence. From this area came the finest stone for building and the timber needed for ship construction. By the 1580s, revenues from the Província exceeded those of Goa itself and were by far the most profitable possessions of the Portuguese Crown in the East.[64] Although there were administrative problems with the Estado da India, these years would be the height of its authority. Eventually, the Estado succumbed to attacks by the Dutch and uprisings by locals where the factories were located, and the Portuguese seaborne empire would face threats from every direction.

King Manuel I died in 1521 and his son, John III, did not share his father's vision for North Africa. By this time, the Portuguese had to abandon ambitions of expanding in Morocco and retrenched. It was increasingly difficult, dangerous and costly to maintain the Portuguese gains, let alone extend a presence in North Africa.[65] It forced the king to abandon fortresses and eventually evacuate Asilah and Ksar-es-Seghir. Portugal reduced their possessions in Morocco to Ceuta, Tangier and Mazagão, upgrading the defences of these cities while they continued to attract caravan business.[66]

Ksar el-Kabir and the Succession Crisis

King Sebastian succeeded his grandfather, John III, in the summer of 1557. His obsession was becoming a soldier and reinstating the neo-Reconquest in North Africa. In 1574 he visited Ceuta and Tangier, which only increased his zeal for a military crusade.[67] An opportunity presented itself in 1576, following the deposition of the reigning Sultan with Ottoman backing and his replacement with an uncle. The deposed Sultan requested help from Christian monarchs to back his restoration. King Philip II of Spain judiciously turned him down, but his maternal nephew, Sebastian, enthusiastically determined to back the ex-Sultan's cause.[68]

Sebastian went to North Africa with an army of possibly 15,000 troops, comprising a mixture of men ranging from raw recruits to the flower of the Portuguese nobility. The invasion force also contained Castilians, Italians, Irish Catholics and even German Lutherans and Dutch Calvinists. On 13 July 1578, the entire expedition reached Tangier and the garrison there augmented the army. Their destination was al-Arish, and the council met to decide whether the troops should go by sea or overland. The selected overland route involved the fording of two creeks and the crossing of the Loukkos River north of Ksar el-Kabir, with a turn back towards the coast.

The army made their way into the interior, and before long, conditions became unbearably hot. Temperatures may have exceeded 104 degrees Fahrenheit (40 degrees Celsius). They believed the enemy to be many miles away, but with Sebastian's delayed stay in Tangier, the opponent mustered and brought in more forces. The Sultan monitored the movement of Sebastian's army and set a trap in the region between the second creek and the Loukkos River.

On 4 August, the attacks began. After six hours, with many men and nearly all the leaders captured, it became obvious the situation for the Portuguese was hopeless. Sebastian, who may have had three horses killed from under him, died valiantly after refusing to surrender. Ksar el-Kabir was undoubtedly the greatest military disaster the Portuguese suffered in the course of their overseas expansion. Historians consider this battle the definitive end of the neo-Reconquest era.[69]

The Unification of the Iberian Peninsula

For the family of Catherine of Braganza, this was a critical turning point. Sebastian's lack of a direct successor led to several potential heirs contesting the succession to the throne of Portugal. This led to the union of the Iberian Peninsula, sometimes known as the *Domínio Filipino* or the Spanish Captivity. The repercussions of the union of the Crowns would cause the restoration of the Braganza family to the monarchy in the next century.

The prosperity of the town of Tangier declined after Ksar el-Kabir and the citizens continually complained to the government. They were looking for a more extensive commitment from Portugal, resisting the government's efforts to scale down.[70] There is no doubt they maintained Tangier at a loss to the Crown.[71] The families of the town opposed any thought of withdrawal, and they kept Tangier long after it should have been relinquished.[72] Tangier would feature prominently in Catherine of Braganza's dowry.

After the death of Sebastian at the battle of Ksar el-Kabir, his immediate successor was his uncle, Cardinal Henry, a son of King Manuel I. Old, sick and childless, Henry worried about appointing a legal successor and avoiding civil war.[73] Normally, the crown would pass to his nephews, the grandchildren of King Manuel, because there were no descendants left from King John III.[74]

There were plenty of candidates who could assert their claim to the Portuguese throne.[75] Manuel had two sons who had descendants. His son Luis never married but had an illegitimate son named Antonio, who was the Prior of Crato. Another son, Duarte, had two surviving daughters: Maria was the wife of Alexandro Farnese, (the future Duke of Parma and governor of the Netherlands) and she had a son named Ranuccio. The other daughter was Infanta Catarina of Guimarães, married to John, the sixth Duke of Braganza.

The daughters of King Manuel also had issue. These included King Philip II of Spain and Emanuele Filiberto, Duke of Savoy. Obviously, Ranuccio had the most lawful claim, but he was only 9 years old and his father, being the governor of the Netherlands, could not challenge his sovereign, Philip II. Catarina, Duchess of Braganza was next in line and posed the most serious threat to Philip II. Antonio, Prior of Crato had the benefit of being the only male heir of a male descendant of King Manuel. He worked hard to prove his father had legitimised him and convinced many of the Portuguese people, making him a popular choice.[76]

The most viable candidate was Philip II of Spain. He might not have had the utmost legal argument for this claim, but he had strength and determination with an army to back him up. He commissioned his ambassadors and spies to bribe, threaten and lobby those who had a say in the succession and those who had survived Sebastian's African campaign, along with the chief entrepreneurs of Portugal who supported him. These merchants expected great profits from potential cross-border commerce and protection by the Spanish fleet for their trade routes.[77]

The rest of Portugal preferred Antonio, Prior of Crato, although the Cardinal did not like him and favoured Catarina of Braganza. Fearful of Philip II of Spain, the Cardinal-King summoned the Cortes to decide the matter and did his best not to cooperate in facilitating their decision. Realizing Portugal was a hopelessly divided country, he appointed five governors to form an interim regency before dying of tuberculosis on 31 January 1580.[78]

Because most of the people preferred Antonio, his faction declared him king.[79] Catarina's husband, the Duke of Braganza, had a great deal of support from nobles and churchmen, but acted cautiously, recalling how his ancestor had lost his head in 1483. He was also reluctant to surrender his luxurious residence. King Philip II, unwilling to concede, dispatched troops under the command of the Duke of Alba with specific orders to seize Portugal by force.[80]

Antonio had himself proclaimed king in various Portuguese cities while the Spanish army invaded, reinforced by the Spanish fleet hovering along the coastline. The Spanish army marched to the Tagus River in a few weeks and the Duke of Alba landed in Cascais, just west of Lisbon. They routed the improvised and outnumbered army of Antonio at Alcântara, and the Spanish entered Lisbon.[81]

Antonio's forces put up some resistance at the gates of the city, but Alba forcefully marched into the capital. Antonio fled to England, then France, and would persist in stirring up trouble. Philip had some of Antonio's followers executed as a deterrent and pacified the rest of the country in a few months.[82] In 1581, the Cortes met at Tomar and proclaimed Philip II of Spain, King Philip I of Portugal.[83]

The Aftermath of the Union of the Crowns in Iberia

Shortly before the union of the crowns, the financing of the India fleets and the operation of the royal spice monopoly had become too much for the Crown to manage. Beginning in 1575, the government contracted out the pepper monopoly to an association of merchants. Twenty-five years before the founding of the Dutch East India Company (*Vereenigde Oost-Indische Compagnie* or VOC) and the English East India Company (EIC) the trade with India had effectively passed from the Portuguese Crown into the hands of a consortium of bankers and financiers.[84]

For most of the sixteenth century, the major profitable items of the Portuguese seaborne expansion were slaves, followed by gold and spices. Eventually, spices took first place, followed by gold and slaves. Spices was a general name for many products, including sugar, with various uses. They had always been rare and expensive, but the use of spices became more extensive in pre-Renaissance Europe. Because of the huge profits, merchants appreciated and coveted spices and their quest would have a significant effect on individuals, societies, and countries.[85]

After the union of the Iberian Peninsula, the Portuguese trade expanded and became more profitable. Exports to India included gold and silver coins, silver and copper in bars or objects, lead, mercury and some coral.[86] By the mid-sixteenth century, the most important products of the Portuguese seaborne empire included the gold of Guinea, southeast Africa and Sumatra; sugar from Madeira, São Tomé and Brazil; pepper from Malabar and Indonesia; mace and nutmegs from Banda; cloves from Ternate, Tidore and Amboina; cinnamon from Ceylon; gold, silks and porcelain from China; silver from Japan; horses from Persia and Arabia; and cotton textiles from Cambay and Coromandel.[87] These were all places the Portuguese sailed to and controlled.

Other imported items included ivory, skins, musk, livestock and gum from Africa, along with an enormous diversity of rare, beautiful, and exotic merchandise from Asia. Demand for these items by the courts and the bourgeoisie of Europe increased. The Orient produced soft textiles such as silk, furniture made of precious woods, different varieties of china and pottery, and works of art.

They took these valuable commodities to Lisbon, and redistributed them to the Mediterranean and Atlantic in exchange for goods needed for Portugal, such as metals, cereals, textiles, and naval stores.[88] From the 1450s until the end of Portuguese dominance in Asia, the spice trade never ceased to grow. The monopoly the Portuguese Crown owned on the spice trade generated a net profit of eighty-nine per cent. This goes a long way in explaining the allure of India and the incredible efforts made by the Portuguese to control Asia's maritime commerce.[89] In the era after the reign of King Philip I of Portugal, western India was the heart of the commercial activity of the Estado da India and the royal monopoly on pepper the *raison d'être* for the entire enterprise.[90]

After 1600, the operations of the monopolies reverted to the Crown, and they made no further private contracts. However, private trade continued to rise. By the early seventeenth century, the volumes of Crown pepper were much reduced and private traders were increasingly remitting their wealth to the Portuguese Crown in diamonds and other jewels. The Portuguese were also importing Indian cotton cloth in vast quantities, an item not a part of the Crown monopoly.

In the early seventeenth century, for the first time, other Europeans, such as the Dutch and the English, were a whole new threat and challenging Portugal's claims of commercial monopoly and sovereignty of the sea.[91] Soon after the defeat by England of the Spanish Armada in 1588, Portugal faced devastating attacks by the Dutch and English, defeat in Sri Lanka and unsustainable losses of their ports and factories.[92] These struggles with the English and Dutch would last until shortly after Catherine's marriage to King Charles II of England.

The Portuguese Crown had mustered and organised the resources of labour, shipping, armaments and capital and could sustain the enterprise over a long period. This allowed the Crown to build up an elaborate network of support. Without a similar infrastructure, it was next to impossible for any other country to use the sea route to trade regularly with the East. What they required would be a state effort, comparable to that of the Portuguese Crown, which could mobilise and direct resources over a long period or the creation of some private body with the resources to undertake operations on a similar scale.[93]

Enter the EIC and the VOC. The English East India Company was a corporation dedicated to trade that had gone through several transformations, starting from the reign of Queen Elizabeth I. We will hear more about the EIC later. On 20 March 1602, the foundation of the *Vereenigde Oost-Indische Compagnie,* or the United East India Company, also known as the Dutch East India Company, took place. It was a privately managed, for-profit company with the powers of a sovereign state, which could make treaties, establish ports, appoint governors, dispense justice and wage war[94] and would become the largest commercial enterprise in the world.

In the beginning, the VOC was the greatest threat to the Portuguese seaborne empire. This long colonial war devolved into a global fight for the spice trade in Asia, for the slave trade in west Africa and for the sugar trade of Brazil.[95] Reasons for Dutch success against the Portuguese included superior economic resources, an expert workforce, more professional and competent naval commanders, and outstanding sea-power. Lack of ships, lack of discipline and inadequate military training put the Portuguese at a disadvantage.[96]

Until the restoration of the Portuguese monarchy in 1640, the Portuguese and the Spanish allied against the Dutch.[97] The Dutch went to war with Spain in 1602, starting with a policy of concentrating attacks on Portuguese territories overseas, rightly recognising Portugal as the weaker partner in the Dual Monarchy. They strong-armed their way into control of the cloves, mace and nutmegs in the

Moluccas, of the cinnamon of coastal Ceylon and the pepper of Malabar.[98] After an uneasy truce between Spain and the Netherlands in 1609, Portuguese trade with India recovered and reached new heights.[99]

Beginning in 1609, the European wars of the Habsburgs drew Portugal into their orbit. The 1620s were the last decade of prosperity for the Portuguese commercial system.[100] War with the Dutch resumed in 1621. East Asia was a theatre of war and one of the war's major casualties.[101] The Dutch mounted major expeditions, sometimes expelling the Portuguese altogether, as they did in Macassar and Japan.

Their successful blockade of the Straits of Malacca from 1634 to 1640 effectively forced Portugal to finally surrender in 1641.[102] In 1639, the Dutch gained the monopoly of European trade with Japan and by 1663, the Dutch also displaced the Portuguese in obtaining most of the carrying trade in Asian waters between Japan and Arabia. Following the founding of the Dutch West India Company in 1624, they first assailed Brazil that same year. In 1630, they invaded Pernambuco. Within fifteen years, the Dutch controlled the greatest and richest part of the sugar-producing northeastern coastal districts of Brazil, reducing by half the sugar production available to Portugal.[103]

They attacked Portuguese settlements in east and west Africa and set up their own factory at the Cape of Good Hope in 1652.[104] The English East India Company carved out their position from within the existing Portuguese Empire as well. They captured the base at Hormuz in the Persian Gulf in 1622. In 1626, the EIC raided Bombay.[105] With the inroads made by the Dutch alarming the English as much as the Portuguese, they ratified an Anglo-Portuguese Truce at Goa in 1635.[106]

Besides the overseas troubles, Portugal also suffered social and economic deprivations at home beginning in 1620. The population declined because of disease, immigration and famine.[107] Portugal fought many wars for fifty years, from 1618 to 1668. The empire felt the strain, and the claim to a monopoly over the trade between Europe and the East proved impossible to maintain.[108] After this, the eastern empire lay in ruins, trade with the south Atlantic survived and Portugal fell a generation behind the rest of Europe in terms of economic, administrative and military modernisation and development.[109]

In 1621, King Philip IV of Spain had ascended to power. King Philip appointed as his minister in Portugal the Spanish grandee, Gaspar de Guzmán y Pimentel, first Duke of Sanlúcar, third Count of Olivares, known as the Count-Duke of Olivares. Olivares wanted to challenge the commercial supremacy of the Dutch and involved Portugal in these efforts. The war went well for Spain at first, but the tide turned in 1628. The fighting and the financial obligations were becoming unsustainable. Olivares developed plans to increase the contribution made by Portugal and other parts of the Spanish Crown to the war effort. Portugal suffered from drought and famine and the war brought into focus the negative consequences of being interconnected to the Spanish monarchy. In 1637, a revolt broke out among the peasants and artisans in Evora and quickly spread to the rest of the kingdom.

The Portuguese recognised the union of the Crown with Spain as the primary reason for the attacks by the Dutch on their overseas dominions and, to a lesser extent, the attacks by the English. Anti-Spanish feeling spread. The misfortunes of the Portuguese against the Dutch during the first forty years of the seventeenth century were one of the principal reasons for the rebellion against the Spanish Crown in 1640.[110] Increasingly popular resentment toward the landowning nobility accompanied this. All the turmoil combined to threaten a revolutionary state of affairs.[111]

Considering these ominous conditions, explained more in depth in the next section, the Portuguese people were ready to expel the Spanish and restore their own monarchy. In searching for a suitable candidate, they selected John, eighth Duke of Braganza and sent a delegation to ask him to be their new king. The duke, being the richest landowner in Portugal, and thoroughly enjoying his family life, at first was reluctant to accept. But after negotiations, along with the strong urging of his wife, he agreed to become King John IV of Portugal. This was two years after the birth of his daughter, Catherine of Braganza.

Rise of the House of Braganza

As we have seen, the House of Braganza has its origins in the Portuguese royal House of Aviz, through King John I's illegitimate son, Afonso, by his mistress Inês Peres. He was born sometime between 1371 and 1377, before King John married Philippa of Lancaster. Afonso and his sister Brites (or Beatriz) were older half-siblings of Prince Henry the Navigator, Pedro and King Duarte. Afonso would be very influential during his father's reign. King John seemed to esteem him as much as his favourite legitimate son, Prince Henry[112] and Queen Philippa lobbied to have Afonso elevated to the nobility.

His mother raised Afonso in Leiria, where he received an excellent education. The king knighted him in the summer of 1398. After receiving a papal decree from Rome in 1401, his father legitimised Afonso.[113] A month later, he made a brilliant marriage. His wife was Beatriz Pereira, the sole heir of the Holy Constable Nuno Álvares Pereira, the hero of the Battle of Aljubarrota. The Constable gave the couple all of his possessions north of the Douro River. King John approved the passing of the title of Count of Barcelos from Pereira to Afonso.[114]

The title came from an ancient town between the Douro and the Minho rivers in the northern portion of Portugal and included lands near Neiva and Faria. Under the Celts, the location of the Braganza patrimony, called Bragantia, was in the high mountains of Trás-os-Montes and considered a provincial backwater.[115] The count extended and enlarged the ducal castle at Barcelos.[116] Afonso and Beatriz's children were born at their residence in Chaves. They had Alphonso, Count of Ourem, Fernando of Portugal (the future second Duke of Braganza), and Isabel, who married her cousin John, a younger legitimate son of King John I.[117]

Afonso recruited soldiers and was present in the conquest of Ceuta in 1415. In 1432, King Duarte solicited advice from his brothers. He enquired if he should expand the Portuguese territories in North Africa or support Castile against the Moorish kingdom of Granada. Barcelos argued against any war plans. Duarte went ahead with the invasion in North Africa and, as we have seen, this resulted in the disaster of 1437.

King Duarte died of the plague in 1438 and his will designated his wife, Queen Eleonor, as regent for their young son, King Afonso V, with Barcelos as her most significant supporter. Eleonor was not Portuguese. Even worse, she came from Aragon and as time passed, hostility against her and her regency intensified among the nobility. Eventually, Prince Henry brokered a compromise, allowing Eleonor and the king's uncle, Prince Pedro, to act as joint regents.[118]

This arrangement quickly deteriorated and became unsustainable. By 1439, the Lisbon town council demanded Pedro become sole regent, and the Cortes soon reinforced this attitude. Pedro reluctantly agreed. The state of affairs created by the decision put Barcelos in opposition to his half-brother, especially after Queen Eleonor fled to Castile. Barcelos, isolated on his estates in the north, could not help her.

During Prince Pedro's regency, he ruled with integrity from 1439 to 1446. Eventually, his support base eroded, and the opposition rallied around Barcelos. As the count's support grew, Prince Pedro sought reconciliation and endowed Barcelos with the title of Duke of Braganza in 1442.[119] The territorial aggrandisement of the House of Braganza rapidly continued thereafter, and the Braganza family would assert potent influence over the king.

By now, the first Duke of Braganza reigned over fifty domains, which included towns, castles, villages, fortresses, fields and country manors. His palaces were nearly as sumptuous as the king's, and he had the equivalent retinue to match. He also commanded an army, with the ability to muster 10,000 men-at-arms, and 3000 mounted troops.[120]

In 1448, the hostilities came to a breaking point when Prince Pedro married King Afonso V to his own daughter, in opposition to the Duke of Braganza, who had offered his granddaughter as a bride. Also, Braganza expected to be named Constable of Portugal and Prince Pedro blocked the appointment. Once King Afonso reached his majority and assumed power in his own right, instability and civil war resulted between the supporters of the two men. As we have seen, Pedro lost his life during the Battle of Alfarrobeira on 20 May 1449, dying with an arrow through his heart.[121]

The House of Braganza was now at the pinnacle of its authority over the king. He favoured them with even more titles of nobility, grants of money, and positions of power in his government.[122] The Braganzas had no interest in west Africa or in the concerns of the commercial towns,[123] and the last ten years of the first duke's life were peaceful. He died on 15 December 1462, in his palace at Chaves, a year after the death of his eldest son. His second son, Fernando, inherited the dukedom, which comprised nearly the entire patrimony of the Holy Constable Nuno Álvares Pereira.

Duke Fernando I married Joana de Castro, Lady of Cadaval and together they had four sons to carry on the Braganza legacy. He was one of the nobles who advised King John I against going to Ceuta in 1415. In 1437, he advised King Duarte not to attack North Africa in accord with his own father. But Duarte appointed him Constable of the Nobles, and he consented to taking part in the second disastrous expedition.

Upon his return to Portugal, Duke Fernando argued against surrendering Ceuta to the Moroccans and served as one of the leaders of the opposition in the Cortes. The Cortes urged the king to find another mechanism to release the hostage, Prince Fernando, but as we have seen, this never happened. The duke served as governor of Ceuta from 1445 to 1450.[124] In 1455, King Afonso V gave him the new title of first Marquis of Vila Viçosa. In 1458, Fernando I took part in the expedition to Ksar-es-Seghir, commanded by King Afonso V. Fernando I died in 1478.

Fernando I's eldest son, also named Fernando, was born in 1430 and King Afonso V thought highly of him. He remained popular with the nobility and fought by the king's side during his expeditions to Morocco. Afonso V made him first Count of Guimarães in 1464 and Duke of Guimarães in 1475. He became the third Duke of Braganza in 1478 upon his father's death, inheriting all of his father's titles. The House of Braganza now reigned as one of the most powerful noble houses in the Iberian Peninsula. The castle of Vila Viçosa served as Duke Fernando II's primary residence.

During the rest of Afonso's reign, royal lands, offices, pensions and other benefits were bestowed on the nobility at the highest rate since the reign of John I, causing the alienation of the wealth of the Crown. An increase in illustrious titles, used for the first time in Portugal, included marquis, baron and viscount, with the bulk of the titles being given to the House of Braganza.[125]

These gifts strengthened the dominance of the nobility and concentrated authority in the hands of a few great magnates, mainly Prince Henry and the successive dukes of Braganza. In addition, the Braganzas had extensive interests in Castile and were the acknowledged champions of the nobility.[126] They totally dominated King Afonso's regime. Following the death of Prince Henry in 1460, the members of the House of Braganza were by far the richest and most powerful in Portugal, with their control competing with that of the Crown itself.

When Afonso's son, Prince John, reached his majority, he effectively co-ruled with his father. In the agreed arrangement, King Afonso ruled at home and John was in charge of the overseas territories. Because the Braganzas and other nobles were so powerful, Prince John concentrated his efforts on conquests in Morocco and on the acquisition of the Castilian crown.[127] He resented the fact his father gave out so many titles to the nobility. At the time of the death of King Afonso, John complained there was nothing left for the Crown.[128]

Prince John became King John II in 1481. One of the first things he did was force the nobility to swear a new oath of personal loyalty to himself and put in motion a stringent process of verifying titles and privileges.[129] He intended to constrain the nobles with what they considered a humiliating form of fealty. John required confirmation of all grants of lordships and jurisdictional privileges, demanding the examination of the documents issued by the king authorising the gifts. They carefully scrutinised the paperwork.[130] In addition, the king implemented measures requested by the people and the Cortes which directly threatened the nobility's feudal privileges.[131]

John was an autocrat by nature, protective of his power and filled with an ardent conviction for absolutism.[132] The king made it clear there would be no ambiguity, and he was their unequivocal superior. After the oath taking ceremony at Evora in 1481, the royal orator spoke, asserting the subject's duty to be obedient to the king. This unmitigated demonstration of power aroused great resentment among some nobles and engendered immediate opposition to the king.[133] They relied on Fernando II, third Duke of Braganza, to lead the resistance.[134]

Braganza could easily raise an army of 13,000 men, making a showdown inevitable. By 1482, the duke and his supporters were deep in a conspiracy to remove King John II.[135] The backlash by the upper nobility took the form of a widespread intrigue, including Castilian involvement, initiated by Braganza.[136] The duke sent written messages to Queen Isabel of Castile, but due to careless security, one of the duke's retainers betrayed the plotters.

King John retaliated by having Braganza arrested along with other suspects, and they arraigned the duke on twenty-two counts of treason. The king formed a specially made up court where Braganza underwent a brief trial. They convicted him and publicly beheaded him on 20 June 1483 at Evora, in the heart of the Braganza patrimony.[137] The duke's co-conspirators, including his brothers and two of his sons, fled to Castile. King John had gotten rid of the strongest feudal family, making an example of them to intimidate the rest of the nobility. He confiscated all the Braganza castles, estates, lands and lordships, and abolished their titles. The entire ducal patrimony reverted to the Crown for the rest of the reign.[138]

The death of King John's only son, Afonso, in a riding accident in 1491, compelled him to name his queen's younger brother, Manuel, as heir to the throne.[139] He became king upon the death of John II in 1495. When Manuel ascended the throne, the upper nobility, who had been in a state of open warfare, needed sensitive handling.[140] John II had marginalised the Braganzas, but Manuel understood he needed their support for personal and political reasons.

Manuel agreed to reconcile with the House of Braganza and allowed them to return from exile with full reinstatement. Jaime, the fourth Duke of Braganza, obtained a pardon for the entire family from the king, allowing them to regain their dynastic wealth. The government forced those who had supported John II and received grants of portions of the Braganza estates to relinquish them in return for compensation from the Crown. The Duke of Braganza once again became the premier grandee of Portugal.[141]

Duke Jaime, traumatised by the death of his father, refused to live in the castle of Vila Viçosa. He constructed a new palace beginning in 1501 to the east of Lisbon. Expanded and improved under successive dukes, this palace would feature prominently in the life of Catherine of Braganza. Jaime helped to reconcile relations between the nobles during the reign of King Manuel. In 1513, he led an army of 18,000 men on an expedition to North Africa where he conquered the city of Azemmour and captured and fortified nearly all the Moroccan coast west of Gibraltar.[142]

Jaime married Leonor Pérez de Guzmán as his first wife. She was the daughter of the Spanish third Duke of Medina Sidonia. The couple had two children. Isabel married Duarte I, Duke of Guimarães. Isabel's daughter was Infanta Catarina, who married the sixth Duke of Braganza and had a claim to the throne of Portugal in 1580. The second child, born to Jaime and Leonor in 1510, was Teodósio.[143]

Teodósio became the fifth Duke of Braganza in 1563. King John III endowed him with the additional title of Duke of Barcelos.[144] Highly educated, he loved artistic culture, especially sculpture and painting. He married his first cousin, Isabel of Lencastre, as his first wife by whom he had a son, John I, later the sixth Duke of Braganza. John served as Constable of Portugal and became a Habsburg Knight of the Golden Fleece in 1581. He married his cousin Catarina [see above, granddaughter of the fourth Duke of Braganza] in 1563.

In the previous section, we discussed the succession crisis after the death of King Sebastian following the Battle of Ksar el-Kabir. Infanta Catarina of Guimarães was one of the many claimants of the Portuguese throne, and she had a powerful case. As the daughter of Duarte, a younger son of King Manuel I, she claimed the daughter of a younger son (herself) took precedence over the son of an elder daughter (King Philip II of Spain). And, she argued, she was married to the premier noble in Portugal who descended from King Manuel's sister.[145]

Philip of Spain had begun his campaign for the throne of Portugal even before King Sebastian left for North Africa, as he expected the ruinous outcome of the expedition. He wrote letters professing his enduring affection for the Portuguese people.[146] After all, his mother was a Portuguese Infanta. He paid many bribes to the notables of Portugal and although many did not want Spanish rule, support for Philip slowly grew.[147]

The aging Cardinal-King Henry preferred the Duchess of Braganza's claim, and in the summer of 1580, there was a brief, last-minute movement by some Portuguese patriots to transfer their allegiance to Catarina and her husband.[148] Philip offered the duke and duchess the whole of Brazil and the title of king if they would renounce their claim to the Portuguese Crown. Catarina, being a woman of high abilities and grand ambition, advised her husband to refuse Philip's offer.[149]

They declared King Philip of Spain, King Philip I of Portugal. He travelled to Lisbon in December 1580, where the bishops and prominent nobles greeted him. Through a representative, the Braganzas swore allegiance to Philip as the lawful king of Portugal.[150] The Duke of Braganza remained the premier grandee of the realm.

The sixth duke died in 1582. John and Catarina's eldest son, Teodósio II, became the seventh Duke of Braganza. Teodósio grew up at court and he was present in Africa for the battle of Ksar el-Kabir when King Sebastian died. Sebastian sent Braganza behind the lines for his safety. The enemy took the duke as a hostage but later safely released him with no ransom demanded.[151]

The seventh duke was a loyal servant to King Philip. Because of his fidelity to the Crown, Philip endowed him with many lands and titles, including Constable of the Realm. Teodósio married Ana de Valasco y Girón. The couple's eldest son, John, was born in 1603. Duke Teodósio possessed a fiery and impetuous nature and, despite his outward loyalty to the Spanish king, privately nursed a hated of the Spaniards, whom he viewed as usurpers of the Portuguese Crown.

He tried to instill this antipathy into his son John, reminding him the Portuguese Crown belonged to him by right. By imparting his own ambition to his son, the seventh Duke of Braganza hoped John would gain the courage and spirit necessary to seize the throne of Portugal, if the opportunity ever presented itself.[152] John would become the eighth Duke of Braganza upon the death of his father in 1630. He is the father of Catherine of Braganza, queen of England, Scotland and Ireland.

At first, the union of the crowns of the Iberian Peninsula had more benefits than drawbacks.[153] The first two Philips had ruled with the cooperation of the Portuguese nobility, and this lasted into the mid-1630's.[154] But eventually, the situation deteriorated. The Spanish Crown did not completely honour its pledge to acknowledge the integrity of Portuguese institutions, although they respected the essentials of the agreement.

There was no military occupation. As time advanced, they disregarded Portuguese interests more and more, and tended to appoint more Spanish officials to offices in Portugal than Portuguese.[155] Overseas losses to the Dutch intensified. The dissatisfaction with Spanish rule strengthened well into the reign of King Philip IV of Spain.[156]

Military and financial pressures on the Portuguese Crown throughout the late 1620s and early 1630s became relentless, along with major challenges overseas such as losing Hormuz in the East and Pernambuco in Brazil in the West. King Philip IV's minister, Olivares, wanted to mount an expedition to recover Pernambuco and needed millions of cruzados. The means of raising the money included the rigorous collection of Crown debts and raising prices on the royal monopoly on salt, effectively doubling its price. Olivares also raised several forced loans in Lisbon, provoking discontent.[157]

Resistance rose against the regime. In 1631, Olivares ordered twenty-five per cent of all emoluments paid by the Crown, other than salaries, suspended until he raised the required funds. Many of the elite felt deprivation upon the loss of this income. Then in March 1635, over constitutional objections, Olivares increased the excise taxes by twenty-five per cent and levied a special tax on wine and meat. Subsequently, in 1637, he declared a new tax on both capital and income.[158]

These fiscal demands set the stage for an explosive confrontation. Since the government relied on profits derived from royal trade monopolies, taxation in Portugal had been relatively light.[159] Because the people were used to low taxes, they felt these new forced revenues were unreasonable. The Portuguese tolerated raised taxes to defend the borders of Portugal, but found it unbearable to do so for overseas campaigns. There were those who believed the nobility should contribute more. All of this increased social and political tensions.[160]

Olivares courted the Braganzas, promoting marriage links between this noble house and his own family, the Guzmáns. In 1632 he brokered a match between John, eighth Duke of Braganza and Luisa Maria Francisca de Guzmán y Sandoval, daughter of the eighth Duke of Medina-Sidonia. In the beginning, this marriage appeared to have a political advantage for the Spanish, but the Duke of Braganza remained aloof from court and maintained his own interests via proxies in the councils of Portugal. By the time of the last crisis, Luisa would prove to be an aggressive and determined advocate of Portuguese independence.[161]

Besides objections to the excess taxes being levied, there were political factions forming among the nobility. The situation became explosive and disturbances erupted in Evora in August 1637. Initially, Olivares declined to intervene, expecting local officials to contain the rebellions. Within weeks, the trouble spread into southern Portugal and even extended north of the Tagus River. Local nobility, including the Duke of Braganza, showed little interest in forcefully suppressing the rebels and only did what was necessary to pacify the situation. Eventually, Olivares gathered Castilian troops on the frontier, which intervened in the Algarve and Alentejo. By the summer of 1638, they restored order.[162]

After these disruptions, the restlessness in Portugal continued to simmer, going nowhere because of a lack of leadership and direction. The people resented the nobility, but they viewed the Olivares regime as the principal oppressor, and anti-

Habsburg sentiment became widespread.[163] They naturally viewed the eighth Duke of Braganza, with his convincing claim to the throne, as a rival to the Habsburg king, but he persisted in remaining secluded in his palace of Vila Viçosa.

Olivares would humour the duke, periodically trying to lure him away from Portugal or to bring him into the government's service. John remained cautious and refused to let Olivares' flattery persuade him. When Olivares offered him the post of Governor of the Arms of Portugal with command of the army, he found the proposition difficult to refuse and reluctantly consented.

The long-awaited expedition to Pernambuco in Brazil departed, but accomplished no real gains. There were other concurrent military engagements in Europe threatening the sovereignty of Portugal. Catalonia was in rebellion and the French, at war with Spain, were threatening to attack Portugal. Olivares wanted to make one last ditch effort to secure a better position from which to negotiate honourable terms for peace with the French and the Dutch. He asked for 8000 men to send to Italy.

Many protested the Portuguese had no obligation to fight outside of Portugal, but the Habsburg government ignored these objections. The nobles began levying troops with the Duke of Braganza in command. Unintentionally, Olivares had given an opportunity and cover for the organisation of conspiratorial action against the existing Spanish government by the Portuguese army.[164]

In May 1640, the Portuguese army received orders to put down the rebellion in Catalonia. Fear intensified as Olivares' summons to Spain seemed to be a subterfuge meant to gain control of the Duke of Braganza,[165] with Duchess Luisa becoming especially alarmed. Matters reached a turning point, and the nobles decided they were ready to act.[166] About a month later, some nobles approached Braganza with the idea of a revolt in Portugal against Habsburg rule, viewing the duke as the natural leader of Portuguese society.[167]

The Restoration of the Portuguese Monarchy and Independence from Spain

Because of the Spanish regime's fiscal and military policies and Portuguese resentment against Olivares and other ministers, Braganza had known since 1635 he would receive overwhelming popular support if he showed any interest in claiming the crown, just as his father had predicted. He remained restrained and did not allow a coup after his summons to Spain. But his last remaining doubt departed when Olivares demanded the Portuguese follow the Spanish king into battle against the Catalans. Braganza agreed to accept the Portuguese crown.

The duke judiciously stayed on the sidelines, anticipating the outcome of the coup. Olivares issued the last order for the Portuguese troops to go to Spain. Some went, but the majority did not. Braganza's agent and steward of his household, Dr John Pinto Ribeiro, negotiated with a group of nobles and officials to put in place everything necessary for the upcoming coup. On the morning of 1 December 1640, the conspirators assembled in the Terreiro do Paco in Lisbon, and forced their way into the palace.[168]

The vicereine, Margaret of Savoy, widowed Duchess of Mantua and Philip IV's cousin, along with her hated secretary, Vasconcelos, cowered inside the palace. The rebels overpowered the viceroy's guards and killed Vasconcelos. They compelled the duchess to order the Castilian garrison stationed in São Jorge Castle not to interfere and sent her back to Spain. Within hours, the rebels had control of Lisbon and the central government with minimal resistance and bloodshed.[169] Restoration of the Portuguese monarchy delighted all social classes.[170] The duke was praying in his chapel when, on 3 December, he received a formal offer of the crown.[171] The *coup d'état* restored Portugal's traditional order and customary government.

A ceremony of acclamation for King John IV of Portugal took place on 15 December 1640, before a large gathering of dignitaries and nobles. There would be no coronation. During a ceremony in 1646, King John dedicated his kingdom to Our Lady of the Conception and crowned her queen of Portugal. Since then, no Braganza has ever worn a crown. In portraits, the crown rests nearby on a table.[172] King John called the Cortes into session and, following his swearing in, they voted to give him the funds for the struggle against Spain.[173] Pro-Braganza propaganda quickly started flowing out of Portugal, justifying the coup.[174]

Chapter Two

Early Years and Marriage

Catherine's Early Years

As rebellion against Spain gained traction and the whispering of revolution began, the Duke and Duchess of Braganza lived in their palace of Vila Viçosa, about 117 miles to the east of Lisbon. The couple began their family, starting with the birth of a son, Teodósio, in February 1634. A daughter, Ana, died shortly after birth in early 1635. Joanna, Princess of Beira, was born nine months later and then Catarina Henriqueta de Bragança (her name in Portuguese) appeared on 25 November 1638. A son, Manuel, died in infancy, followed by Afonso in 1643 and Pedro in 1648, both of whom would become king of Portugal.

They baptised Catherine on Saturday, 12 December 1638, in the ducal chapel of the palace with Anthony de Brito e Sousa, dean of the chapel, officiating. Her godfather was Francisco de Melo, fourth count of Tentugal, third marquis of Ferreira, a member of the Council of State and of War, a minister of Dispatch, and butler to the duchess. He would serve as marshal after the acclamation of the duke as king.[1] Many nobles from the family of Braganza and their supporters attended the baptism.

The Infanta Catherine, named after Saint Catherine of Alexandria, on whose feast day she was born, grew up in a peaceful and sheltered environment in a kind and loving atmosphere in the care of her nurse, Marian of Lancaster. Her entire family adored her, and people instantly took to her when they met her. She was especially close to her father and her brother, Teodósio.[2] The duke lived happily in his luxurious palace, managing his estates which encompassed one-third of the entire kingdom.

He remained as far away as possible from the turmoil in the government of Portugal[3] and the intrigues of his friends, living the life of a country gentleman, devoting himself to his wife and children. A pleasure palace with every imaginable amusement, at Vila Viçosa they passed the hours in sporting and feasting with a company of those who enjoyed the wholesome pastimes and recreations of the countryside.[4]

The duke was a generous patron of music for which nearly all the monarchs of the House of Braganza had a true and discriminating passion, besides showing authentic talent and ability as performers. Music dominated the life of the ducal court, where there was a comprehensive music library. The duke collected music and had an acknowledged reputation as a composer and musical scholar.[5] When he became king, his support of the Lisbon opera made it the best in Europe outside of Italy. His children, especially Catherine and his son Pedro, would consolidate this position.[6] The Braganzas showed a great passion for the sport of hunting and Catherine inherited this love of the chase.

During Catherine's early years, her father had several meetings with his steward, Dr John Pinto Ribeiro, besides others, to discuss a coup and the restoration of the Portuguese monarchy. The duke had deliberated on the prospect of ascending the throne with his wife, an enthusiastic supporter. These meetings culminated in a critical discussion on 25 November 1640.

On this date, they celebrated with a splendid second birthday party for Catherine at the palace. The pageantry of the festivities concealed the actual intention of the gathering of the many friends of the duke and duchess. Shortly before this party, the Habsburg vicereine's government had summoned the duke to Madrid to discuss his mission in leading troops in his capacity as commander of the Portuguese army, to counteract a rebellion against Spain in Catalonia.

He made his excuses to the government in Lisbon as long as he could without being arrested for disobeying orders. Either the duke made an appearance in Madrid, or the intended coup must go forward immediately. Now, with a party of 150 gentlemen, most of them heads of families, with all of their servants, along with 200 citizens and operatives in attendance, discussions took place on the restoration of the Portuguese monarchy.[7]

The duke hesitated to take up the call to arms on the side of Spain as he had everything to lose and nothing to gain from doing so. During the birthday party, they asked if he would definitively and categorically consent to becoming king of Portugal.[8] With the duchess by his side, she persuasively pointed out to him the hazards of leaving Portugal and going to Spain, insisting he risked death. The story of her holding up the Infanta Catherine and asking him if he would deny making her a royal princess is probably apocryphal, but Luisa convinced him and the duke agreed to being proclaimed king if the planned coup proved successful.[9]

The nearly effortless overthrow of the Spanish government took place in Lisbon on 1 December. On 25 December, ten days after her father's acclamation as king of Portugal, Catherine left Vila Viçosa and moved to Lisbon with her mother, her brother Teodósio and her sister, Joanna. They settled into their new residence of the Ribeira Palace on the banks of the Tagus River.

We first hear of Catherine when she was 3. It was recorded that she suffered from quinsy, a suppurative inflammation of the tonsils. In later years, she says they treated her ailment with oil from the lamp of the Immaculate Conception of the Blessed Virgin of Vila Viçosa and she recovered.[10] The next we hear of Catherine is her attendance at the baptism in the Royal Chapel of her brother, Afonso, on 13 September 1643, along with her mother and her sister.[11]

Portugal in the seventeenth century lacked the sophistication of other parts of the world. There was no such thing as religious tolerance. The Jesuits supported King John IV's bid for the throne and the Catholic Church exercised its power not only through bishops and the papacy, but through the Inquisition, which set up for business in Portugal in 1537 in the form under which it would operate for the next 200 years. The Inquisition extended its power over the monarch, and the population at large, and would have a profound influence on King John IV's court and Catherine's life.[12]

The routine of the Portuguese court was austere, sombre and monotonous with strict, highly regulated and formal etiquette and ceremony. The nobles were stiff and solemn. They secluded women in severe and rigorous privacy. Well-born girls were intentionally preserved from the contamination of the world, shut up like nuns until they found husbands. Duennas fiercely guarded them, forbidding the girls even to speak to a man outside of their family.[13]

Catherine, along with every other daughter of the House of Braganza,[14] was no exception to the enforcement of these stringent precepts. They gave her an education equivalent of that taught in a convent. There is some evidence she received her education in a convent very near the royal palace. An English agent in Lisbon, Sir Francis Parry, wrote in a letter to Sir Robert Southwell in London in 1679, mentioning that the convent where Catherine received her education was just inside 'the great gate that goes to Aeleantara' [Alcântara] and calls it the place where the 'Marquera de Mira' had recently retired. He mentions that Catherine, at that time queen of England, was a patron of the convent.[15]

Parry most likely meant the Dominican Convent of the Holy Sacrament, which opened in 1620 and accommodated women of the high nobility who lived in great austerity.[16] The Convent of the Holy Sacrament of Alcântara is mentioned again by Conde de António Maria José de Melo César e Meneses Sabugosa in his book *Donas de Tempos Idos., fourth edition* [*Ladies of Time Gone By...*]. He states Catherine knew little of the political unrest and economic struggles of Portugal. She 'had during her childhood but a vague notion, as she had been educated in a convent in Alcântara, to whose seclusion she considered retiring when, many years later, she became a widow'.[17]

It is unclear if Catherine lived in the palace and the nuns taught her there, or if she actually lived in the convent during her education. It is also possible they took her to the convent, if not daily, at certain intervals. As she patronised the Convent of the Holy Sacrament and considered withdrawing from life and retiring there as a widow, it seems likely this is where she received her education.

Her mother thoroughly supervised her instruction.[18] Besides learning to read and write in Portuguese and Spanish, she mastered needlework and embroidery, singing holy music and attended endless religious services.[19] The nuns taught her excellent manners. The young princess spent hours in prayer, went to Mass, learned obedience and submission, played with her brothers and sister, embroidered altar cloths, and strolled in the gardens of the palace.[20]

Catherine was plump and very petite, with beautiful hands and delicate small feet, just like her mother. She had her mother's olive complexion and brunette hair, which was described as abundant, dark and shining. Her eyes were angelic in their size and in the splendour of their very dark pupils and she had a fleshy mouth with protruding teeth which were seen often as she never stopped smiling.[21] According to the standards of the day, she was not a great beauty, but neither was she ugly. However, she exhibited a special charm and a mournful smile which revealed a natural, inherent kindness. Innately serious minded,[22] she appeared thoughtful and very focused, maybe even tending towards mysticism.[23]

Quiet in manner, dignified and self-possessed, when she spoke she had copious amounts of wit and spirit in her talk. Catherine inherited her good nature and sweetness of disposition from her father.[24] She seemed to inherit from her mother an obstinate will, determination and an unusual, highly developed capacity of comprehension. Acutely conscious of her dignity as a royal princess, she knew full well she was due to receive the full obligatory ceremony requisite of her position.[25] In fact, Catherine was utterly spoiled and did not take kindly to being crossed. Crossing her rarely happened. But she was never known to do anything mean or ignoble or ever say anything spiteful regarding anyone.[26]

Catherine's biographer, Lillias Campbell Davidson, says that Queen Luisa, despite her wisdom and political acumen, categorically miscalculated considering Catherine's fate. Early on, she may have marked Catherine as the bride of the king of England, but gave her an education woefully inadequate for the position of queen. They never gave her tutorials in the English language, in the skills of diplomacy and tact, or in foreign royal courts or courtly intrigue. She knew nothing of men and their habits and received no instruction in the use of womanly charm for the acquisition of power over her immediate circle, let alone her adopted kingdom.[27] It would not be long before this glaring omission in Catherine's upbringing would come into brilliant focus once she reached England.

During the initial years of King John IV's reign, he claimed his rise to the throne of Portugal came through his legitimate descent from King Manuel I and maintained the Spanish Habsburgs were the usurpers. He faced a great deal of opposition from a large group of nobles and churchmen who continued to back the Habsburgs. His own support came from the authorities of local towns, the minor nobility, the lower clergy, and most significantly, the Jesuits who were the original supporters of the restoration of the Portuguese monarchy.[28]

King John could not recover Brazil from the Dutch or concentrate on the ports in Africa and Asia while continuing to resist head-on the looming threat of annexation by Spain. The House of Braganza sold its gold, silver and jewels in order to raise funds.[29] The pressing task at hand for the new monarch was to expel the Spanish from Portugal and to confirm the kingdom's liberation. One of the first orders of business concerned getting recognition of the House of Braganza as the authorised regime of Portugal and to appeal to foreign powers for aid.[30]

Eduardo Brazão has remarked, 'It is impossible to study the political history of Portugal without the framework of its diplomatic history'.[31] King John had no interest in an offensive war with Spain and knew diplomacy meant peace for the Portuguese.[32] None of the Catholic entities in Europe would recognise the new Braganza dynasty as the government of Portugal. Only France remained sympathetic because of their hatred of Spain. This state of affairs compelled the king and queen to seek mutual relations with the Protestant nations.[33]

Queen Luisa believed firmly in the high value of an English alliance.[34] King Charles I of England was the first monarch to recognise the new government of Portugal. The contents of a new treaty signed with England in 1642 allowed Portugal to recruit ships and men and granted the English merchants the same privileges as the Dutch. But when civil war broke out in England, the treaty had no practical value. Despite this state of affairs, the king of Portugal broached the idea of a marriage between a Portuguese Infanta and the son of King Charles I in 1644.[35]

In 1650 and 1651, the English parliament passed a series of Navigation Acts, resulting in highly protective measures which were the basis for the success of English commercial capitalism. These acts struck at the Dutch shipping trade. In 1652, the rivalry between England and the Dutch resulted in a war lasting two years.[36]

One of the relevant and enduring consequences of this war, along with the establishment of the Protectorate in England under Oliver Cromwell, was the strengthening of the alliance between England and Portugal, allowing the two countries to confront the Dutch together in different locales around the globe. The English valued their access to Portuguese ports and were looking to expand their trade with Portugal and its overseas possessions. Conversely, Portugal badly needed English shipping and the protection of the English fleet. This state of affairs resulted in the Anglo-Portuguese Treaty of 1654, 'arguably the most important treaty in the history of Anglo-Portuguese relations'.[37]

Overwhelmingly favourable to the English,[38] the treaty had no requirement for the English to commit to the defence of Portugal. It allowed Portugal to recruit soldiers and hire ships in England. The treaty confirmed privileged status to the English merchant community in Portugal and the islands, allowing them to establish their own factories and to appoint a judge conservator to handle all judicial cases involving English merchants.

For all intents and purposes, this allowed English factories in Portugal extraterritorial status and, on paper at least, access to Portugal's colonial markets. The ultimate result of this historic agreement allowed the English to establish themselves as the prevailing capitalist class in Portugal.[39] In addition, King John IV could move closer towards obtaining the international guarantees upon which he believed the future of Portugal depended.[40]

As Catherine grew up, John IV's court at Lisbon became the focus for political activity and national culture. He was a modest man who was not interested in exaggerated ceremony and elaborate displays of conspicuous consumption, usually dressing in black. Furniture and tapestries were conveyed from Vila Viçosa to adorn the Ribeira Palace to give it a semblance of royalty. King John held public audiences on Wednesdays and Fridays and received the noblemen on Saturdays. Occasionally, he would sit in the high court, gaining a reputation as a lover of justice. He engaged in diplomacy and could build a military of modest strength, all while maintaining a balanced domestic policy.[41]

The king was robust because of his pursuit of hunting when he was duke. As king, more than ever, he pursued his musical interests while composing pieces for his chapel. The dominant personality in the family, Queen Luisa, guided the first twenty years of the Braganza dynasty. She had an authoritative presence and more than once historians described her as majestic.[42] As Francis Gribble says in his story of the Braganzas, the women were the men in the family[43] and Queen Luisa personified this.

The year 1653 was not a happy one for the entire family. Catherine's beloved brother, Teodósio, died in May. She mourned his death.[44] Teo had been full of promise and the country's expectations for him had been rising. They described him as having good judgement and a fear of God, with a generous, pious, modest and brave personality.[45] A clear sign of her closeness to Teo is demonstrated in her will as Catherine asked to rest eternally by the side of her brother.[46] In November, her sister Joanna, Princess of Beira, died. They buried both Teo and Joanna in the church of the Jerónimos Monastery in the parish of Belem in Lisbon.

King John suffered from dropsy for some time, along with gout and kidney stones, and he grew weaker and more ill. Knowing he would die, and his wife would most likely pursue an English marriage for Catherine, he issued letters patent on 1 November 1656, granting Catherine a dowry. Given to her and all her successors were the island of Madeira, the city of Lamego, the village of Moura, and the marsh of Magos. These and other sources of income made Catherine rich in her own right and allowed her to have a separate household. If she married outside the kingdom, the letters stipulated she must give up these holdings in return for the equivalent in just rewards from the Crown.[47]

John IV died on 6 November and was buried in the Church of St Vincent de Fora in Lisbon, ushering in the tradition of this monastery serving as the mausoleum of the House of Braganza. The king's request for Teodósio's and Joanna's remains to be moved from the Church of Belem to St Vincent, would not be fulfilled while he lived.[48] Catherine's brother, Afonso, became king, although King John knew his son was not capable of fulfilling his monarchical duties. As a child, Afonso contracted meningitis,[49] and the illness left him physically and mentally incapacitated.

Afonso had not yet reached his majority. Infighting resulted between those who sought control of the new king and the Crown patronage. One faction favoured an alliance with France. As long as hostilities raged between France and Spain, France was Portugal's natural ally and did not pose as much of a threat to Portugal's overseas possessions and commerce. To cement this alliance, Francisco de Melo e Torres[50] would eventually broker a marriage between King Afonso and a French princess, Maria Francisca of Savoy, in August 1666. During these negotiations, they also discussed the idea of a marriage between Catherine and King Louis XIV.[51]

King John put in place provisions for Queen Luisa to act as regent for Afonso. The queen presided as the head of the faction at court who remained deeply suspicious of France. She believed the French would willingly trade Portugal to Spain in return for peace. This faction committed to following the belief of John IV that Portugal's only hope of survival lay in adhering to an English alliance.[52] Queen Luisa assumed the reins of government and would hold them for the ensuing ten years.[53] The war with Spain dragged on. There were some decisive battles in the conflict, but neither country could win the entire campaign.[54]

Following the death of her father, her income now established, Catherine finished her studies and left the convent. She had the ability to assert her freedom, but she chose to await a husband, living a sheltered life in the gloomy and austere Ribeira Palace, under the supervision of her mother. Surrounded by her mother's old, devout ladies and a grave and boring nobility concerned primarily with maintaining its prerogatives,[55] the events of Catherine's life during this time remain obscure as the historical record rarely mentions her.

The Negotiations for Catherine's Hand in Marriage

Portugal had its own unique version of the French Salic Law with a twist. A Cortes was allegedly summoned to Lamego in 1143 during the reign of King Afonso Henriques of the royal House of Burgundy. The result of the meeting, legislation known as the *Actas das Cortes de Lamego,* ratified the rules of succession to the Portuguese throne.[56] There is a passage in this set of articles regarding the inheritance of the Portuguese throne by a woman.

Articles IV and V state: 'If the King of Portugal should leave no male issue, his daughter shall be our queen, provided she marry a Portuguese nobleman, who, however, shall not bear the title of king till after the birth of a male child. In presence of the queen, he shall always be placed on her left hand, and shall not be permitted to wear the regal crown'.

Article VI: 'This last law shall always be strictly observed, and the king's eldest daughter shall never espouse any but a Portuguese nobleman, lest the kingdom should become subject to a foreign prince. Should the king's daughter infringe this article and become the wife of a prince or nobleman of another country, she shall not be acknowledged queen; and this, because we will not suffer our people to be ruled by a king who was not born a Portuguese, since it is our subjects and countrymen alone, without any foreign aid, who shed their blood in our service, and by their valour raised our country to regal dignity'.[57]

Later historians have agreed this document is undoubtably a forgery with a clear nationalist intention. For political purposes the Braganzas invoked the *Actas* to reinforce the restoration of the family to the Portuguese throne.[58] These articles would justify Catarina, Duchess of Braganza's stronger claim to the Portuguese throne in 1580 over King Philip II of Spain, as she was the daughter of Edward, a younger son of King Manuel I, whereas Philip was descended from a daughter of Manuel I.

Not only did it justify the Braganza claims to the throne, but it would also have serious consequences for future royal Infantas in relation to their marriages. These *Actas* were used to rationalise incestuous unions between cousins and even uncles and nieces. Queen Luisa, in pursuing her plans to marry her daughter to the future king of England, ignored these purported guiding principles. With two brothers, the likelihood of Catherine becoming queen of Portugal remained minimal. Besides, at the time of King John IV's death, Luisa needed allies to ward off annexation by Spain and was well aware of the value of her daughter as a commodity on the European royal marriage market.[59]

As Catherine awaited her fate, political machinations went on for years behind the scenes. There were several candidates for her hand in marriage. Catherine's only concern would have been that the marriage ceremony did, in actuality, take place and that the reputation, prestige and dignity of Portugal suffered no negative consequences.[60]

In February 1641, King John IV sent an embassy to King Charles I of England. Antão Vax de Almada and Francisco de Andrade Leitão departed for London, where they received a positive welcome at the English court. They negotiated the Treaty of Peace and Commerce on 29 January 1642. The terms of this treaty certified English recognition of Portuguese independence and the legitimacy of the Braganza monarchy. The two Portuguese ambassadors left for Lisbon and The Hague. Antonio de Sousa de Macedo, the secretary of the Portuguese embassy, remained in England during the first English Civil War and acted as Charles I's agent in procuring guns and ammunition.

In the struggle between King Charles I and Parliament, civil war broke out by the end of 1642. King Charles I left London for Oxford, taking his two eldest sons,

Charles and James, with him. Several battles ensued, and the king and princes had to keep moving across Britain.[61] In 1644, Sousa de Macedo sought an audience with the king in Oxford. While there, the English Secretary of State approached him and asked to discuss the marriage of the Prince of Wales with an Infanta of Portugal. Macedo declined, saying he had not received instructions to do so. The secretary insisted that King Charles requested him to raise the subject. On hearing this, Macedo relented. This is the first recorded conversation discussing the idea of marrying Prince Charles to a Portuguese Infanta.[62]

Catherine's name was not mentioned specifically at this point in the discussions. The Infanta Joanna was 7 years old, and Catherine aged 4.[63] Macedo wrote to John IV in Portugal, bringing up the subject. Charles I expressed interest, but the most important object of any agreement would be the right of the bride to worship as a Catholic and religious freedom for Catholics in general in England. Macedo reiterated to King John that he had refused to talk any further, saying he had received no further instructions from Portugal.

The religious issue was the most troublesome sticking point regarding any negotiations, and Portugal dropped the idea. It is a point of contention among historians who first proposed a marriage for the Prince of Wales with a Portuguese Infanta during this time frame. Macedo was very close with Charles I and either of them could have brought it up.[64] In a letter written to Richard Fanshawe, then England's minister in Lisbon, just months after his wedding to Catherine, Charles II recalled that Antonio de Sousa de Macedo, 'who served the King of England, Charles I, with great zeal, had been the first to speak of the happy marriage which has just taken place'.[65]

John IV dispatched other embassies to all the main courts of Europe. In seeking diplomatic relations and Portuguese independence, marriages were continuously discussed. Several candidates came forward for Catherine's hand after the death of her sister Joanna. It is uncertain when the match with Don Juan of Austria, bastard son of King Philip IV of Spain, first merited consideration. It may have originated in Madrid during negotiations of a twenty-year truce where they also discussed the option of Don Juan of Austria ruling Brazil. We can garner all of this from a few small paragraphs in documents from France's ministers in Lisbon, Francis Lanier and the Chevalier de Jant, and from the Viscount of Santarém's notes in his *Quadro Elementar*.[66] But this alliance gained no traction.

Cardinal Richelieu, prime minister of France, ratified an alliance with King John IV on 1 February 1641. The cardinal aimed to compel Spain into four major but interconnected conflicts against France, the Dutch Republic, Catalonia and Portugal.[67] Richelieu's successor, Cardinal Jules Mazarin, continued the policy of supporting the rebellions against Philip IV in Catalonia and Portugal, allowing large numbers of Spanish troops to be otherwise occupied and unable to fight in the Netherlands.[68]

Another French marriage for Catherine came under consideration with the suitor being Francis de Vendôme, Duc de Beaufort, a sailor in the French navy and the second son of César de Bourbon, the illegitimate son of Henri IV and his beloved mistress, Gabrielle d'Estreés. They discussed a double marriage proposal with Catherine's brother Teodósio marrying Anne Marie Louise d'Orleans, known as 'Grande Mademoiselle'. Anne Marie Louise was the daughter of Gaston, Duke d'Orleans, the brother of King Louis XIII of France.

However, Gaston was against this proposal as he wanted Anne Marie Louise to marry the exiled king of England, Charles II and the Duke d'Orleans refused the match. The alleged bastardy of the Duc de Beaufort was another factor taken into consideration.[69] Ultimately, Beaufort conspired against Cardinal Richelieu, and they dropped the proposal. Beaufort never married.

When Cardinal Mazarin came to power in France after the death of Cardinal Richelieu, he found it politically expedient to take control of the narrative and began an offensive to marry Catherine to King Louis XIV. This became the chief focus of his foreign policy for the next four years, allowing him to play Portugal against Spain and vice versa. On 23 February 1655, Mazarin's envoy, the Chevalier de Jant, arrived in Lisbon.

They conducted negotiations with de Jant and the king's ministers along with Frei Domingos do Rosario.[70] This was Daniel O'Daly, an Irishman born in 1595 (died in Lisbon on 20 June 1662). He was the confessor to Queen Luisa, who also employed him as an ambassador extraordinaire, granting him an important role in Portuguese politics and diplomacy.[71] Queen Luisa herself engaged in the negotiations with de Jant. She told him there was no princess more suitable for the king of France than her daughter Catherine. She was gentle, submissive and obedient and if there was no king in Europe for Catherine, then she would retire to a convent.[72]

On 7 September 1655, a French treaty was agreed upon, with Portugal promising not to conclude peace with Spain without including France. They sent Rosario to France in October to ratify the treaty, arrange the marriage of Catherine with Louis XIV, and get further validation of the alliance with France.[73] Rosario found the atmosphere in Paris hostile and only gained an audience with Mazarin at the end of the year.

Mazarin informed Rosario he had exceeded his powers and instructions. The State Council demanded to see an accredited ambassador from Portugal before the matter could proceed any further. In July 1656, Rosario realised the futility of his mission and returned home.[74] De Jant allowed Rosario to make a second trip, fully invested with the powers necessary to make a match between Catherine and Louis XIV. Again, Rosario was rebuffed. The death of King John IV, on 5 November 1656, ended this round of negotiations.[75]

In June 1657, Louis XIV's special ambassador, the Count de Comminges, carrying secret instructions, came to Lisbon along with Rosario to offer condolences to Queen Luisa on the death of her husband and to congratulate King Afonso on his accession to the throne. Luisa believed they would complete final negotiations for the marriage but became angry when the French made further unreasonable demands.

Over the next two years, Comminges alluded to a marriage for Catherine during the dialogue taking place with the Portuguese commissioners, allowing Queen Luisa to remain hopeful. Comminges wrote to Mazarin saying Catherine was 'very beautiful and majestic, and that if her hair were well styled and she well dressed, few beauties in the French court could compare with her'. He continued, noting Catherine was 'the delight and the darling of the entire Kingdom'.[76]

By February 1660, Mazarin recalled the ambassadors from Portugal to France as they were no longer needed. The Treaty of the Pyrenees, ratified on 7 November 1659, established peace between France and Spain, and deliberately did not include Portugal. Instead of Catherine marrying Louis XIV of France, he would marry the Spanish Infanta Maria Theresa, his mother's niece. No aid would come from France, leaving Portugal politically isolated.

After nineteen years, Portugal was still fighting for independence from Spain and defending their empire from the Dutch. Spain, no longer at war in Catalonia, could concentrate all its efforts on overtaking Portugal. The Pope had still not recognised Portugal's independence or the restoration of the Braganza monarchy. The government in Lisbon rightly believed Spain, who enjoyed the support of the papacy, would become more vigorous in attempting to reconquer Portugal.[77] Now, more than ever, Portugal's survival as a nation depended on her relationship with England.[78]

Restoration of the Stuart Monarchy in England

After a contentious civil war in England, the execution of King Charles I took place at the end of January 1649. His eldest son, King Charles II, in exile on the Continent, would wander through much of Europe for ten years, looking for financial and military support for his restoration to the throne of England. This became less likely as the years rolled on. In the meantime, Oliver Cromwell's Protectorate ruled England with Parliament.

Cromwell died in 1658 expecting his son Richard to govern in his place. But Richard's rule never gained traction and he ended up in exile. At that moment, General George Monck, the great military tactician of the English Civil Wars and Oliver Cromwell's protégé, made it clear he would support the restoration of the Stuart monarchy. A Royalist in the early part of the civil conflict, Monck later formed a personal loyalty to the Cromwells.[79]

Following the death of Oliver Cromwell, Queen Luisa still maintained negotiations with Cardinal Mazarin for the marriage of Catherine to Louis XIV.

In order to cover all her bases, she sent the dependable ambassador, Francisco de Melo e Torres on a secret embassy to General Monck. De Melo approached the General, putting forth the idea of Catherine marrying King Charles II. Monck agreed to advocate for the Portuguese match.[80]

In February 1660, General Monck convened a new parliament to discuss the restoration of the Stuart monarchy and initiate negotiations with Charles. On 1 May 1660, Parliament voted to approve the restoration and proclaimed Charles king on 8 May. The people greeted him with wild enthusiasm on the day of his return to England. As he established his government, one of Charles' first orders of business was to secure the succession. The people wanted Charles to marry a Protestant. At first, he looked to make a match with Henrietta, daughter of the Prince of Orange. But Henrietta's mother rebuffed his proposals, a humiliation he would never forgive or forget.[81]

The English Marriage Treaty

There are many opinions on who first proposed the marriage between Catherine and Charles II after the Stuart Restoration. Frei Domingos do Rosario may have met Charles II on one of his visits to France during Charles' exile. The Count of Schömberg passed through England on his way to Portugal to become the leader of the Portuguese military. Charles' mother, the dowager queen Henrietta Maria, wanted her son to marry a Catholic. Whoever first brought up the match, Francisco de Melo e Torres, ambassador to Whitehall, facilitated the marriage negotiations.[82]

According to Portuguese sources, it was Dom João da Costa, Conde de Soure, the Portuguese ambassador to France, who first suggested the marriage of Catherine to King Charles II when he recognised the Stuart Restoration was a fait accompli. Costa wrote to Queen Luisa and de Melo recommending a revival of the English negotiations. Luisa, eager to pursue the idea, wrote to de Melo suggesting not only should Charles marry Catherine, but proposed that Charles' younger sister, Henriette Anne, marry Catherine's brother, King Afonso.[83]

However, the queen gave no further instructions for any additional bargaining. Soure suggested, since Queen Luisa had offered the French one million cruzados and agreed to cede Tangier for the marriage of Catherine to Louis XIV, then de Melo should proceed with these as bargaining chips for the English marriage.[84] Events in England would eventually propel the negotiations into high gear.

During the exile of King Charles and his brother James, Duke of York, they stayed in the Low Countries at the court of their sister Mary, who was the widow of William II, Prince of Orange. James met and fell in love with Anne Hyde, one of Mary Stuart's ladies-in-waiting and the daughter of Charles' lord chancellor, Edward Hyde, first Earl of Clarendon. Anne had charmed and captivated James, so much so he wanted to marry her. She knew how to fan the flames and James may not have had entirely honourable intentions. However, in either August or November 1659, at Breda shortly before the Stuart Restoration, the couple exchanged vows before the appropriate witnesses and consummated the marriage, all without the king's permission.

The dowager queen, Henrietta Maria, was furious over this ill-advised marriage. She believed the match to be beneath James and he undoubtedly lost a crucial opportunity to make a more politically advantageous marriage for the newly restored Stuart monarchy. Henrietta Maria came to England from exile in France to see what she could do to mitigate the damage of James' rash act. Despite Henrietta Maria's efforts, Charles allowed the marriage to stand as Anne was heavily pregnant.

Following an official English wedding ceremony, Anne gave birth to a son who sadly would not survive. Henrietta Maria was very close to her nephew, King Louis XIV of France, so it is highly likely Louis had discussed the marriage of Catherine of Braganza and Charles with his aunt. The family debated the marriage during her sojourn in England. The dowager queen, a Catholic herself, aimed to bring all her children into the Church of Rome. She hoped Charles would convert with the help of a Catholic wife.[85]

Queen Louisa and King Afonso gave Ambassador de Melo instructions to begin serious discussions for the match. Father Richard Russell, an Englishman educated in Portugal, assisted him. Russell would act as secretary to de Melo and become the primary intermediary between the Portuguese ambassador and the English ministers.[86] De Melo called on the Earl of Manchester, lord chamberlain to King Charles, suggesting a wife be found for the newly restored king.

De Melo pressed his case by mentioning: 'there was in Portugal a princess in beauty, age, and person very fit for him, who would have a portion suitable to her birth and quality. She was indeed a Catholic and would never depart from her religion; but she had none of the meddling activity, which sometimes made persons of that faith troublesome when they came into a country where another mode of worship was practised. She had been bred under a wise mother, who had carefully infused another spirit into her, and kept her from affecting to interfere in State affairs with which she was unacquainted, so that she would be content to enjoy her own religion, without concerning herself with what others professed'.[87]

De Melo continued, stating 'he had authority to make the proposition to the King, accompanied with such advantages as he thought no other power in Europe could offer'.[88] The terms of the arrangement were substantial: a dowry of two million cruzados, the port of Tangier, free trade with Brazil and the East Indies, among other concessions. In return, de Melo asked that Catherine be allowed to worship in peace as a Catholic and that England promise protection for Portugal from Spain and the Dutch.[89]

The Earl of Manchester met with the king to discuss the terms offered by de Melo on behalf of the government of Portugal. Charles needed funds and found the offer tempting. He told Manchester he would consider it. Charles consulted with his chancellor, the Earl of Clarendon, who advised caution, objecting to Catherine because she was Catholic and asking Charles to consider a Protestant wife. Charles told him there were no suitable Protestant prospects available. He agreed to meet with the Portuguese ambassador.

During an audience with the king on 11 September 1660, de Melo reiterated the terms he discussed with the Lord Chamberlain. He also promised the surrender of the port of Bombay in India. Charles convened a secret council for further discussion. He informed the assembly he considered the enormous amount of cash being offered extremely attractive and asked his ministers about the significance of the port of Tangier. Two of his admirals, the Earl of Sandwich and Sir John Lawson, knew the port and spoke highly of it. They agreed the port would be of immeasurable strategic value for trade in the Mediterranean[90] and they considered Bombay interesting, but not of as much tactical consequence as Tangier.

At the time of these talks, there were ongoing commercial negotiations being carried out in the open with Portugal. England, eager to maintain good relations with Spain, conducted the marriage portion of these negotiations in secret with the king through the Earl of Manchester.[91] Father Richard Russell rapidly became close to King Charles, his ministers and others of influence at Whitehall. There was so much confidence in him, he was the only other person who had information about the covert negotiations for the marriage treaty.[92] The Spanish ambassador only knew about the terms of the trade agreement.[93]

Discussions were ongoing and by the end of October, Charles had agreed to the marriage with the only remaining requirement being the guarantees from Portugal. On 16 October, Charles issued a proclamation declaring confirmation of the commercial treaty with Portugal, allowing for the continuance of the amity and commerce between the two countries. The marriage remained secret.[94] Charles supplied de Melo with two ships and he sailed for Lisbon on 24 October in order to conclude the details. He received great acclaim at court, and King Afonso endowed him with the titles of first Marquis de Sande and Conde de Ponte for his services.[95]

The Earl of Bristol had recently been to the Spanish court and overheard rumours that Charles was considering marrying the Portuguese Infanta. Bristol passed this information on to the Spanish ambassador, Baron de Batteville. It troubled the ambassador that Charles would entertain an alliance with Spain's lost satellite of Portugal, and he sought an audience with Charles to dissuade him from the alliance. Unable to make any headway with the king, De Batteville began spreading rumours, casting aspersions about Catherine, saying she had deformities and suffered from poor health. He said everyone in Spain knew Catherine could have no children, although he had no way of knowing if this was true.[96]

Rumours flew about that Clarendon had worked to persuade Charles to marry Catherine, knowing full well she was barren, and therefore allowing the children of his daughter Anne, Duchess of York, and Charles' brother, James. to inherit the throne. Again, he had no way of knowing if Catherine was infertile. It does not appear the king took anyone's advice regarding his marriage, but the rumours seemed to agitate Charles.

King Philip IV of Spain offered to provide Charles with a Protestant bride and treat her as his own daughter, bestowing on her the equivalent of the Portuguese dowry. Charles was very familiar with Spanish diplomacy, having made an alliance with Spain in 1656 during his exile, the terms of which included a cash payment and an income to Charles and his two brothers, James and Henry, Duke of Gloucester.

This money, when it did come, was slow and soon in arrears. Charles knew full well Spain could not pay the promised dowry. De Batteville threatened Spain would declare war on England and he would desert his post as ambassador. Charles told him he had no right to dictate who he would marry and he was welcome to leave.[97] As a result, the marriage negotiations with Spain went no further for the rest of the year.[98]

Charles had no intention of alienating Spain because he wanted to maintain commercial and trade relations. The rumours about Catherine's health dismayed him and he had not heard from the new Marquis de Sande or Portugal for months. The Earl of Bristol, under the influence of de Batteville, pressured Charles forcefully enough to influence the king to dispatch him to Italy to report on two Protestant princesses from Parma as prospective brides.[99]

Queen Luisa kept the negotiations concealed as much as possible, especially the preparations for the delivery of Tangier and Bombay.[100] The Catholic Portuguese would resent the sacrifice of Bombay and Tangier, even though there was no likelihood Portugal could develop these two possessions any further in the current circumstances.[101] The secession of the two cities would be a continuation of a long trend in Portuguese overseas policy of retraction and reduction of the profitless commitments of North Africa and of making Brazil a priority over the Estado da India for the kingdom's limited resources.[102]

Neither city had much economic value to Portugal, but a powerful party in Lisbon opposed the ceding of Tangier as it had symbolic importance. Catherine's father had confided to the French envoy at Lisbon he would gladly abandon the heavy burden of trying to sustain Portuguese India if he could find an honourable way of doing so. But the rest of the country was proud of the Estado da India and willing to sacrifice to maintain it.[103]

Prince Henry the Navigator's association with Tangier remained strong. His expedition in 1437 had resulted in the disastrous loss of his brother, Prince Fernando, to the Moroccans. Bombay, with its exceptional harbour, had been the port of gathering for many Portuguese armadas. Its potential was increasing as a thriving settlement for Portuguese immigrants. They believed, in the hands of the

English, Bombay would eventually eclipse the Portuguese trade in Bassein and Goa.[104]

Finally, the Marquis de Sande returned to England to complete the treaty but met with coldness from the king. De Sande began handing out bribes to the king's counsellors, cultivating and buying the goodwill of General Monck and many others. Chancellor Clarendon, the Lord Treasurer, and the Earl of Southampton and de Sande convinced Charles of the weakness and lack of resources of Spain, assuring him Spain would not declare war.[105] De Sande told Charles the compilation of the dowry by the Portuguese, already underway, neared completion.[106]

At this critical moment, King Louis XIV's minister, Cardinal Mazarin, died and Louis inserted himself into the English negotiations. In March 1661, probably with the consensus of King Charles' mother, Louis sent Charles a letter, touting Catherine's fine qualities and declaring he almost married her himself. Louis sent a secret envoy to extend an offer of French aid to pay for the soldiers being sent to Portugal as part of the treaty negotiations. Louis had a vested interest in keeping Portugal independent of Spain for the foreseeable future, and these overtures by the French king made the Portuguese marriage even more attractive to Charles.[107]

When de Sande arrived at Whitehall to complete the negotiations, he took a portrait with him which Father Russell had brought from Portugal. Catherine's biographers have debated over the identity of this painting, and there are three theories. One possibility is a canvas from the collection of Horace Walpole in his home at Strawberry Hill, sold off during the dismantling of his household. Virginia Rau argues it was another portrait, now in Lisbon, which in the beginning of the twentieth century hung in the gallery of the Duke of Fife.

Another prospect is the work of the Dutch artist Dirck Stoop, which is currently in the National Portrait Gallery in London. The Stoop portrait is the most likely choice, as the artist was in Portugal at the time and recorded many events there and in England during the Stuart Restoration.[108] When Charles viewed this portrait, he stated, 'This person cannot be unhandsome!'.[109] Charles finally consented to the alliance and the marriage. His coronation took place on 23 April 1661, and Clarendon gave a speech announcing the Braganza marriage on 8 May.

Consequences of the Marriage Treaty

The signing of the Articles of Marriage took place on 23 June 1661 at Whitehall, by de Sande, Clarendon, and others. (See Appendix I, *Articles of Marriage between his Majesty and the Lady Infanta of Portugal, 1661.*) The beneficiaries of the treaty were Portugal, France and England. Portugal had insured its own survival with guarantees of aid from England in the fight for independence from Spain. France received a guarantee that Spain lacked allies and would be forced to continue its war with Portugal. England gained much needed funds for the Exchequer, a royal bride in Catherine of Braganza and valuable commercial advantages, all at little or no cost.[110] After his marriage to Catherine, Charles worked to negotiate an end to the Spanish-Portuguese war and to improve relations between England and Spain. This would be an important principle of his personal foreign policy until the Treaty of Lisbon in 1668.[111]

After the Treaty of the Pyrenees of 1659, Spain tried to reconquer Portugal. As with the prior wars, it played out in sieges and counter-sieges and lasted from 1661 to 1668. At one point the Spanish invaded, coming down from the mountains in 1663 and capturing Evora, Portugal's third largest city.[112] The English provided infantry, cavalry and artillery while English ships kept the seas surrounding Portugal safe. Portugal engaged a mercenary general, the Count of Schömberg, to take control of the armies and train forces. By 1667 the Portuguese won several significant victories against Spain and evicted all invaders.

King John IV and Queen Luisa's faith in the English alliance paid off handsomely. During the peace negotiations in 1668, Spain, and eventually even Rome, acknowledged Portugal's independence.[113] The three Anglo-Portuguese treaties of 1642, 1654 and 1661 secured the commercial command of the English in Portugal. These strong commercial ties resulted in an even more robust and long-lasting bond between England and Portugal.[114]

There would be no proxy marriage. Because the union involved a Protestant and a Catholic, they needed no papal dispensation. Rome had not yet recognised the Braganza dynasty, so in effect they considered Catherine the daughter of a duke. Neither party concerned themselves with these details.[115] England had recognised the sovereignty of Catherine's family from the first day of the restoration of the monarchy in Portugal, and this alliance with England gained the prestige of an inter-dynastic match of the first order for the new Braganza monarchy.[116]

Following wine and dinner to celebrate the signing of the treaty, de Sande received some letters written by Charles in Spanish for Catherine and her mother. Charles' letter to Catherine read:

My Lady and Wife,

Already, at my request, the good Count da Ponte has set off for Lisbon; for me, the signing of the marriage has been great happiness; and there is about to be dispatched at this time after him one of my servants, charged with what would appear necessary; whereby may be declared, on my part, the inexpressible joy of this felicitous conclusion, which, when received, will hasten the coming of your Majesty.

I am going to make a short progress into some of my provinces; in the meantime, whilst I go from my most sovereign good, yet I do not complain as to whither I go, seeking in vain tranquility in my restlessness, hoping to see the beloved person of your Majesty in these kingdoms, already your own, and that with the same anxiety with which, after my long banishment, I desired to see myself within them, and my subjects, desiring also to behold me amongst them, having manifested their most ardent wishes for my return, well known to the world. The presence of your Serenity, only wanting to unite us, under the protection of god, in health and content, I desire.

I have recommended to the Queen, [Luisa] our lady and mother, the business of the Count da Ponte, who, I must here avow, has served me in what I regard as the greatest good in this world, which cannot be mine less than it is that of your Majesty; likewise, not forgetting the good Richard Russell, who laboured on his part to the same end.

The very faithful husband of your Majesty, whose hand he kisses.

Charles Rex
London, 2nd of July 1661.

To the Queen of Great Britain, my wife and lady, whom God preserve[117]

Catherine replied: 'I give myself reciprocally with much joy, and could find it in my heart to give it over and over to Your Majesty'.[118]

With the conclusion of the Articles of Marriage, many English writers went into overdrive with descriptions of the ceremony at the Portuguese court, her journey and arrival in England and her wardrobe. Regarding Catherine's character, emotions and feelings, there is nothing written.[119] Thomas Maynard, a merchant from Devon appointed the first English consul to Portugal by Oliver Cromwell in 1656, wrote about his impressions of Catherine to Sir Edward Nicholas, the Secretary of State.

Maynard says: 'About four days ago since arrived in this port three merchant ships, who brought the news of His Majesty's intentions to make the Infanta Queen of England (the welcomest news that ever came to the Portuguese people), and confirmed by the King's and by the chancellor's (Clarendon) speeches. There is no doubt His Majesty hath made both nations very happy in his choice. The Infanta is a lady of incomparable virtue, of excellent parts, very beautiful, and of an indifferent stature, being somewhat taller than the Queen, His Majesty's mother'.[120]

He writes again: 'We shall be extremely happy in a Queen. She is as sweet a dispositioned princess as ever was born, a lady of excellent parts, but bred hugely retired. She hath hardly been ten years' time she was not out of doors, until she heard of His Majesty's intentions to make her Queen of Great Britain, since which she hath been to visit two saints in the city, and very shortly she intends to pay her devotions to some saints in the country'.[121]

After the ratification of the marriage treaty, they referred to Catherine as queen of England at the Portuguese court. She appeared more often in public. Charles sent her some silks and tailor-made suits[122] along with a miniature portrait of himself by Sir Richard Fanshawe, the king's ambassador to Portugal. She practised how to walk in English shoes with high heels[123] and Father Russell tried to teach her a little English as she awaited the fleet to take her to England.[124]

Clarendon insisted Tangier be in English hands before the marriage, as he feared the Portuguese would either lose it or go back on their word.[125] Item II of the Articles of Marriage required Portugal to surrender the port of Tangier to England and Edward Montagu, first Earl of Sandwich, sailed to take control of Tangier from the Portuguese before returning to Lisbon to convey Catherine to England.[126] In September, he was in Lisbon working on the arrangements for the royal wedding, and he departed to take possession of Tangier in October. He administered the evacuation of the Portuguese from the port and awaited the English garrison.[127]

After delivering Tangier to the new governor, Sandwich sailed for Lisbon on 18 February. When he arrived, he made a spectacular ceremonial entrance into the city, followed by meetings with Queen Luisa, King Afonso and Catherine herself. Then, the long-drawn-out negotiations over the payment of Catherine's dowry began. On March 19, to Sandwich's dismay, he learned only half of the two million cruzados were on board ship to England. He also discovered bills of exchange for future cargoes figured in as part of the dowry.[128] He complained to Queen Luisa the bills of exchange were outside the treaty's terms, which stipulated the dowry payment comprise money, jewels, sugar and other merchandise.[129] (See Appendix I – *Articles of Marriage between his Majesty and the Lady Infanta of Portugal, 1661*, Item V.)

Queen Luisa attributed the shortfall to the expenses of the war with Spain. The earl's disappointment with this news was great, but he had already taken possession of Tangier and met with Catherine and her family. They agreed to a compromise after several rounds of negotiation. The merchandise would travel with the English fleet, be delivered to a designated representative of King Afonso VI in London, and exchanged with the delivery of the proceeds in coin to the king. Portugal agreed to pay the second half of the dowry portion within a year.[130]

Catherine surrendered her claims to the island of Madeira, and for Lamego and Moura to the Crown. In return, she received five hundred thousand cruzados.[131] Following the conclusion of the negotiations for the delivery of the dowry, and four days before she departed, Catherine received all the English residents in Lisbon and they had the privilege of kissing her hand, the supreme ceremonial rite of the Braganza court.[132] By 23 April 1662, everything was ready for Catherine's departure. Sandwich's flagship, the *Royal Charles* waited at the mouth of the Tagus River to receive her on board.

Catherine Departs Lisbon

The morning of 23 April, Catherine emerged from the antechamber of her mother's apartments in the Ribeira Palace, followed by her two brothers, King Afonso and

Infante Pedro. Behind them was a long and imposing procession of the grandees of Portugal, the officers of the household and the court nobles. Catherine wore the traditional costume of Portugal comprising a wide hoop skirt made of a rich material with farthingale, huge bishop sleeves, a deep lace collar, a stiff stomacher and a long ostrich feather in her hair.

The entire party made their way down the Tudescos Chamber to the balcony at the top of the stairs leading to the Chapel Pateo, the appointed place for Catherine to make her final leave-taking with her mother.[133] Being a dutiful daughter, Catherine begged permission to kiss her mother's hand. But Catherine was no longer her daughter but the queen of England, so Queen Luisa would not allow her to humble herself before the queen mother of Portugal.

Luisa formally embraced Catherine and gave her a blessing. Neither one of them showed any emotion but the courtiers, grandees and duennas surrounding them openly wept.[134] Following this, Catherine and her brothers descended the grand staircase and they escorted her to her coach. She turned back to her mother and made a deep curtsey. The queen blessed her again and retired from the scene before Catherine even entered the coach. Catherine sat in the right-hand seat, Afonso by her side, and Pedro sat with his back to the horses.

The royal coach and procession of English and Portuguese nobles along with many guards made its way to the cathedral. Cannons boomed from the fortresses and ships, and the bells of the cathedral and monastery chimed. Music and dancers filled the streets, ornamented with silks, tapestries and triumphal arches.[135] The cortege reached the church at 9 o'clock where they celebrated a special benedictory Mass in the beautifully decorated cathedral.

As the coach arrived, Lord Sandwich, followed by Pedro and then Catherine led by King Afonso, entered the great door. The king and Pedro dropped to their knees to kiss a cross under a canopy held by six priests. Catherine took her seat in the place of honour in the church, while the English Protestants strolled in the shady cloisters during the Mass.[136] Following the singing of the *Te Deum*, the entire party returned to their coaches.

The stately royal train made its way to the Terreiro do Paço and the quay through streets hung with silks, damasks and cloth of gold. Part of the cavalcade included effigies of Catherine and King Charles in robes of state and jewels.[137] The effigy of Charles bore the regalia of his coronation. The people yelled joyful shouts of triumph. As they neared the Terreiro do Paço, at the waterside, the coach bearing Catherine and her brothers entered the docks by a garden nearby where a special door had been cut through the wall for their entrance.[138] Everyone else left their coaches and walked through another door into the same garden and made their way to the brilliantly adorned pier, hung with flying flags and pennons.

Everyone who had escorted Catherine ceremoniously kissed her hand with great reverence. People offered to kiss King Afonso's hand, but he refused, as he did not want to detract from the glory of Catherine's day. The fleet awaited Catherine in the bay. It included fourteen men-of-war, among them the *Royal Charles* and the Vice-Admiral's ship the *Gloucester*. The *Montague* carried the new queen's entourage. The three deck ships flew the English standard, and the *Royal Charles* had the royal ensign. Beside the quay lay a splendidly appointed barge with the Portuguese royal standard.

Afonso led Catherine to the barge of state. Pedro, Lord Sandwich and the English gentlemen of Catherine's new household, the Portuguese ambassador, the Marquis de Sande and four other Portuguese grandees boarded the barge. Other nobles and duennas followed in high-prowed boats. As the barge drew away from the quay, the artillery boomed a salute from the forts in the hills which the ships in the bay answered. Many gondolas accompanied the barge along with other small highly decorated boats, filled with the nobility and others, along with musicians, dancers and various performing artists.[139]

Catherine came up to the side of the *Royal Charles* which had a crew of six hundred and eighty brass cannons. She was legally in England once she boarded the ship. Afonso formally handed her over to Lord Sandwich, who accompanied her to the specially prepared cabin. Decorators had covered the wooden bulkheads with crimson velvet embroidered with gold. The cushions, stools, chairs and cloths of state were also of red velvet and gold and the portholes had curtains of damask and taffeta. There was a bed of white taffeta in a red and gold frame.[140]

She said her last farewell to her brothers in this room. Other ladies kissed her hand and departed, leaving her alone with members of her new household. Court etiquette dictated she remain in her cabin, but she defied the rules and made her way back to the deck. Afonso indicated she should return below deck, but Catherine disobeyed him. She followed her brothers to the top of the ladder and watched as they descended into the royal Portuguese barge. The king again motioned for her to return to her cabin and she reluctantly obeyed.

The *Royal Charles* should have sailed, but the winds took to blowing strongly against the fleet and they remained moored in the Tagus River for two days. People of the city took this opportunity to continue the celebrations and rejoicing by bringing gaily decorated craft into the bay. At night there were fireworks. Guitars played and the sound of love songs drifted over the water. Catherine remained in seclusion with her ladies in her cabin. No one visited her. Her mother dispatched messages, declaring her sympathy over the delay.[141]

On the evening of 24 April, Afonso and Pedro joined the river carnival celebrations. They arranged for several talented nobles of the court to accompany them in barges with their musical instruments. Surrounding the *Royal Charles*, they serenaded Catherine with various carols, sonnets, madrigals, canozoni, and epithalamiums, all specifically composed in honour of her nuptials.[142]

The wind calmed during the night and although the conditions were not ideal, Lord Sandwich put to sea. Catherine emerged from her cabin to take one last look at sunny Portugal and watched Lisbon fade from view. But before the flotilla had crossed the river's bar, the winds intensified with the rain falling in torrents. The waves were so high, water broke over the decks of the ships. Everyone became seasick and several of the ships suffered damage. The storm lasted thirteen days.

Arrival in England and Marriage – Union of Two Restored Dynasties

At last, the ships reached the English coast between the Lizard and Land's End and sought shelter in Mount's Bay. The people welcomed Catherine with salvos of artillery and fireworks, but she felt too ill to make an appearance. After two days, the fleet headed to Portsmouth and dropped anchor off the Isle of Wight. The news arrived at Portsmouth that the fleet had appeared. Charles' brother James, Duke of York, awaiting the summons, boarded his ship, setting out with five frigates to receive and welcome Catherine on behalf of the king.

As soon as James came in sight of Sandwich's ships, he sent his secretary to ask permission to wait upon Catherine and kiss her hand. Catherine immediately dispatched the secretary with the answer that a delay would be painful to her.[143] James boarded his private barge accompanied by several nobles and members of Catherine's new household, all wearing full court dress. The Marquis de Sande with other Portuguese grandees stood on the deck of the *Royal Charles* to receive James.

Catherine wore an outfit made of white cloth trimmed with silver lace in the English fashion for the meeting. She waited in the innermost presence chamber of her cabin, replete with a throne and canopy. James entered the room and dropped to his knees. Catherine came forward and raised him to his feet. She then returned to her throne and sat down. Using her almoner and interpreter, Bishop Richard Russell, she offered a few ceremonial remarks in Portuguese, acknowledging James' equally official welcome spoken in English.

Formalities out of the way, Catherine motioned for James to sit in an armchair on her right, but this he modestly refused. She then pointed to a tabouret (high stool) outside the canopy on her left, which he cordially accepted. They began speaking in Spanish together and James assured her of his brotherly affection for her and his desire to always serve her. Catherine was gracious, dignified, self-possessed, and seemed very pleased,[144] and Catherine's gentleness and kindness impressed James.

The interview being over, all the English nobles were introduced to Catherine and kissed her hand. Then she presented the Portuguese grandees to the English. James received them with great courtesy. It was time to end the ceremony and

Catherine stood up and walked toward James. He tried to stop her, protesting that she must remember her rank. Catherine replied she wished to do out of affection what she was not obliged to do. This response delighted the duke. Catherine had made an excellent first impression.

Charles was delayed in greeting his new bride, detained in London with the business of parliament and with his mistress, Barbara Villiers, Countess of Castlemaine[145] and it would be a week before he arrived in Portsmouth. James visited Catherine on board the ship every day and it was the beginning of a long-standing friendship.[146] On 14 May, word of the fleet's appearance sailing up the Solent arrived. Catherine disembarked from the *Royal Charles* and James handed her from the barge to the steps to shore. Wearing English-style clothing, she seemed jubilant.

Her gilded state coach made its way through the streets of the town so the people could see her. It conveyed her to the residence of the Governor of Portsmouth, known as the King's House.[147] Catherine received her new ladies-in-waiting here and sat down to write a letter to Charles. The next day she asked her ladies to assist her in choosing the best clothes to please the king.[148] Catherine and Charles exchanged letters until his arrival in Portsmouth on 20 May.

Once Charles freed himself from his duties in London, he rode with all speed to Portsmouth. After Charles changed his clothes, the long-awaited meeting of the couple took place. Catherine had fallen ill with a cold and had a sore throat. Although recovered, she met Charles in her bed and the meeting went well. Catherine fell deeply in love with Charles. Even though she was not feeling her best, her kindness and graciousness impressed the king. Charles wrote to Clarendon, saying of Catherine that although she was not a beauty, her eyes were excellent good and there was not anything in her face that in the least degree could shock anyone.[149]

Catherine felt well enough for the marriage to take place the next day. She insisted on a Catholic ceremony and Charles consented.[150] Her almoner, Lord d'Aubigny, who was a secular priest, performed this secret Catholic service in her bedchamber to the satisfaction of Catherine. The only witnesses were the Marquis de Sande, three Portuguese nobles and a couple of Catherine's Portuguese women.[151] They kept the Lord Chancellor in the dark about this wedding as Clarendon, as well as the people of England, would object to a Catholic ceremony.

Catherine knew it was her duty to take part in a Protestant rite of marriage. The parish church of St Thomas's in Portsmouth, heavily damaged during the English Civil War, was considered unsuitable for a royal wedding. Preparations began for the ceremony in the governor's presence chamber of the King's House.[152] In the afternoon, Charles led Catherine by the hand into the chamber where they sat on a throne with two seats under a canopy.

Sir John Nicholas, Secretary of State, read the marriage contract aloud. Afterwards, Charles took Catherine by the hand and Gilbert Sheldon, Bishop of

London, began the Church of England marriage service. Charles pledged his troth and Catherine gave her consent. The bishop made the declaration of marriage and pronounced them man and wife.[153] Charles took Catherine by the hand and led her to his apartments. All her ladies and the leading people of the court assembled in the room to kiss Catherine's hand and offer congratulations.

The bride and groom signed the wedding register, written in letters of gold on a vellum page. It reads:

> Our most gracious sovereign lord, Charles II, by the grace of God, king of Great Britain, etc., and the most illustrious princess donna Catherina, infanta of Portugal, daughter to the deceased don Juan, king of Portugal, were married at Portsmouth upon Thursday the 22 May 1662, being the fourteenth year of His Majesty's reign, by the right reverend father in God Gilbert, lord Bishop of London, dean of His Majesty's chapel-royal, in presence of several of the nobility of his Majesty's dominions and Portugal.[154]

On 23 May, Charles wrote to Catherine's mother:

> Being now freed from the dread of the sea and enjoying in this springtime the company of my dearest wife, I am the happiest man in the world and the most enamoured, seeing close at hand the loveliness of her person and her virtues, not only those which Your Majesty mentioned in your letter – simplicity, gentleness and prudence – but many others also. These things oblige me to think of the interests and procure the tranquillity of her beloved country, as will be seen by my deeds and by the orders and powers which I give to my ambassador, whom, on arriving at Hampton Court, I shall dispatch to that of Portugal. And I wish to say of my wife that I cannot sufficiently either look at her or talk to her. May the good God preserve her to me and grant Your Majesty long years of life, in which to be a comfort to us both.[155]

Chapter Three

Married Life, Pregnancies and Troubles

The French Tradition of 'maîtresse en titre'

Catherine was about to come up against a century's old tradition of the French kings, a situation for which her sheltered upbringing initially made her ill-equipped to handle. In the mid-fifteenth century, the Valois French king, Charles VII, began a new trend by naming his voluptuous and stunningly beautiful mistress, Agnes Sorel, *maîtresse en titre* or 'titled mistress'. This gave Agnes a privileged public and quasi-official status, and the position would evolve down through the centuries.

The woman given this status received titles, castles, gifts, jewels, land and income. Some mistresses used the position to influence politics and some did not. She could act as a confidante to the king, helping, guiding and inspiring him. It was possible for the official mistress to serve on his council, go on diplomatic missions and dispense patronage by influencing the king.

The position of *maîtresse en titre* relegated the king's wife to bearing the king's heirs, educating her children, running her own royal household and taking part in designated rituals and ceremonies at court requiring the queen's involvement. Sometimes, the children of the king and queen and the illegitimate offspring of the mistress lived and grew up together. The queen and the mistress would mingle together in the same social network at court. There are some instances in history where the mistress had a position in the queen's household, obliging the queen to pay for her upkeep and forcing her to be in close contact with the mistress on a day-to-day basis.[1]

Following Agnes Sorel in the position we find Francoise de Foix, Madame de Chateaubriant, the first official mistress of King Francis I, who appropriated all of Queen Claude's official duties at court. Once out of favour, de Foix's replacement was Anne de Pisseleu d'Heilly, Duchess d'Étampes. King Henri II of France had one of the most famous titled mistresses, Diane de Poitiers, Duchess of Valentinois. Twenty years older than the king, de Poitiers wielded substantial power and influence at court.

When Charles VII appointed Agnes to the position of *maîtresse en titre*, writers usually commented on it as atypical. By the seventeenth century, they considered it a conventional practice. King Henri IV was so enamoured of his mistress, Gabrielle d'Estrées, he placed her and her sister on his council and relied on her advice in many areas of politics and government. The king would have married her had she not died giving birth to his child just a few days before the wedding. Henri IV's grandsons, Charles II of England and his cousin and contemporary, Louis XIV of France, would take this French tradition to new heights, to the detriment of their queens.

The Honeymoon

Catherine did not know what was in store for her right away. She had fallen in love with Charles and for a few short weeks, the king exhibited his best behaviour. They did not spend their first night as husband and wife together due to Catherine's illness and Charles' exhaustion, having slept very little the night before while travelling to Portsmouth. Also, as he wrote to his sister Henriette Anne, Catherine was in her menstrual cycle.[2]

The couple lingered in Portsmouth for a few days to allow Catherine to complete her recovery and for enough carriages to arrive to take the entire party to London. The king went hunting during the day and joined Catherine in the evenings. Catherine had brought with her from Portugal an undisclosed number of musicians and singers and they would play and sing. There were banquets and feasts, and Charles christened a new ship *Catherine*. The Earl of Manchester received orders to entertain the Portuguese retinue lavishly. Charles focused his attention on Catherine, determined to be a loyal and faithful husband.[3]

Catherine's lord chamberlain, Philip Stanhope, second Earl of Chesterfield, wrote to a friend of his impressions of the new queen. He stated: 'Now as for the queen, of whom I know you desire the description, you may credit her being a very extraordinary woman; that is, extremely devout, extremely discreet, very fond of her husband, and the owner of a good understanding. As to her person, she is exactly shaped, and has lovely hands, excellent eyes, a good countenance, a pleasing voice, fine hair, and, in a word, is what an understanding man would wish a wife'. He expressed his doubts that Charles would return her affection.[4]

On 27 May the king and queen left Portsmouth to make their way to Hampton Court Palace. Crowds gathered to see them pass as they spent the first night in Guildford and the second night at Windsor Castle. They arrived at Hampton Court late at night. Staged celebrations began commemorating Charles' birthday and the anniversary of his restoration to the throne. Many people gathered to greet the new queen and ceremonial introductions took place. Those who congratulated her and kissed her hand included the Lord Chancellor, Edward Hyde, Earl of Clarendon, judges, counsellors of state, foreign ministers, many of the nobility, gentry and ladies of the court.

Next up was an audience with her sister-in-law, Anne Hyde, Duchess of York and then more courtiers such as the Duke and Duchess of Ormonde, the diarist John Evelyn, the Lord Mayor and the aldermen of London. Everyone watched Catherine closely, commenting on every little detail. They observed her at dinner and were amazed she used a fork.[5] While dining in public the first evening, the hall became so crowded and hot, Catherine hurriedly left the room as her makeup began to run off her face with sweat.[6]

Also noticed were her Indian cabinets. John Evelyn notes in his diary entry for 9 June 1662 'the Queen had brought over with her from Portugal such Indian cabinets as had never before been seen here'.[7] The cabinets were curiously inlaid with ebony, mother-of-pearl, ivory and silver. Besides the cabinets, Catherine displayed lacquer chairs and various intriguing pieces of decorative porcelain.[8] Eventually, her introduction of these novelties would spread throughout the court and then into English society. (See Chapter 8.)

After living with the stifling Portuguese etiquette guided by its moral and religious principles, the gaiety, splendour and decadent atmosphere of the Stuart court seemed to overwhelm Catherine. She simply lacked the appropriate behaviour necessary to handle the painful change required for her to engage and take part. Her Portuguese retinue did not help the situation, objecting to any manifestation of her behaviour they considered as flouting proper Portuguese decorum.[9] The only mechanism available to her allowing her to cope involved retreating to her chapel in devotion and prayer.

Catherine received a cool reception by the English courtiers. She was Catholic and her behaviour did not add to the radiance of the court. The French count, de Grammont commented 'The new Queen gave but little additional brilliancy to the court, either in her person or in her retinue' however, he noted 'in the end, she was pretty successful'.[10] Pepys says that although Catherine 'be not very charming, yet she hath a good, modest and innocent look which is pleasing'.[11]

This aspect of Catherine's image rarely appeared at the Restoration court and seems to have been one of the principal features that attracted Charles to Catherine. Sir John Leeke's daughter Dorothy, a relation of the Verney family of Buckinghamshire, confirmed this look. She wrote to one of her Verney cousins: 'My sister says the queen is very handsome, and I hear very strict in her carriage, and all that is with her modest and reserved. I hope it will work upon some of our wild ladys to make them more grave'.[12] Dorothy's hope was not to be realised.[13]

The Marquis de Sande had to persuade Catherine to accept the customs of her newly adopted country, asking her to spend less time in her chapel and more time mingling with the courtiers. Another part of the equation had to do with the language barrier. Catherine received tutoring in English by Father Russell, but either he did not do a proper job or Catherine had difficulty learning the language, or a combination of both. It took some time for her to understand and get comfortable speaking English. But Pepys notes in his diary on 1 January 1664, she now 'spoke very pretty English' and by the end of 1663, was prone to coining quaint alien phrases to the amusement of her hearers.[14]

Both the king and queen lived their lives out in the open compelling Catherine to tolerate being under prying eyes all day long, with every move and gesture exposed to interpretation by the gossips at court. It took her some time to be at ease with the free and intimate manners of her adopted home. Pepys believed she had 'spirit enough' and noted she ignored Charles' irregular little pleasures: 'seeing that she do no good by taking notice'.[15] The Count de Grammont described her as 'a woman of sense, who used all her endeavours to please the king, by that king obliging behaviour which her affection made natural to her…'.[16]

Catherine had the wherewithal to realise she needed to change her behaviour. For the first six weeks of the marriage, Charles continued to be courteous and attentive towards her. Catherine found she enjoyed his company and accompanied him during the evening to balls, concerts and plays. She actively took part in walks through the gardens and parks next to Hampton Court and enjoyed boat trips down the Thames and observing the traditional English pastimes of cockfights and bear-baiting. During Charles' reign, festivities at court would begin on St Catherine's Day, the queen's birthday, and continue through the English winter until Charles' birthday on 29 May. Catherine gradually dropped her Portuguese inhibitions, adopted the manners and dress of the English women,[17] and joined in the animated activities of the court.

In the evening she played cards, a pastime in which she took great pleasure. Cards and dice were popular at court. The Venetian game of basset would customarily be played by ladies and gentlemen in masks to avoid being recognised and became a favourite form of gambling during the English Restoration era. While gambling was an aspect of basset, Catherine and Charles did not play for high stakes. She also played ombre, an intimate card game for three players, which she had learned in Portugal in her youth. When she was not playing cards, Catherine listened to music and attended the soirees held in the palace escorted by her husband. Unable to partner with Charles in dances just yet, she resolved to learn so she could take part.[18]

The Honeymoon Ends

Inevitably, Charles' respectable behaviour did not last long. Lady Castlemaine initially remained in the shadows, but she determined to regain her influence with the king and increased the pressure by upping the ante. Pregnant with Charles' child and now separated from her husband, Roger Palmer, Charles could not resist temptation and visited Castlemaine, spending his evenings at supper with her as he had done before his wedding.

It is unclear who informed Catherine of Castlemaine's identity as Charles' mistress. Perhaps her mother, politically astute and well-informed, told Catherine about her before she left Portugal. Or maybe the Portuguese ambassador or someone in Catherine's Lisbon entourage let her know. It is also entirely possible Catherine had observed Charles' behaviour and knew exactly what was going on, just as Pepys had observed in his diary.

It did not take long before the strain of her journey, the gloomy weather and her efforts to adapt to her new surroundings finally took their toll. She became ill and the Venetian ambassador says she took to her bed. He also noted how disgusted she was by the court, that she was accosted by too many people, unable to get used to the food and refused to drink anything but water, which was not a healthy thing to do in England.[19] Catherine had also been told Castlemaine had given birth to a son on 18 June.

Catherine recovered from her illness and returned to enjoy the pleasures of the court. But her situation deteriorated once again when, as a part of her campaign, Castlemaine insisted on being given an appointment in the queen's household. Charles consented to her request. Long-held tradition established that it was entirely up to the queen to appoint whomever she wished to these positions. Charles presented a list of suggestions to her with Castlemaine's name given, probably presuming Catherine did not know who she was. But by now, she knew full well about her and she crossed his mistress' name off the list.

Her stance in the matter both surprised and offended the king. He furiously demanded an explanation. To convince her to change her mind, he stated he had ended the affair and offered Castlemaine the position as a favour to her family for services rendered to the Crown. It stunned Catherine he would even suggest placing his whore in her household and she truly believed the idea was an egregious insult. Being accustomed to having her way since childhood, she would not back down. Charles found Catherine's obstinance shocking. He promised to have nothing more to do with Castlemaine and agreed for the moment.

Catherine had grown accustomed to the king bringing courtiers to her for an introduction. In July, Charles entered her apartments with a woman on his arm and presented her to the queen. Because of the shakiness of Catherine's English, she had trouble understanding the woman's name but proceeded to greet her according to custom. When she eventually realised it was the infamous Lady Castlemaine, Catherine became hysterical, grew pale and dissolved into tears with blood streaming from her nose. She then fainted and had to be carried away.

It astounded the entire court. Catherine's reaction embarrassed Charles and he angrily let her know. He intimated the only way Catherine could repair the situation was to admit Castlemaine into her household as one of her ladies of the bedchamber. He promised he had not engaged in sexual relations with Castlemaine since the day of his wedding and he would be entirely faithful to her. Catherine adamantly refused.

Catherine withdrew from court, the honeymoon being over. The Earl of Clarendon was the only one to stand up and defend the queen and Charles requested his intervention. Clarendon's first meeting resulted in Catherine tearfully breaking down. During a second meeting, Clarendon seemed more amiable, and Catherine agreed to be dutiful and pleaded with Clarendon for his help. But Clarendon said the king would not back down. She must take Lady Castlemaine into her household. Catherine declined and, to Clarendon's amazement, threatened to return to Lisbon.

After Clarendon relayed the details of their conversation to the king, Charles went to Catherine's rooms and there was a vociferous royal row in Spanish. Catherine repeated her threat to go back to Portugal. The entire court heard the fight and the couple did not speak to each other for several days. Clarendon persisted and tried again with Catherine, but she remained steadfast.

Charles' favourite younger sister, Henriette Anne, whom he called by the pet name of Minette, wrote to him from France where she lived with their mother, admonishing him for his behaviour. In her letter she said: 'But to speak seriously, I beg you to tell me how the Queen has taken this. Here people say that she is in the deepest distress and to speak frankly I think she has only too good reason for her grief'.[20]

Despite the reprimand from his sister, Charles had no intention of backing down. He criticised Catherine about the payment of her dowry being in arrears and short of the agreed amount. He insulted the Marquis de Sande and threw in prison the man responsible for selling the merchandise that comprised the Portuguese dowry, Duarte da Silva, the queen's financier.[21] In addition, he now threatened to dismiss all of Catherine's Portuguese servants.

Catherine's Aquatic State Entry into London

Catherine received a temporary reprieve from this intense state of affairs when, on 8 August, the dowager queen, Henrietta Maria, arrived from Paris to meet her new daughter-in-law. Catherine and Charles put aside their differences to present a genial face before the queen mother at Greenwich. In her entourage, she brought James Crofts, the king's eldest illegitimate son by his mistress, Lucy Walter, with whom he had an affair while in exile on the Continent.

Catherine tried to kneel and kiss the dowager queen's hand, but Henrietta Maria would not allow it. She eagerly greeted Catherine, took her in her arms and kissed her. She blessed Catherine, embraced her and held her hand frequently during her visit, remarking on her beauty in front of others.[22] Henrietta Maria promised to be her ally. Charles would be on his best behaviour during his mother's entire visit.

The dowager queen's residence in London, Somerset House, was under renovation, so she lodged at Hampton Court until the completion of construction. On 11 August, Henrietta Maria arrived there and Charles led Catherine by the hand to greet her. Catherine welcomed her warmly with open arms. The two queens and the Duchess of York all sat under a magnificent canopy. Charles and the Duke of York remained standing and interpreted the conversation for the women. Henrietta Maria spoke no Spanish or Portuguese, and Catherine spoke no French and little English.

After dinner, the family went to Catherine's apartments and her musicians played for her mother-in-law. Henrietta Maria remained at Hampton Court for several weeks and the entire family got along well for the duration of the visit. The two queens spent much time in each other's company and shared their Catholic devotions.

Preparations were in the works for Catherine's state entry into London on 23 August. There would be no coronation for various reasons. Catherine was Catholic and would not take part in a Protestant service. The Braganza family, as we have seen, made the deliberate decision to have no coronations, and Europe had not yet fully recognised the new Portuguese dynasty as legitimate. In addition, King Charles eschewed large public ceremonies related to his marriage.[23] In contrast with the lavish ceremonials staged in Lisbon to celebrate the conclusion of the marriage treaty and Catherine's departure for England, the hastily put together London pageant lacked spectacle.

On the day of the celebrations, the king and queen, accompanied by the Duke and Duchess of York, the Countess of Suffolk, Charles' cousins, Prince Rupert and his brother Prince Edward, departed Hampton Court aboard a gilded brig at 2 o'clock in the afternoon. The ladies of the queen's bedchamber, the lord steward and the lords of the king's household followed in more brigs and an immense crowd watched the procession from the banks of the Thames. Eight miles from London the king and queen left the brig and boarded a larger and more opulent river-going vessel having glass windows and a red and gold canopy, which took them to Putney, three miles from London, where they transferred to the royal state barge. This impressive vessel had been decorated with the royal arms and a cloth of gold canopy and was propelled by twenty-four oarsmen, all clad in scarlet.

John Tatham, a dramatist and poet of the City of London, created and designed the pageantry which he titled the *Aqua Triumphalis*. He had staged earlier events for the Lord Mayor of London and had presented a pageant in July 1660 to celebrate the restoration of King Charles.[24] His restrained creation for this occasion visually lacked focus on the king and queen. The Lord Mayor had directed the livery companies to create some kind of pageantry relating to their own significance and mystery (referring to their trade or occupation).[25]

The aldermen made the deliberate decision to celebrate their occupations rather than the monarchy or the marriage, largely because of political circumstances and attitudes. The City guild companies did not show a willingness to spend much of their money for sumptuous public display. Besides the funds provided by individual companies, the City spent more than five hundred pounds for the pageant. They also gave Catherine a little over twelve hundred pounds.[26]

Despite this, the splendour of the occasion was clear from eyewitness accounts and based on the engravings of the artist Dirck Stoop.[27] According to these visual documents, they decorated vessels in the aquatic pageant like Roman temples. The royal barge, positioned in the centre of the back row, was not the grandest of the vessels.

There were some visual elements alluding to the Anglo-Portuguese alliance, including banners or shields with the arms of England and Portugal on them, and a motto referring to Portugal's colonial empire. On the Merchant Tailors' entry for the pageant, there were several figures in Indian dress.[28] Other guild barges bore huge carved and gilded figures, emblematic of their liveries. There were thrones, arches and 'inventions'. Music could be heard from the water and on the shore. There were peals of ordnance from the Tower and the ships while the people gave shouts and acclamations.[29]

John Evelyn describes the event in his diary. 'I was spectator of the most magnificent triumph that ever floated on the Thames, considering the innumerable boats and vessels, dressed and adorned with all imaginable pomp, but, above all, the thrones, arches, pageants, and other representations, stately barges of the Lord Mayor and Companies, with various inventions, music and peals of ordnance both from the vessels and the shore, going to meet and conduct the new Queen from Hampton Court to Whitehall, at the first time of her coming to town. In my opinion, it far exceeded all the Venetian Bucentoras, &c, on the Ascension, when they go to espouse the Adriatic. His Majesty and the Queen came in an antique-shaped open vessel, covered with a state canopy, of cloth of gold, made in form of a cupola, supported with high Corinthian pillars, wreathed with flowers, festoons and garlands. I was in our new-built vessel, sailing amongst them'.[30]

Pepys also witnessed the event. 'I offered eight shillings for a boat to attend me this afternoon, and they would not, it being the day of the Queen's coming to town from Hampton Court. So we fairly walked it to Whitehall, and through my Lord's lodgings we got into Whitehall garden, and so to the Bowling Green, and up to the top of the new Banqueting House there, over the Thames, which was a most pleasant place as any I could have got; and all the show consisted chiefly in the number of boats and barges: and two pageants, one of a King, and another of a Queen, with her Maids of Honour sitting at her feet very prettily: and they tell me the Queen is Sir Richard Ford's daughter. Anon came the King and Queen in a barge, under a canopy, with ten thousand barges and boats I know, for we could see no water for them, nor discern the King nor Queen. And so, they landed at Whitehall Bridge, and the great guns on the other side went off. But that which pleased me best was that my Lady Castlemaine stood over against us upon a piece of Whitehall. But methought it was strange to see her Lord [her husband] and her upon the same place walking up and down without taking notice one of another...'[31]

Even Lady Castlemaine inserted herself into the spectacle. Besides the *Aqua Triumphalis*, they popularised the royal marriage with the production of decorative objects, such as plates, embroidered boxes, designs on paper and other handcrafted items with depictions of Catherine and Charles. This is the first instance of a royal marriage being marketed for public consumption.[32] Later that night, the festivities ended with fireworks and bonfires.

The Crisis Resumes and Catherine Makes a Resolution

Catherine moved into her apartments at Whitehall and Castlemaine was back at court. Item seven of the marriage treaty required that Catherine and her whole family [household] 'shall enjoy the free exercise of the Roman Catholic religion, and to that purpose shall have a chapel, or some other place set apart for the exercise thereof, in all the royal palaces where she shall at any time reside, in as full a manner, to all intents and purposes, as the Queen mother now living enjoyed the same, and shall have such chaplains and ecclesiastical persons in number and quality about her, as the said Queen mother hath had, with the same privileges and immunities'. The chapel at St James Palace, which had been used by Henrietta Maria, had been dismantled after the death of King Charles I. Charles ordered the reconditioning of the chapel as soon as they proposed the Portuguese marriage.[33]

When Catherine first arrived in England, she most likely had a private oratory at Hampton Court Palace. Once the repairs were finished at St James, Pepys gives us a description of Catherine's first visit. 'To the parke; the Lord's Day. The Queen coming by in her coach going to her chapel at St James's (the first time that it hath been ready for her), I crowded after her, and I got up to the room where her closet is, and there stood and saw the fine altar, ornaments, and the fryers in their habits, and the priests come in with their fine crosses, and many other fine things. I heard their musique, too, which may be good, but it did not appear so to me, neither as to their manner of singing, nor was it good concord to my ears, whatever the matter was. The Queen very devout; but what pleased me best was to see my dear Lady Castlemaine, who, tho' a Protestant, did wait upon the Queen to chapel. By and by, after masse was done, a fryer with his cowl did rise up and preach a sermon in Portuguese, which I not understanding, did go away, and to the King's Chapel, but that was done; and so up to the Queen's presence-chamber, where she and the King were expected to dine; but she staying at St James', they were forced to remove the things to the King's presence, and there he dined alone'.[34]

By now, Charles had given the order to dismiss Catherine's Portuguese entourage. He offered no explanation to her brother, the king of Portugal. Catherine implored Charles to allow her to keep a few servants.[35] Charles agreed. The sister of the Marquis de Sande, Mary Drago of Portugal, the Countess of Penalva, was elderly and blind and allowed to stay, along with some of Catherine's kitchen staff, and the priests of the queen's chapel who were also musicians. In response, Catherine sought refuge in the Catholic chapel at Somerset House.

Lady Castlemaine ruled at court as the official *maîtresse en titre,* living in rooms at Whitehall. The king dined with her regularly. Castlemaine would visit Catherine every day, entering her bedchamber and carriage, following her to the chapel and patiently listening to long sermons in Portuguese, as Pepys had witnessed. She did all this, although she had not yet received a position in the queen's household in any sanctioned or official capacity. Charles no longer slept with Catherine and the court left her alone with the Countess of Penalva and her much reduced staff, shunned and locked out of court life. Courtiers were completely disregarding Catherine, recognising she had no influence.

Instead of having some sympathy for a young woman ill-equipped in the ways of the world and plunged into an alien domain, the king backed her into a corner, isolating her from court and depriving her of her entourage and her support system. The unrecognised Braganza dynasty made it impossible for her to seek diplomatic aid. But Catherine was very clever. Her travails had allowed her to realise her own innate dignity, pleasing personality, and fun-loving nature.

Catherine realised Charles preferred his mistress over herself and the queen mother appears to have convinced her to accept the inevitable as well. Her instinct for self-preservation forced her to deal with Castlemaine and Charles' son, James Crofts, who was turning out to be a thorn in her side. One day, as Castlemaine arrived in her chambers, Catherine publicly acknowledged her, and in the future, she tolerated the mistress, taking solace in always knowing she was the queen and Castlemaine the servant.[36]

From this point forward, she started an agenda of reinserting herself into the amusements of the court to regain her husband's favour and esteem all over again. During the first eight months of their marriage, Charles had advised Catherine 'to follow the Queen Mother of France's example and go in masquerade before the carnival be done'.[37] Henrietta Maria had been an avid actor and dancer, taking part in masques during the reign of her husband.[38] Catherine followed his advice and made a resolution to join in the entertainments, balls and masquerades which Charles obviously relished.

While Catherine's mother-in-law was ensconced in Somerset House, she held drawing room gatherings called 'circles' in the evenings, reviving a tradition from the days of her husband's reign.[39] Catherine would attend these gatherings and the one on 7 September 1662 was witnessed by Samuel Pepys, who observed the entire royal family. Rumours were flying around that Catherine was pregnant. During this familial scene, Charles told his mother Catherine was with child. Catherine replied, 'You lie!', much to Charles' amusement.[40]

Catherine remained at odds with Charles over the Castlemaine affair but by the end of 1662, she began to imitate Henrietta Maria by staging her own 'circles'. In the beginning these events were sparse in attendance as Catherine was still being shunned by the court and had little influence. Her gatherings were not as convivial as her mother-in-law's were as she probably adhered to the habitual sombre Portuguese etiquette.

As Catherine became more relaxed, attendance improved and after Henrietta Maria departed for France, and as Catherine regained influence over her husband and with courtiers, her circles would begin to sparkle and vibrate. The queen's circles were confirmed as the principal court meeting place for courtiers, visitors and members of the royal family.[41] The meetings were initially held in Catherine's presence chamber at Whitehall.

This chamber imposed a certain formality as Catherine sat on a throne on a raised platform under a velvet canopy of state embroidered with the royal arms. Sometime later, about 1664, Catherine moved the circle to the more informal withdrawing room. The Lord Chamberlain supervised the presence chamber, used for the most ceremonious audiences. The withdrawing room, considered a private room, was overseen by her mistress of the robes. As long as Catherine was at court for the rest of the reign, these evening circles in the royal 'drawing room' would remain the key social event at the English court well into the twentieth century and Catherine presided almost daily over the most important and well-attended social assembly in England.[42]

Within a few years, the French ambassador reported to Louis XIV that no self-respecting member of the court ever missed an evening in Catherine's circle. Members of society, from the private gentleman to public ministers congregated in her drawing room. The meeting started around the end of the day and lasted until 8 o'clock in the evening when people departed for supper. The room itself faced the terrace overlooking the Thames and people would move out onto the terrace on warm summer evenings. There were curtains on the windows and tapestries on the walls with very little furniture, until tables and stools were brought in to play cards.

Visitors would be ushered into the room before the queen seated on her chair at the wall, and they would stand in a circle in front of her. As new people entered and bowed to the queen, she would acknowledge them with anything from a frosty nod to a warm embrace.[43] Usually, well over 100 people would attend from all walks of life. It was common for the king and the Duke of York to frequently drop in during the course of the evening. Catherine's ladies, including the maids of honour, along with noblewomen and unmarried beauties could be seen attending.

Noblemen, such as the Duke of Buckingham or Monmouth, and men of business, like the Earl of Sandwich, vice admiral of England, would appear along with foreign diplomats and dignitaries from overseas. Any ladies and gentlemen who looked respectable would gain entry, with no invitation required. In fact, the circle was one of the few royal events where men and women could mingle freely.

Lively discussion would ensue, with rumour and news mixing with court gossip. Along with sensational topics, serious information could pass between attendees, relating to politics, diplomacy and international relations.[44] Business, as well as affairs of state, could be discussed with informality here, with a great deal of discretion. The king or the Duke of York could pull someone aside into a quiet alcove and have a word about politics or patronage.

In addition to being a forum for social and political conversation, these circles served as useful ceremonial and symbolic purposes. People used them for public demonstrations of loyalty, favour and inclusion, to show respect to their majesties and their royal highnesses.[45] In turn, they allowed the royal family to demonstrate publicly whom they favoured and shunned.

The primary reason people came to these circles was easy access to the king. They were a respectable court gathering at which the most reputable person could appear but one that gave Charles greater freedom than he had in his own apartments. Since Catherine hosted, those duties were left up to her and he could wander in at any time and mingle freely, tell amusing stories, whisper promises to aspiring courtiers or have political discussions in a window embrasure.[46]

Catherine began staging theatricals of her own. There is evidence in the Lord Chamberlain's records of livery orders for 'the Queenes Comoedians' and for specifically named actors. These records begin in December 1661 and appear intermittently until 1669.[47] Clearly Catherine patronised her own troupe of players early in her marriage.[48] The queen's apartments included at least one room large enough for private theatricals.[49]

Her presence chamber regularly appears to have been used for the queen's music, with records showing music seats being borrowed from the Hall Theatre.[50] In October 1662, the Clerk of the Works noted the building of a stage in the queen's guard chamber (presence chamber) along with an elevated dais for the king and queen to sit on. This may have been for the puppet show Pepys reports he viewed at Whitehall.[51]

They celebrated her birthday in November with many outstanding festivities. Charles opened a ball held at Whitehall on New Year's Eve dancing a *branle*, partnered with the Duchess of York. Catherine did not know the dances such as the *coranto* and *branle,* but after this she pledged she would learn them so she could take part in the future. Castlemaine would outshine all the beauties at court during these days, wearing more brilliant diamonds and jewels than even the queen.

Relations Between the King and Queen Improve and Charles Takes on New Mistresses

Shortly after Charles' restoration to the throne, he appointed a new dancing master, a Frenchman named Jerome Francis Gohory (Gehors). In the summer of 1663, the king appointed Gohory to the position of groom of the queen's privy chamber.[52] He may have given Catherine dancing lessons before this appointment because John Evelyn notes he witnessed the king and queen dancing at a court ball on 5 February 1663.[53]

On 11 May 1663, the French visitor, Balthasar de Monconys, wrote of the queen's 'petit bal en privé' at which 'L'on commença le bal par un branle comme en France, & ensuite l'on dança des courantes & d'autres danses; le Duc d'York commença avec la Reyne' adding 'Quand elle ou le Roy dansoient, toutes les Dames demeuroient debout'.[54] [Translation: 'little ball in private' during which 'We started the ball with a *branle* as in France, & then we danced the *corante* & other dances; the Duke of York began with the Queen'. 'When she (the Queen) or the King danced, all the Ladies remained standing'.]

Presumably, Catherine took her lessons from Gohory, and she had obviously learned both the steps and the etiquette of the court ball quickly.[55] She learned to dance to please her husband and discovered she loved it. Charles wrote to Minette: 'My wife hath given a good introduction to such a business for the other day she made … her chaplains dance country dances in her bedchamber'.[56]

Despite all of Catherine's efforts, Charles continued dining with Castlemaine and there was a distance between them. Castlemaine invited the charming Frances Stewart to one of her dinners with the king. Stewart arrived in England from France in the queen mother's entourage, and Charles was very taken with her.

In February 1663, Charles resolved to elevate his son Crofts to the title of Duke of Monmouth. Catherine was fond of Crofts, but she objected to his elevation to the peerage as she hoped to provide the king with an heir herself, and she viewed his elevation to the title as being just short of legitimising him as his successor. She voiced her objections to Charles in anger, but she resigned herself to the fact that fits of passion were not working to her advantage.

In April, the Duke of Monmouth married Anne Scott, daughter of Francis Scott, Earl of Buccleuch. After his marriage, they would call Crofts by the name of James Scott. Catherine appointed the new duchess to a position as one of her ladies of the bedchamber. Three days after the wedding, a magnificent ball took place at Windsor attended by the entire court. Catherine opened the ball, dancing with the Duke of Monmouth, followed by a dance with Charles.

The House of Lords accused Lord Chancellor Clarendon of high treason during this time. One charge against him related to his support of the marriage of the king and queen. Several lords in parliament alleged that because the queen had not spoken the customary marriage vows during the public Church of England ceremony, the marriage was invalid. They also implied they knew the king had married in the Catholic Church, which was illegal in England.

The Earl of Bristol tried to implicate Clarendon in some correspondence Catherine had entered into with Rome, allegedly intending to spread her religion in England. Catherine, with the sanction of the king, wrote letters to Pope Alexander VII and Cardinals Orsini and Baroorin in October 1662. In these letters, she requested 'prayers for the kingdom I have entered' but there is no mention of converting England to Catholicism.[57] The letters clearly show she sought the Pope's recognition of Portuguese independence from Spain.[58]

The Earl of Bristol pressed the issue even further by sending two priests to Lisbon to determine if any evidence existed of the queen's infertility. When Charles found out about it, he had the priests arrested upon their return to England. The king sent Bristol into exile while threatening him with more severe punishment. Judges deliberated over the evidence regarding Clarendon's alleged crimes and determined they did not amount to treason.

The Opening of the Restoration Theatres with Female Actors

After his restoration to the throne of England, Charles brought with him a love of drama and literature. The theatre would become a particular hobby for him.[59] In July 1660, Thomas Killigrew, who had been in exile with the king, used his influence to get a royal warrant giving him permission to set up a playhouse and presenting him with a theatre monopoly in London along with Sir William D'Avenant, an established theatre impresario since the reign of the king's father. D'Avenant already held a patent issued for a theatre in 1639, but Killigrew wanted in on the action.[60]

In a petition addressed to the king dated October 1660, a troupe of players mention they had come to an agreement with Killigrew to act under his management along with women.[61] It was customary for men or young boys to play women's roles during the Elizabethan and Jacobean eras. Some women appeared on the stage during Charles I's reign and also during the Commonwealth of Oliver Cromwell, even though the Puritan Protector banned theatricals. Commercial theatre never regularly employed women in any capacity until the Restoration.[62]

Two licensed theatres opened. Killigrew oversaw the Theatre Royal, patronised by the king, and D'Avenant opened the Duke's Theatre, patronised by the Duke of York. Charles was the first English sovereign to attend in any frequency a public playhouse, with his first appearance occurring at the opening of the Duke's Theatre on 28 June 1661. Charles had a private playhouse at Whitehall, but his primary interest was in the public theatres.[63]

It would be two more years before King Charles II issued a patent to Killigrew in which he stated 'and we do likewise permit and give leave that all the women's parts to be acted in either of the said two companies for the time to come may be performed by women'.[64] Charles had witnessed women on the stage many times during his exile on the Continent.[65] Regardless of when the first actress actually appeared, the fact remains that from the construction of the first theatres of D'Avenant and Killigrew, we find female actors were immediately and fully established on the stage and the boy actors had vanished.[66]

On 20 December 1661, Killigrew took a lease on a plot of land between Drury Lane and Bridges Street and opened a new theatre.[67] In the spring of 1663, the King's Company opened the new playhouse which later became the Theatre Royal. The theatre now offered evening entertainments and the king first viewed the actresses Nell Gwyn and Moll Davis, both of whom would later become his mistresses.

Efforts to Become Pregnant and Catherine's Near-Fatal Illness

Charles realised he needed to have an heir. Her doctors advised Catherine to take the waters at Tunbridge Wells to facilitate conception and she dispatched her officials to the Chancellor of the Exchequer to obtain the funds for her journey. They were told her £40,000 annual pension had already been paid out.

It incensed Catherine that she had been credited with a sum she had never received. She immediately notified the parliamentary commission they had only given her £4000, all of which she had spent on maintaining her household since her arrival in England. Her musicians, servants and laundresses' salaries were in arrears, and she was down to only six uniforms for her eight pageboys.

In early June 1663, news arrived in England of the Portuguese victory at the Battle of Ameixial [Battle of Estramoz in Spain]. The Portuguese had won with the help of 2000 English troops. Catherine's brother, King Afonso VI, had no money and compensated the English army with snuff. Catherine agreed to surrender her funds and Charles agreed to send her £40,000 to help pay the troops, which pleased Catherine and considerably improved the harmony in their relationship. They appeared in public more frequently.

Catherine visibly seemed more relaxed. At a parade in Hyde Park, Catherine and her mother-in-law witnessed the king inspecting the Royal Guards. Pepys noted in his diary in July Catherine was looking 'very pretty'[68] and in August Catherine appeared 'very debonair'.[69] The king and queen rode in a carriage in Hyde Park, hand in hand. She wore her hair loose and dressed more fashionably. Castlemaine's influence appeared on the wane as Catherine garnered more respect at court.

Despite Catherine's good fortune, Charles became more obsessed with Frances Stewart. Catherine knew about her, but interestingly, Stewart held out and did not allow the king to have sexual relations with her, driving Charles to distraction. Castlemaine exhibited more concern about Charles' interest in Stewart than Catherine. The queen's only mission was to stay healthy, get pregnant, and carry the child to full term. The money for her trip finally arranged, Catherine departed for Tunbridge Wells with Charles and most of the court.

They stayed for a month. All during the summer, the Duke of Buckingham and the Earl of Bristol plotted the impeachment of the Earl of Clarendon in the House of Lords once again. News of Catherine and Charles' secret Catholic wedding had leaked to the public and one article of impeachment once again included an attack on this marriage ceremony. Charles had Buckingham, Bristol and Sir Henry Bennet, Earl of Arlington, banned from court and ordered the Lords to toss out the impeachment suit. Charles stated whether they had a private wedding ceremony should concern no one as he considered his marriage a private affair. He adamantly considered the public Church of England ceremony more than sufficient, swearing Catherine was his lawful wife.

Catherine failed to get pregnant after the course of her water treatments. Her physicians advised her to go to Bourbon in France, but such an arduous and expensive trip in her condition was out of the question. On the advice of Alexander Frazier, royal physician to King Charles, Catherine went to Bath instead. Frazier's wife worked as a dresser for the queen from 1662 and her daughter, Carey Frazier Mourdaunt, worked as one of Catherine's maids of honour.[70] The court moved to Bath and Catherine stayed in the house of Dr Pierce, who was treating her. Dr Pierce was a great friend of the diarist, Samuel Pepys, and the source of much of the information, which he recorded in his journal, about Catherine and her health.

Catherine and Charles made an official visit to Bristol accompanied by the Duke and Duchess of York, the Duke of Monmouth, Prince Rupert and other courtiers. The City greeted them with impressive ceremony and outstanding entertainments. One evening, Charles knighted four gentlemen, and the town presented Catherine with a purse containing thirty pieces of gold, which went a long way in relieving her financial difficulties.

Catherine still had not conceived when the court returned to Whitehall. To make matters worse, she succumbed to a virulent fever around the middle of October and a rumour circulated she had died.[71] Pepys heard she had a 'spotted fever'[72] which could have been measles or chicken pox. The Marquis de Sande spent many hours sitting near the queen and he witnessed Charles' tenderness towards Catherine.[73] The king stayed by her side for the duration of her illness and visibly wept, although he continued to dine with Castlemaine every night and persisted in pursuing Frances Stewart.

Despite enduring every remedy prescribed by the doctors, Catherine became delirious. At one point she expected to die and told Charles 'she willingly left all the world but him'.[74] She requested her remains be sent back to Portugal and buried in the Braganza family crypt and said farewell to her husband, pleading with Charles to continue his support of Portugal in the country's fight for independence from Spain. She then received the last rites of the Catholic Church.[75]

In her distress, Catherine talked of children. She believed she had given birth to an ugly son. Charles assured her the boy was beautiful. At another point in her illness, she believed she had three children and her daughter resembled Charles. When the doctor woke her up to take her tonic, she asked him how the children were.

By the beginning of November her health improved. Pepys mentions she recovered because of a cordial concocted by Sir Francis Prujean, president of the College of Physicians, which allowed her to get the required rest she needed. It is mentioned by both Pepys in his diary and Charles in a letter to his sister, Minette, that the fever had abated, but Catherine remained weak and raved and talked nonsense.[76] He wrote again on 20 November to say Catherine mended slowly and was still so weak she could not stand upon her legs.[77]

During a meeting with the French ambassadors in her bedchamber, Charles had to repeat the conversations in her ear as Catherine experienced deafness from the fever. This finally subsided, and she regained her strength. By the end of November, she was well enough to attend chapel. Her birthday celebrations were more subdued than usual and in December, Charles wrote to Minette she was much better. They held a ball in her chamber and Charles asked Minette to send Catherine some images to add to her prayer book.[78]

By the beginning of 1664, while grateful Catherine had fully recovered from her near fatal illness, Charles was by now in hot pursuit of Frances Stewart. Castlemaine had fallen from favour and announced her conversion to Catholicism. Catherine did not believe for one moment Castlemaine did this for 'conscience sake'. Frances Stewart, having splendid rooms in Whitehall, was officially the latest *maîtresse en titre* and accorded the same respect previously given to Castlemaine.

Stewart held off on submitting to sexual relations, despite the furious pressure put upon her by the king. This forced Catherine to hesitate and have someone scout out her own chambers before she entered, fearing she would find Stewart and the king together or the king propositioning her ladies of the bedchamber.[79] Despite this state of affairs, Catherine tolerated Stewart, chiefly because she was Catholic and joined Catherine in her chapel for Mass. Frances had publicly prayed for Catherine's recovery during her illness. Frequently, after Sunday Mass, Catherine and Frances were seen walking in the park together.

Catherine enjoyed the company of her master of the horse, Edward Montagu, and several courtiers complained to Charles that Montagu was in love with Catherine and often touched her hand. In response, Charles had him sacked, which angered

Catherine. She refused to name anyone as a replacement to his post as long as Montagu was alive. Catherine was savvy enough to never jeopardise her position as queen by taking a lover. It is most likely Montagu served as a good friend to Catherine, and she would always remain loyal to those who were members of her service.

Catherine Gains Influence at Court

With her newfound confidence, Catherine gained traction in practising the duties of queenship. This manifested itself as religious, cultural and artistic patronage, actively promoting Catholic Baroque culture. It was about this time Catherine introduced to English ladies the fashion of utilising shading fans from the Iberian Peninsula to keep cool and preserve their pale complexions. These fans would replace the masks, customarily worn outdoors by English women. All the fashionable ladies at court were having themselves painted by the top portrait artist, Sir Peter Lely. Lely, née Pieter van der Faes, born to a Protestant Dutch family in 1618, had emigrated to England. By 1650, he had established the most prominent practice as a portrait painter in the kingdom.[80]

King Charles appointed Lely as his principal painter in October 1661 and granted him a pension of two hundred pounds. In the 1660s, Lely painted the beauties of the court, including the Duchess of York, Castlemaine, Frances Stewart and Charles' sister Minette, among others. It satisfied Catherine to have Lely paint her during this decade.[81] But by the 1670s, Catherine no longer sat for Lely and patronised the Catholic Flemish painter Jacob Huysmans.

Catherine, Castlemaine and Stewart all sat for portraits by Huysmans. In 1664 the clique surrounding the queen spread the report that Huysmans 'exceeded' Lely. The queen patronised Huysmans because of his Catholicism, but she may have wanted to distance herself from Lely who was the painter of choice of Castlemaine. Huysmans called himself the 'queen's painter'. He painted two striking portraits of Catherine between 1662 and 1664. The first depicted her as a shepherdess. References to love and fertility surround her image. Pepys viewed the painting in the artist's studio during a visit on 26 August 1664[82] and it endures as one of Huysmans most important portraits.

Sometime between 1664 and 1670, Huysmans portrayed the queen as St Catherine of Alexandria, with a martyr's palm in her right hand and her left resting upon the broken wheel upon which they had tortured the saint. The painting was a nod to Catherine's birthdate on the day of the feast of the saint. These portraits establish how she altered her Portuguese-influenced hairstyle of the curled foretop and the tight ringlets on the side of her head to the long flowing hair down to her shoulders.[83] Her pearl necklace appears in many of her portraits. Catherine also employed Huysmans in other ways. The art historian, Vertue, reports Huysmans most important work could be seen over the altar of Queen Catherine's chapel at St James', which he painted during the restoration of the building.

In 1665, Catherine ordered construction of an addition to the chapel called the 'Fryery' [Friary].[84] This religious house, built to the east of the chapel, included a large garden, refectory, dormitory, chapel, and library, with cells for the religious.[85] Completed in 1667, the community accommodated a Father Guardian and twelve friars[86] from Catherine's household from the order of St Peter of Alcantara, known as the 'Arabidoes'.[87]

A Spanish Franciscan friar, St Peter wanted to reform the order and live even more simply than the original monks surrounding St Francis. Peter of Alcantara had spent some time in Portugal before his death in 1562 and the Pope would canonise him in 1669. The monks who inhabited the Friary were open to criticism because of their lack of sophistication, but their simplicity may have been what appealed to the queen.[88] Samuel Pepys took a tour of the new buildings and found the rooms pretty with the windows giving a view of the garden.[89] The Friary no longer exists.

It was in Catherine's court that the English could learn Portuguese. Richard Stevens, the son of the page of the queen's bedchamber, John Stevens, would translate and publish several historical books about Portugal, including the works of Manuel de Faria y Sousa, allowing the English to learn more about the country. These publications would pave the way for the future Treaty of Methuen in 1703, which allowed for the consolidation of English trade with Portugal, especially for the wines imported from Douro, beginning in the 1660s.[90]

With her increased efforts in religious, cultural and artistic patronage, Catherine gained confidence and now felt more at liberty to indulge her interests in her adopted country's affairs. In March, the king and queen opened parliament. The king compelled Catherine to meet the Spanish ambassador. Portugal was still fighting for its independence from Spain and Catherine persisted in being obstinate. During the meeting, she refused to hear him address her in Spanish. The ambassador had every right to speak in his native tongue, but she forced him to speak to her in French and the episode nearly caused an unpleasant diplomatic incident.

Troubles with the Dutch and the Build-Up to War

The rivalry in trade at sea between England and Holland escalated. The Dutch, with their strong merchant navy, posed a threat to England's supremacy over America and the East. Charles passed a bill in parliament asserting only English ships could carry English goods, resulting in a direct threat to Dutch interests. In the build-up to war, the English shipyards were busy manufacturing new vessels.

The Earl of Sandwich received orders to take the navy to sea. Catherine, having grown up near Lisbon harbour, enthusiastically observed the preparation and the launching of the ships. She even presented a small frigate named *Hope* to the naval fleet. Charles was also passionate about nautical matters, so they could share this pursuit together. In July, Charles, Catherine and Henrietta Maria travelled to Gravesend and then Chatham to inspect the fleet and watch the navy sail to confront the Dutch.

In October, Catherine and the king went to Woolwich to a ship launch. She took the state barge while Charles and the Duke of York went by land. After lunch, Charles and his men sailed to the Nore, where the Thames meets the North Sea. While Catherine made her way back to Whitehall, the weather took a bad turn, and the waves rocked her barge so violently, her ladies became sick. Soaked to the bone, Catherine ordered the barge sail to Woolwich where she and her ladies boarded the king's coaches and made their way back to London, forcing the king to find another form of transport. Instead of being angry with Catherine, it amused Charles.

The relationship between the king and queen now stood on solid ground. The king enjoyed studying astronomy and engaged in scientific experiments in his own personal laboratory at Whitehall. Catherine took part in his scientific pursuits. At the end of the year, they saw a comet in the night sky. Charles was very curious about the phenomenon and Catherine joined him on several nights to observe the comet. In the spring of 1665, the plague appeared in London and the English declared war on the Dutch [second Anglo-Dutch War].

Catherine told Charles he could use her allowance to help fund the war. During the Battle of Lowestoft, a victory for the English, London heard gunfire from the encounter as the plague killed many during the summer. Henrietta Maria departed for France. Catherine and Charles went to Hampton Court to avoid the plague, but some servants succumbed to the disease and a reduced court moved to Salisbury. Charles went to inspect the navy at Portsmouth, and Catherine continued on, receiving a warm welcome. The Salisbury mayor presented her with two silver flagons and Catherine enjoyed her stay in the town immensely. The French ambassador remarked she hunted every day and played bowls in the evenings.[91]

Catherine's former master of the horse, Edward Montagu, died in battle and Catherine informed the chancellor she wished Charles to name his replacement. With their relationship going so well, Charles wanted to avoid any arguments and referred the choice back to Catherine. At an impasse, they both agreed Clarendon could act as arbiter and he appointed Edward Montagu's brother, Ralph, to the position to everyone's satisfaction.

Charles became ill with a 'collique'[92] which caused Catherine some anxiety. He soon recovered, and the court moved to Dorsetshire for a few days before he opened parliament in Oxford. Catherine lodged in Merton College while Charles tended to business. Much to her delight, Catherine discovered she was pregnant. With Charles attentive and loving, Catherine believed she would at last provide the king with an heir.

As winter arrived, the plague subsided, and the court prepared to return to London. Charles departed, leaving Catherine in Oxford for a few more weeks. As she prepared to travel to Hampton Court, she experienced a miscarriage, confirmed by her physician on 5 February 1666. At least Catherine knew she could get pregnant. Back at court, during the second week of February, Pepys observed Catherine at court, playing cards and looking very pretty and well.

Castlemaine had given birth to another child of the king. Charles had a cold and Catherine rebuked his mistress for keeping him up for all hours of the night. Castlemaine retorted Charles must have been with someone else because he left her house early. Charles overheard the exchange and, furious with Castlemaine for disrespecting the queen, ordered her to be banished from court. Disgruntled, Castlemaine threatened to publish the king's private letters. But they were soon reconciled.[93]

Queen Luisa, Catherine's mother, had died on 27 February, but the news did not reach London until the end of March. They did not inform Catherine right away to spare her feelings. Once she learned of the event, she was devastated and the entire English court went into mourning. In June, another pivotal naval battle resulted in a loss for the English, with many men dying. English ships were lost and captured and the English government had run out of funding for the war.

Catherine spent the summer taking the waters at Tunbridge Wells, trying to get pregnant. Charles was with her, but spent his time in pursuit of Frances Stewart. To entertain the court, Catherine sent to London for a theatre company to present some plays. Moll Davis and Nell Gwyn were among the troupe of actors.

The court returned to Whitehall at the end of the summer. By now, the plague and the war with the Dutch had crippled the entire country, ruined English trade, and put the nation on the verge of financial collapse. Charles sent his diplomat, Sir Robert Southwell, to Catherine's brother Afonso to ask for the rest of her dowry. Included in the exchange was a veiled threat: England would withdraw their protection from Portugal. But Afonso did not have the money, and they dropped the subject.[94]

The Great Fire of London and the Aftermath

In the early morning of 2 September, panicked cries of fire arose in London. The blaze had originated in a baker's shop in Pudding Lane and ran to the east, raging for three days and burning down everything in its path. The king and the Duke of York were highly visible, carrying water to put out the flames, surveying the damage and issuing orders, getting very little sleep or rest.

Old St Paul's Cathedral was damaged beyond repair. The roof melted with the heat of the flames and the lead dribbled down into the interior of the church and onto the streets.[95] The fire resulted in the destruction of many houses, churches and businesses. Catherine anxiously awaited news of the fire at Whitehall. On 5 September, as a precaution, the households of Catherine and the Duchess of York were preparing to leave Whitehall for Hampton Court Palace the next day, creating much confusion.[96]

By 6 September, the tamed fire had died down. Charles rode into a makeshift camp for the homeless at Moorfields to tell the people of London there was no foreign or Catholic plot to burn the city, strongly emphasising the fire was entirely an act of God. The government provided coal, bread and navy biscuit for the poor and the dispossessed.

The king issued orders for the rebuilding of London. Charles commissioned the distinguished and celebrated architect, Sir Christopher Wren, to design and reconstruct many of the churches in London, along with an improved version of St Paul's Cathedral. During the fire, Charles evacuated some valuable items to Hampton Court Palace for safety and he put Catherine in charge of overseeing the return of these items to London. One day, while Catherine dressed as a cavalier and prepared to go horseback riding, the king, the diarist John Evelyn and the Duke of York entered her bedchamber to discuss the fire damage and Evelyn's plans for an entirely new design for the capital. She remained to listen to the conversation and view the plans.[97]

In October, they made preparations in her presence chamber for music and a 'drollery'. Carpenters erected a stage and seating, and they made holes in the ceiling for the hanging of branches.[98] In a clear sign London was recovering from the disastrous fire, the theatres reopened in November. Catherine's birthday ball on 25 November, celebrated at Whitehall, was a superb success. Many of the ladies, especially Castlemaine, sparkled with copious jewels. Only Catherine remained unadorned as she continued mourning for her mother's death. During the ball, Catherine would take Charles' hand before the entire assembled elite at court and lead fourteen other couples in the favourite court dance, the *branle*, in which kissing was a part of the routine.[99]

The House of Commons blamed the Great Fire on the Catholics, which the king strongly rejected. Despite this, in November, they issued a proclamation giving the Roman Catholic priests and the Jesuits a month to leave the kingdom. Magistrates began arresting those who did not comply with the order.

Chapter Four

Catherine's Independent Life

Whispers of Trouble

The year 1667 did not begin on a positive note. People were whispering that the king desperately needed an heir, that Catherine was barren, and that the king should divorce her. Charles, fully aware of how Catherine suffered in her many efforts to enhance her fertility, refused to believe she knew she was incapable of having a child before she married him. To his credit, he declined to put the entire responsibility on Catherine. In the nobles continued search for someone to blame for the lack of an heir, Clarendon became their premier target. The Portuguese marriage had never been popular and the English held Clarendon liable. He had also recently sold the port of Dunkirk to the French, which angered the English people.

While Charles remained loyal to Catherine, he romantically pursued Frances Stewart. She was thankfully less arrogant than Castlemaine, but she required the relationship to remain platonic, deliberately fanning the flames of Charles' passion. Rumours were flying about court suggesting Charles would divorce the queen and marry Stewart. Exasperated with the king, Stewart entertained the attentions of the Duke of Richmond as a suitor. It is unclear exactly how Charles found out about it. Charles may have come upon the couple in Frances' bedroom, or the two lovers may have apprehensively approached him for permission to marry. As a result, Charles ordered Richmond into exile.

Stewart went to Catherine, revealing all she really wanted was a man who had honourable intentions so she could marry and have a home and family. Catherine appealed to Charles, telling him the Duke of Richmond would be a suitable match for Frances. Charles agreed, but required the duke to prove he was worthy of the match and had sufficient wealth to maintain the marriage. He commissioned Clarendon to look into the duke's financials, expecting the chancellor would find something irregular to halt the union. But Clarendon found nothing out of the ordinary.

Frances eloped with Richmond and when Charles learned she had secretly married the duke, he was furious and banned the couple from court. Frances sent back all the gifts the king had given her and vowed never to return to court 'except if it were to kiss the hand of the queen who had been so kind to her'.[1]

By now, Charles was actively and openly philandering with the actresses Moll Davis and Nell Gwyn. Davis would dance suggestively in front of the queen.[2] Catherine and Charles occasionally attended the theatre together where Davis and Gwyn would perform. This would not have been a comfortable situation for Catherine, watching the king's mistresses act.

During the summer, the Dutch attacked again with English ships burned and destroyed in the Medway. The victory by the Dutch forced the king to contemplate starting peace negotiations. Within a few weeks, the second Anglo-Dutch war ended. They signed the Treaty of Breda in the Netherlands on 31 July 1667. The English, the Dutch Republic, France and Denmark-Norway were parties to the treaty, but it highly favoured the Dutch.

Besides pressing the king to marry an infertile princess, the blame for the disaster of the war and the subsequent economic problems also fell on the Lord Chancellor. Clarendon saw the writing on the wall and fled into exile in France before his impeachment or dismissal. Catherine, with her newly given authority to appoint members of her own council,[3] chose Clarendon's son, Lord Cornbury, for the post of the queen's chamberlain.[4]

With the dismissal of Clarendon, Catherine lost one of her few supporters and several powerful noblemen filled the vacuum, rising to a place of supremacy in the king's government. They were called the 'cabal' because of their names and titles: Clifford, Ashley (later Lord Shaftesbury), Buckingham, Arlington and Lauderdale. The Duke of Buckingham also rose in power, and he was no friend of Catherine's. Pressured by his cousin, Lady Castlemaine, he was proposing the king rid himself of his barren wife.

The duke's plan called for the secret kidnapping of Catherine and her transportation to America, where she would be well provided for and never heard from again. Charles could then divorce her on the grounds of desertion. Charles declared the plan to be cruel and immediately rejected the idea.[5] A second plan proposed by the duke advanced the notion that Catherine's confessor convince her to retire to a nunnery so parliament could declare a divorce. Charles said only if Catherine agreed to the plan. When they told the queen of this idea, she stated she had no calling for a religious life and she would never leave the man she loved of her own free will.[6]

Catherine remained at court and continued to take part in all the customary and frivolous festivities. She was tired of being pious and pitied.[7] When 'frolics' became a part of the entertainments at court, Catherine would join other masked courtiers in hackney chairs on their rounds of crashing private parties incognito.[8] One of these 'frolics' took an alarming turn when she went on an outing with some of her ladies. As they rode in their hackney chairs, Catherine's chairman failed to recognise her and left to have a drink, forcing Catherine to find another chair to take her back to Whitehall. She had left herself open to being kidnapped or something even worse.

There were many who wanted Charles to abandon her, but she resolved to remain the king's wife, to stay at court and to dance. During her birthday ball that year, she danced all night. In the early months of 1668, Catherine was pregnant again, but by the first week in May, Charles had written to Minette that she had miscarried.[9]

Frances Stewart was back at court and had rooms in Somerset House. She had suffered a bout of smallpox, but thankfully she had no lasting permanent damage to her complexion. Castlemaine was out of favour and given a fine house and pension. Charles focused his attentions even more on the two actresses, Davis and Gwyn. His relationship with Davis was more of a passing fancy, but with Nell Gwyn he formed a more profound and long-lasting connection. Charles enjoyed her company immensely, and he eventually gave her a pension and post as lady of the queen's wardrobe, the duties of which she never fulfilled.

Meanwhile, in Portugal during the year 1668, there were momentous historical events in the works. The Restoration War, which had begun with the accession of Catherine's father to the throne of Portugal, finally ended. Edward Montagu, first Earl of Sandwich and ambassador of King Charles II of England, mediated the Treaty of Lisbon, ratified on 13 February 1668. This was the same Edward Montagu who had escorted Catherine from Portugal to England for her marriage to the king. The treaty ended the twenty-eight-year conflict between Portugal and Spain. Spain recognised the sovereignty of the House of Braganza as Portugal's ruling dynasty and ended the Iberian Union. Portugal finally had its long-sought for independence.

Catherine's brother, King Afonso VI, had been exhibiting erratic and disturbing behaviour for many years and they finally agreed he needed to be declared incapable of ruling and deposed. A *coup d'état* took place, they named Catherine's younger brother Pedro, Prince Regent, and he assumed de facto power. In effect he was king, but he refused to take the title formally being called Governor of the Kingdom[10] while they kept Afonso prisoner until his death in September 1683. Afonso's wife, Maria Francisca of Savoy, had her marriage annulled so she could marry Pedro. Although the people considered the marriage scandalous, it did resolve various pressing issues in the Portuguese government.[11] The Portuguese historian, Malyn Newitt, has suggested Pedro 'did everything to gain the approval for what he did from his sister Catarina, Queen of England'.[12]

The House of Lords made another effort to get a divorce for the king through parliament and once again Charles ordered the issue be dropped. Catherine went to Tunbridge Wells to take the waters. She refused to follow regular court etiquette during her stay and appeared strained and depressed. The stark realisation she lacked the ability to sustain a pregnancy confronted her.

Following in the footsteps of her father, Catherine had employed Italian musicians to support the Portuguese priests in her chapel. In April 1668, she appointed Giovanni Sebenico, who previously worked at St Mark's in Venice, as her Master of the Italian music.[13] Sebenico would leave England in 1673 and be replaced by Giovanni Battista Draghi. These musicians would have a great deal of influence on the young English composer, Henry Purcell. Purcell would compose and publish a set of trio sonatas in 1683, which he described as 'a just imitation of the most famed Italian master'.[14]

Through all of this, Catherine never wavered from her religious and cultural patronage. She did not introduce Italian music to England; her husband had brought a group of musicians from Italy in 1660. However, her patronage of the Italians was so thorough by now, she succeeded in identifying herself with the music they offered.[15] There was no better place to hear the best continental music performed by leading exponents of the much-loved Italian style of singing than in the chapel of the queen.[16]

In September 1668 Pepys writes in his diary: 'So I to Whitehall, and there all the evening on the Queen's side; and it being a most summer-like day, and a fine warm evening, the Italians came in a barge under the leads, before the Queen's drawing-room; and so, the Queen and ladies went out, and heard them for almost an hour; and the singing was indeed very good together; but yet there was but one voice that alone did appear considerable, and that was Signor Joanni' (possibly Giovanni Battista Draghi).[17]

Religious Patronage and the Convent at Hammersmith

Catherine secretly patronised a convent in Hammersmith. She issued an invitation to one of the acolytes of the English nun, Mary Ward, to establish a house in London. The Reformation had created difficult circumstances for Catholic families. Penal laws, passed by parliament, prohibited the creation of Catholic schools in England and made it illegal for parents to send their children abroad for education. Many of these families were determined and willing to break these laws.[18]

Several of these convent schools were on the Continent, but some were opened in England. There were many reasons for the establishment of these schools during what was known as the 'Exile period'. Some orders wanted to educate girls for religious purposes, while others saw it as a means of educating future members. All these convents needed to secure their existence financially and become self-sufficient to maintain their mission.[19]

Mary Ward, born in York in 1585, was a Roman Catholic nun and founder of the Institute of the Blessed Virgin Mary. Through her contacts with the Jesuits of the English College in St Omer, they admitted Mary as a novice with the Walloon

Poor Clares. She later left the Walloon community in 1607 to found a Poor Clare convent for Englishwomen at Gravelines the following year which quickly attracted applicants from England.[20]

She would eventually establish other Poor Clare convents, and additional houses and schools on the Continent (see Chapter 7). She formed her Institute in 1609 to allow women to do for the church what the men had done with the Society of Jesus. Ignatius Loyola, the founder of the Jesuits, had specifically forbidden this. Ward's Institute took shape with the blessing of Pope Urban VIII.[21]

The Mary Ward sisters did not wear habits but dressed as respectable lay spinsters. In England, they were forced to be exceptionally careful not to draw attention to themselves because of the penal laws. The outside appearance of the buildings in which the schools and convents operated resembled ordinary row houses to avoid attracting unwanted attention.[22]

The sisters would become teachers in their own schools with the hiring of additional teachers when needed.[23] Some students in England would go on to other religious institutions or schools on the Continent. Mary Ward's ventures were a success, but due of the novelty of the convents and schools, and because the nuns were not cloistered, they drew censure and opposition, even drawing a warning and suppression from the Inquisition. Eventually, in 1631, the Pope issued a papal bull suppressing the Institute and denouncing its members.[24] They would imprison Ward for nine weeks, but while incarcerated, she received aid from the Pope and was eventually freed.

Upon her release, she petitioned Pope Urban, and he cleared her of the charge of heresy and allowed her to open one of her schools in Rome. In 1639, she returned to England with letters of introduction from Pope Urban to Queen Henrietta Maria of England, wife of King Charles I and Catherine of Braganza's mother-in-law. Ward established herself in London with the help of Henrietta Maria. She later went back to Rome with a young woman from a good English family, Frances Bedingfield. Bedingfield would become Ward's constant companion.

Both women returned to England and Bedingfield remained with Ward in York until her death in 1645,[25] after which Bedingfield went back to the Continent. She returned to England in 1667 after being persuaded by queen Catherine to establish a house in London. In 1668, they opened a school for young women, first in St Martin's Lane and then in Hammersmith, in direct and open violation of the penal laws.[26]

The school required pupils to go to chapel twice a day and employed additional lay teachers to teach French and to supplement the education given by the sisters.[27] Queen Catherine would provide funding throughout the succeeding years and the school would function in plain sight of the authorities, attracting many daughters of prominent Catholic families. The Mary Ward sisters provided the only Catholic schooling for girls on English soil until the late eighteenth century.[28] The penal laws were rarely enforced, but anxiety and anti-Catholic sentiment continued to flare up occasionally. Indeed, the convent at Hammersmith was searched on the orders of Titus Oates in 1680 during the height of the Popish Plot.[29] (See Chapter 5.)

Catherine's Hopes for an Heir Are Dashed

Catherine and Charles went on progress in the fall to Audley End, Euston and Newmarket. Catherine's birthday ball and New Year's celebrations then followed. Their relationship was now one of mutual understanding, and they very much enjoyed each other's company. Charles wrote to Minette in early May that he believed Catherine was pregnant.[30] A month later, he wrote again to say his wife had miscarried.[31] While Catherine recovered, the king dined with her in the evenings. But witnesses saw him climbing the walls of Somerset House to visit Frances Stewart. Stewart remained faithful to her husband, and Catherine rewarded her with a position as one of her ladies of the bedchamber along with assigned lodgings at Whitehall.

Catherine's carefully laid plan to give birth to an heir and surpass Castlemaine and all of Charles' other mistresses had now ended. Castlemaine was basically out of the picture along with Moll Davis, leaving Nell Gwyn as her only rival. Catherine tolerated Nell, and the actress had no intention of embarrassing or insulting the queen. Catherine resolved to be the king's wife and loyal companion and to support him to the best of her ability.

The dowager queen, Henrietta Maria, died on 10 September 1669 in France. Henrietta had been a staunch friend to Catherine, providing her with unconditional support and solid, profitable advice during the early years of her marriage. Catherine mourned the loss of her mother-in-law, but her death would present her with several new opportunities. The ownership of Henrietta Maria's home of Somerset House reverted to Catherine, opening up the possibility for her to retreat from court. Catherine also began receiving the dowry income from the queen dowager, which she would use to increase her patronage of art and music.[32]

In April, Catherine and Charles attended a comedy acted at St James' by the young Princesses Mary and Anne, daughters of the Duke and Duchess of York, with the girls dressed in glorious costumes and covered in jewels.[33] Later in the spring of 1670, Baron Roos introduced a bill in parliament, allowing him to divorce his wife and remarry, permitting the peers to debate the validity of divorce in general.[34] Previously, the Church would grant a divorce and only parliament could authorise the right to remarry.

Charles took great interest in the case, following it closely, most likely as an element of theatre and not as it related to his own situation.[35] While there was a great deal of speculation at the time, there is no evidence Charles seriously considered a new marriage.[36] The Duke of Buckingham actively worked toward a royal divorce, but Charles displayed no interest. He realised he had a compliant wife willing to sanction his chosen lifestyle.

The Secret Treaty of Dover and Minette's Visit to England

For some time, Charles had been engaging in secret discussions with his sister, Minette, and his cousin, Louis XIV of France. Minette was married to Philippe d'Orleans, Louis' brother, and she was very close to her brother-in-law. The correspondence between Minette and Charles suggests it was Minette and Louis' wish to have a formal agreement between the English and the French.

The treaty devised between Charles and Minette in December 1668 was announced to a select group of advisors in January.[37] Following further debate and exchange of the terms, they reached an agreement. Arrangements went forward for Minette to travel to England in May 1670, ostensibly for a long overdue family visit, but in reality for the official ratification of the treaty. The festivities for Minette's visit were conducted in Canterbury, while negotiations were effected surreptitiously behind the scenes.

Francois Auguste M.A. Mignet, the French journalist and historian of the French Revolution in the nineteenth century, summed up the chief terms of the treaty:

> The King of England will make a public profession of the Catholic Faith, and will receive the sum of two million crowns to aid him in the project, in the course of the next six months. The date of the declaration is left absolutely to his own pleasure. The King of France will faithfully observe the Treaty of Aix-la-Chapelle, as regards Spain, and the King of England will maintain the Triple Alliance in a similar manner. If her rights [i.e., Maria Teresa, the Queen of France] to the Spanish Monarch revert to the King of France, the King of England will aid him in maintaining these rights. The two Kings will declare war on the United Provinces [Holland]. The King of France will attack them by land, and will receive the help of six thousand men from England. The King of England will send fifty men of war to sea and the King of France thirty. The combined fleets will be under the Duke of York's [Charles' brother, James] command. His Britannic Majesty will be content to receive Walcheren, the mouth of the Scheldt and the Isle of Cadzand as his share of the conquered province. Separate articles will provide for the Prince of Orange [Charles' nephew, William of Orange, Stadholder of the United Provinces]. The treaty of Commerce which had already begun shall be concluded as promptly as possible.[38]

Charles commissioned the Duke of Buckingham with negotiating the formal treaty of commerce, while Charles collaborated with Minette. The terms relating to the Spanish succession would have later relevance for Catherine when she returned to Portugal as a widow. They signed the secret treaty on 1 June with Colbert de Croissy acting for France and the Lords Arlington, Arundel, Sir Thomas Clifford and Sir Richard Bellings for the English.

It is highly likely Catherine knew the contents of the secret treaty. In the 1660s, Sir Richard Bellings, a Catholic, was knighted and appointed secretary and master of requests for Queen Catherine.[39] Catherine was probably delighted Charles agreed to become Catholic, and Minette had some influence on him in this regard.

Charles may have sincerely intended to become a Catholic in early 1669, but the question of conversion morphed into a device to win the friendship of France. The idea would soon be abandoned when Charles developed an increased interest in war with the Dutch.[40] The king knew full well if he openly declared himself Catholic, it would lead to civil war in England and therefore it was vital for the terms of the treaty to remain confidential.

During Minette's visit, Catherine met her sister-in-law for the first time and they were quickly on the most affectionate of terms. Minette would later comment to her cousin that Catherine was 'a very good woman, not handsome, but so kind and excellent it is impossible not to love her'.[41] Included in Minette's entourage was the young daughter of a Breton nobleman named Louise Renée de Penancoët de Kéroualle. It is unclear if she met Charles during the English visit, but she may have caught Charles' eye with her exquisite appearance. Louise returned to France with her mistress.

Three weeks later, Minette died unexpectedly. As with unexplained untimely death, rumours of poison surfaced. There were many witnesses at her bedside. Some potential causes of her death include acute peritonitis as the result of the perforation of a duodenal ulcer, a ruptured gallbladder, a ruptured appendix or acute intermittent porphyria. Minette herself had cried out they had poisoned her. Her husband and his lover, the Chevalier de Lorraine, were the top suspects. King Louis ordered a public autopsy with several doctors, English and French, declaring openly she had died of natural causes.

Minette's sudden death shocked her brothers Charles and James. The entire court went into mourning and Charles sent the Duke of Buckingham to France for the funeral. Charles remained in a deep depression at Whitehall where he received comfort from Catherine, Nell Gwyn and Frances Stewart. The court then spent the rest of the summer at Hampton Court. Castlemaine's behaviour had become embarrassing, and to mollify her and pay her off, Charles elevated her to the title of Duchess of Cleveland. The Duke of Monmouth caused a headache for his father when he slit Sir John Coventry's nose. The king concealed the entire incident, but the young man's behaviour greatly concerned his father.

During her last illness, Minette had made clear a request for her brother, Charles, to take care of her servants. A 'person of quality', most likely Ralph Montagu, a politician sent on several missions to France, informed Charles in his letters of Minette's wishes and he wasted no time in complying. Henriette de Bordes, who had attended Minette on her deathbed, was in England within a few weeks and given a post as dresser to queen Catherine. In the autumn, Louise de Kéroualle followed, and they gave her a position as maid of honour to Catherine, similar to her post in Minette's household.[42]

Nell Gwyn disliked Kéroualle immediately and openly made fun of her. She recognised a threat to her position when she saw one. Charles still mourned for his sister and initially demonstrated little reaction to Kéroualle's presence.

In February 1671, an elaborate production of the Queen's Ballet, or 'Grand Ballad', was staged in the great hall at Whitehall to mark the passing of the mourning period for Minette. Workers turned the great hall into a theatre with the existing stage enlarged and covered in green baize to make additional space for the queen's music.[43] For these performances, they constructed rails in the queen's presence chamber and the king's guard chamber and its stairs. This was the first of a series of experiments designed to keep people from crowding into the theatre.[44] They also made improvements to the tiring-rooms to make them ready for the queen and her ladies for a second presentation of the masque on 14 February.[45]

John Evelyn attended the same production on 20 February. Expense records for this staging show 165 pounds were spent on bread, beer, wine, fruit, confections, spices, meat, poultry, butter and apples, all of which were served over the three days to the performers.[46] Dancing in the production were Catherine, Frances Stewart, Louise de Kéroualle and the duchesses of Monmouth and Buckingham. Kéroualle drew a lot of attention from the crowds.[47] Her engaging and sweet manner charmed everyone, marking the beginning of her rise as Charles' new paramour.

The History of Somerset House and the Catholic Chapel

In the summer of 1671, most of Catherine's clergy moved to Somerset House so she could worship there in her own Catholic chapel. This move caused some confusion. Reports circulated she would live in Somerset House permanently, but this did not happen. She continued to perform her duties as queen consort and frequently accompanied the king on his many journeys outside of London.[48] For the next fourteen years, she worshipped at both the Somerset House chapel and St James' Chapel.

The Duchess of York was pregnant and became seriously ill, probably with breast cancer. Catherine attended her, sitting by her bedside. Anne of York, and her husband, the duke, had covertly converted to Catholicism, but the king asked them both to keep the conversion a secret. Anne seemed better after she gave birth to a daughter, but on 30 March she became violently ill. Requesting and receiving the Catholic last rites, her conversion was now known publicly. She died on 31 March. Catherine would take the duchess' daughters, Mary and Anne under her care.

Catherine, now 33 years old, painfully realised she could not carry a pregnancy to full term. She had no wish to witness the king's flirtation with his new mistress and did not have it in her to fight off the influence of Kéroualle. With Somerset House now in her sole possession, she made it her home away from court. Kéroualle had settled into sumptuously furnished apartments in Whitehall and assumed the unspoken title of *maîtresse en titre*. She began receiving daily visits from the king.

Old Somerset House was the London home of Edward Seymour, Duke of Somerset and Lord Protector of England during the reign of King Edward VI. Construction began on his magnificent palatial home on the Strand in 1547 and was nearly completed when they executed the duke in 1552. They used the house during the reigns of Queen Mary I and Queen Elizabeth I as a royal residence in London, for grace and favour apartments and a type of government office for holding council meetings. During the reign of the first Stuart king, James I, it was the residence of his queen, Anne of Denmark and often referred to as Denmark House. Queen Anne enjoyed staging masques at Somerset House.

When Charles I, as Prince of Wales, was betrothed to the Spanish Infanta, the chapels of St James', Somerset House and the chapel attached to the Savoy Hospital were designated for her use.[49] The Spanish marriage never materialised and Charles eventually married Princess Henrietta Maria, daughter of King Henri IV of France. In February 1626, the king granted Somerset House to her for life. In 1627, Henrietta Maria employed a bishop, ten Capuchin priests, a confessor and his coadjutor, and ten musicians for her chapel. At the king's expense, renovations were made to the chapel at St James' and the building of another chapel at Somerset House was proposed.[50]

By 1630, the queen convinced her husband to allow for an increase in her ecclesiastical staff to twenty-nine priests and fifteen seculars. These personnel arrived from France in February. Public services soon began in the chapel and drew a multitude of worshippers.[51] Construction began on the new chapel on the site previously occupied by the tennis courts and a few tenements of Somerset House. The building, designed by the talented architect Inigo Jones, was finished and paid for by 1637.[52]

They celebrated Mass with all pomp and circumstance on 10 December 1636. It was the first pontifically celebrated Catholic Mass in nearly 100 years in England. Throngs of people came to receive Holy Communion and the benediction of the bishop. Musicians performed the sacred music, and a French cleric gave the sermon.[53] The chapel would long serve the function of celebrating Mass along with baptisms and weddings for English Catholics and other foreigners. It would fall into disuse during the Interregnum and the Commonwealth, but they held Oliver Cromwell's funeral in Somerset House.

As we have seen, after the restoration of the Stuart monarchy, Henrietta Maria returned to England for a visit. They prepared Somerset House with plans for the reconstitution of the chapel for its original purpose. It had fallen into disrepair and needed renovations.[54] New designs were created by Inigo Jones for the facade of Somerset House as well. Pepys visited the chapel and Somerset House on Ash Wednesday 1664.

> To the Queen's chapel, where I stayed and saw their mass, till a man came and bid me go out or kneel down: so, I did go out. And thence to Somerset House; and there into the chapel, where Monsieur d'Espagne used to preach. But now it is made very fine, and it was ten times more crowded than the Queen's chapel at St James's; which I wonder at. Thence down to the garden of Somerset House, and up and down the new building, which, in every respect, will be very mighty magnificent and costly.[55]

He visited again on 21 January 1665, and wrote:

> Mr. Povy carried me to Somerset House, and there showed me the Queen mother's chamber and closet, most beautiful places for furniture and pictures; and so down the great stone stairs to the garden; and tried the brave echo upon the stairs, which continues a voice so long as the singing of three notes, concords, one after another, they all three shall sound in concert together a good while most pleasantly.[56]

The chapel at the Savoy was also under the queen mother's jurisdiction.[57] During the dowager queen's stay in England, there were many visits back and forth between Whitehall and Somerset House. Henrietta Maria departed not long after they completed the renovations. During her absence, many noblemen and women lived in the manor. Following Henrietta Maria's death, Catherine occupied the state apartments at Somerset House occasionally. Under her guidance, the establishment of the Roman Catholic order was maintained in the chapel, and she would frequently journey from one or another of her outlying palaces to be present for Mass in the chapel.[58] She hired Sir Christopher Wren to redecorate her new home.

Along with the decorative changes being made to the house itself, Catherine instituted a restructuring of her household after 1670. During the first ten years of her marriage, most of her Portuguese entourage returned to Portugal, and she had only English ladies in attendance. Under the groom of the stole, the position held by the Countess of Suffolk, there were five ladies of the bedchamber, four dressers or bedchamber women and six maids of honour.[59] The one remaining Portuguese lady, the countess of Penalva, collected a pension as a friend of the queen.

During her reorganisation, Catherine eliminated the post of lady of the bedchamber in order to avoid any recurrence of the Lady Castlemaine calamity. She placed the bedchamber under the guidance of the Countess of Penalva in an unofficial capacity and gave her a salary of 960 pounds. The Countess of Suffolk kept her position, but Catherine reduced her salary to 300 pounds. Instead of ladies of the bedchamber, Catherine increased the number of dressers to eight in 1671, ten in 1677, twelve by 1682 and fifteen in 1684.

Catherine created a new post of keeper of the sweet coffers, and she added a governess called mother of the maids. This woman supervised all of Catherine's ladies, mostly in an effort to defend them against the unwanted attentions of the king. She appointed another Portuguese lady to aid the blind countess of Penalva and employed an additional four new Portuguese women who were given the position of dresser with increased salaries. All these changes allowed Catherine to maintain a more dominant status in her own bedchamber.[60]

The Rise in Influence of Louise de Kéroualle

Catherine took great pride in managing her own household and her outlook on life improved immeasurably. Her closest companions were Frances Stewart, Duchess of Richmond and Mary Villiers, Duchess of Buckingham. Catherine continued to attend balls and masques and would come whenever Charles requested her presence.

In the fall, Catherine and Charles went on progress. Her escapade at the annual fair of Saffron Walden while the court was at Audley End in October 1671 is well known. Catherine, the Duchess of Richmond and the Duchess of Buckingham rode pinion on horseback behind obliging gentleman. They were all disguised as country lasses in waistcoats and red petticoats and made their way to the fair. Because their strange costumes looking nothing like country folk, they immediately drew the attention of the crowd.

The people followed them right into a booth where Catherine purportedly went to buy a pair of yellow stockings for her beau. With her curious accent, they recognised Catherine as the queen, forcing the women to flee from the scene on their horses, followed by the motley crowd right up to the court gate of Audley End.[61]

The court moved on to Euston Hall, Lord Arlington's residence near Newmarket. Charles and the Duke of York went to Yarmouth, and everyone agreed to rendezvous in Norwich. The royal entourages crossed the city from two different ends and throngs of people greeted them and the parties lasted all night. On the following day, Charles worshiped in the cathedral. Catherine did not attend the Protestant service, so she greeted the people of Norwich and was very well received. The mayor gave her 400 guineas.

A resident of Norwich, only known as T.C., wrote an eyewitness account of the visit to a friend in London, dated 2 October 1671.

> I cannot likewise here forbear to let you know how infinitely gracious her Majesty was to all our City; being pleased to condescend so far as to let almost all sorts of people (of what degree soever) to kiss her hand, ever as she passed along the Gallery, with a most admirable and saintlike charity and patience; so as our whole inhabitants within & without doors ring & sing of nothing else but her praises; continual prayers and tears being offer'd up for her temporal and eternal blessings, by us, who all conclude that if there be a saint on earth, it must undoubtedly be her Majesty; since no eye alive did ever see, nor ear within the memories of man did ever hear of so much goodness, charity, humility, sweetness, & virtue of all kinds to meet in one earthly creature, as are now lodged in her Majesties' saintlike breast.[62]

In early October they were at Blickling Hall and then moved on to Oxnead. The king and queen practised archery there under a leafy oak tree. Both Catherine and Charles were keen bowmen. Archery had ceased to be a national sport with the abandonment of the bow as a military weapon, but there was a revival of the activity with the restoration of the Stuart monarchy. A company of 400 archers under two military officers took part in an archery demonstration in Hyde Park in 1661 and in 1681; the London archers marched to Hampton Court Palace to shoot before the king for monetary prizes.[63] Another society, formed in the late fifteenth century, would practise the longbow in Finsbury fields, just north of the London Wall.[64]

Members of the Honourable Artillery Company founded the Finsbury Archers or the Honourable Fraternity of Bowmen[65] and they established several ongoing competitions. They appointed Catherine the Protector of the Fraternity.[66] In July 1676, the marshal of the society, William Wood, sent to the members of the society a subscription enrolment document, stating the officers and members of the Society of Archers within the cities of London and Westminster 'had determined that the bearer, William Wood, shall have a Silver Badge and wear the same as Marshall to the Queens Majesty's Regiment of Archers', with the names of the various subscribers being listed and the amount of one pound, one shilling pledged by each individual.

They duly purchased the badge and delivered it to Wood. Made of silver, they embossed it with an archer drawing his long bow, with the arms of England and Portugal on the top supported by two bowmen, along with the inscription 'Reginae Catharinae Sagittarii'. The queen was born under the zodiac sign of Sagittarius the Archer. When Wood died in September 1691, the badge, now known as the Catherine of Braganza Shield, remained in the care of succeeding marshals for the society until 1736, when they abolished the office of marshal.[67]

The last captain of one of the competitions for the society, Mr Philip Constable, was in possession of the shield until they dissolved the Finsbury Archers in 1757. Constable joined the Toxophilite Society, established in 1780, and transferred the badge to that organisation.[68] The badge is still in existence and now on permanent loan to the Victoria and Albert Museum.[69]

After several other stops on the progress, the court returned to Euston Hall. Charles took advantage of being close to Newmarket to enjoy the horse races. Kéroualle had been in attendance on Catherine for the entire progress and it is generally acknowledged that during this tour, she surrendered to Charles and had sexual relations. It is unknown if Catherine was still with the royal party when this happened.

The court returned to Whitehall in November, and Catherine retired to Somerset House. She became very ill and Dr Alexander Frazier diagnosed her with an incurable disease, giving her a year to live. It appears stress exacerbated Catherine's illness. Kéroualle, fully installed as *maîtresse en titre,* was having great success in influencing the king. As Catherine lay suffering, Kéroualle attended meetings in her own chambers at Whitehall with Charles and his ministers of state.

Catherine's Independent Life

Catherine's illness proved to not be fatal with her resilience allowing her to recover. She returned to her religious practices, spending many hours in the Somerset House chapel. In the evenings, she played cards and occasionally attended concerts held at court. She carved out a life for herself without her husband. Her efforts in patronising Italian artists and musicians continued unabated, with the added benefit of allowing her to counteract the French influence of Kéroualle.

Hostilities with the Dutch escalated, leading to the start of the third Anglo-Dutch War in April. However, this time the circumstances differed from the prior conflict. England had the protection of Louis XIV based on the secret Treaty of Dover. Charles toured the shipyards to inspect the war fleet. Scheduled in May 1672 to visit Deal, Catherine lobbied Charles to permit her to accompany him to see the fleet.

Charles agreed to her participation, but because her ladies were journeying to the port, they were delayed and soon realised the fleet had already sailed.

She decided to see the enemy vessels which had taken shelter in Dover to avoid a violent storm. Catherine managed to view the ships remaining in port and when she returned to London, she issued orders for the crews of her ships to prepare themselves to serve in the navy where they were desperately needed. A battle took place in early June with no clear winner. The French had come to the aid of the English, and Catherine and Charles inspected the navy and the French ships which had sailed from Rochester. They greeted the Duke of York and the French captains as they returned to shore.

After the death of Anne Hyde, the Duke of York searched for a new wife, finally settling on the Catholic Mary Beatrice, daughter of Alfonso IV d'Este, Duke of Modena, and his wife, Laura Martinozzi, a niece of the former French minister, Cardinal Mazarin. This led to great dissatisfaction among English Protestants as it was clear Catherine would not produce an heir and this marriage further strengthened the duke's position as the king's successor. Nobles allied with the new English chancellor, Lord Shaftesbury, eyed the growing influence of Catholics in the court with apprehension. Their suspicions were reinforced when the Duke of York publicly converted to Catholicism and married his Italian princess by proxy in September 1673. It raised the spectre of a nation ruled by the Vatican, causing great fear amongst the English people.

During the negotiations for the marriage, the Duke of York, with the acquiescence of the king, had promised Mary Beatrice the ability to worship in the chapel of St James'. Charles, in one of his efforts to delay the duke's marriage as long as possible, withdrew his offer of the St James' chapel to the new duchess and compelled Catherine to claim the right to use the chapel belonged to her to gloss over the affront.[70] Because his brother's marriage was unpopular, Charles felt it would be more judicious for the new duchess to worship as inconspicuously as possible.[71] He also did not want a cadre of Italian priests in the palace. This incident would become a source of irritation between Catherine and Mary Beatrice with the new duchess being forced to worship in her own private oratory at court.[72]

Charles put forward legislation in parliament called the Declaration of Indulgence. He hoped to promote religious tolerance and possibly pave the way for the return to Catholicism that he had promised Louis XIV in the secret Treaty of Dover. In March 1673, Lord Shaftesbury, having anti-Catholic views and supporting the claim to the throne of the Duke of Monmouth, encouraged the opposition. Charles withdrew his declaration on the advice of Parliament.

In its place, the House of Commons passed the Test Act which legislated that all those in public office had to swear an oath of allegiance and supremacy and receive the sacrament according to the rites of the Church of England. The intention of the Test Act was to remove all Roman Catholics from civilian and military posts. It also specified if any of the king's servants did not take the oath, they were to be dismissed. The specific target of this law was the Duke of York, who held the position of Lord High Admiral.

Because of his conversion to Catholicism, the law forced the duke to resign his post. In Catherine's case, it compelled her to reduce the number of Catholics in her household, limiting her to employing only nine Catholic ladies. She graciously left open one place for Kéroualle. Pressure increased to remove Catherine's priests in her chapel, but because they were Portuguese subjects, they were deemed to be exempt.

Lord Shaftesbury was no fan of the queen, and his primary aim was to get a divorce for the king and replace Catherine with a Protestant queen. He convinced his party in parliament to propose a motion to pay Charles 500,000 pounds if he agreed to a divorce. Strongly opposed to this motion, Charles forbade any discussion on the issue.

Emboldened by this state of affairs, Kéroualle envisioned herself becoming queen, but Charles had no intention of supplanting Catherine as he had shown over and over. Louise gave birth to the king's son in July and later that year, Charles created her Duchess of Portsmouth, Countess of Farnham and Baroness Petersfield. Charles gave her son the dukedoms of Richmond and Lennox, the title having lapsed upon the death of Frances Stewart's husband in 1672.

Catherine's master of the horse was arrested and imprisoned in the Tower of London after he challenged the Duke of Buckingham to an illegal duel for insulting the queen. Ralph Montagu would prove as loyal to Catherine as his brother Edward had been. King Charles released Montagu after a few days, but the incident served as a reminder that the queen still had enemies.[73]

In November 1673, the new Duchess of York, Mary Beatrice and her mother arrived in England. Charles led her by the hand into Whitehall through a private entrance to avoid any crowds. Catherine met Mary Beatrice at the top of the stairs and embraced her.[74] When the 15-year-old Mary Beatrice met James, his appearance mortified her. Twenty-five years older than her, he had two daughters who were near her own age. She soon overcame her misgivings after realizing he was a good man and grew to love him.

The court snubbed the Italian women when they arrived. Catherine knew all too well what it was like to be Catholic and arrive in a strange new foreign and Protestant country. She left Somerset House to return to court to make the duchess and her mother feel at home. Despite the kerfuffle over the St James' Chapel, she did everything within her power to ease their entrance into society. She sent for a group of Italian musicians to entertain the women. She issued an invitation to Mary Beatrice and her mother to dine with her and allowed the duchess, Laura, to sit in an armchair, a privilege she enjoyed in her own home. Sitting in the queen's presence was a singular honour.[75]

The Calm Before the Storm 1674–1677

Catherine began her patronage of the Italian Catholic painter, Benedetto Gennari the Younger. Born in 1633, he travelled to Paris and worked at the court of Louis XIV. In 1674, he moved to London and worked at court for Catherine, Charles, and the Duke and Duchess of York. He painted portraits of Catherine and Mary Beatrice of Modena. Both women commissioned him to create and paint decorative works for their private worship. Catherine used his presence to strengthen her position as a champion of Italian cultural styles and to counteract the influence of Kéroualle's favourite French painter, Henri Gascars.

She employed Gennari to decorate the queen's chapel at St James' Palace and her chapel at Somerset House. Other employees of Catherine, and aristocrats of the court and the king, used Gennari's decorating services.[76] Gennari's portrait of Catherine, painted in 1674, was a gift to her family in Portugal. Gennari would follow King James II to St Germain, near Paris, following his deposition from the English throne in 1688.

In February, a bill was put forward banning Catholics from sitting in Parliament, entering the king's presence or going to court. The only exceptions allowed were Catherine, the Duke of York, and his wife. Anglican bishops asserted Mass could not be heard anywhere apart from the queen's chapel or those of foreign ambassadors. Renegades plundered the warehouse over Catherine's stables, searching for popish propaganda, and they kept a close watch on all activity at Somerset House. They appointed guards to watch for and apprehend any English man or woman entering the Somerset House chapel.

Satirical songs were being sung about Catherine, showing the people's wish to rid themselves of their barren, Catholic queen. Catherine knew they viewed her with suspicion and it took a toll on her health. She experienced nervous headaches and her physicians prescribed taking the waters at Bath. Kéroualle, who also suffered bad health, joined Catherine. Louise had contracted a dose of syphilis from the king. Because of the growing anti-Catholic sentiments, the people ignored the entire entourage on the way to Bath. None of the sheriffs appeared to accompany the party, and once in Bath, the customary visits of the town mayor and aldermen to Catherine did not happen.

Disrespected openly during her visit, the treatments failed to help her condition, forcing Charles to issue a rebuke. The king reminded the sheriffs of their duty to accompany the queen during the return to London, going so far as to provide her itinerary. From Bath, Catherine went to Bristol and joined the king and court at Windsor for the rest of the summer. She would now spend most of her time at Somerset House, taking pleasure in her gardens and her chapel. If Charles asked for her presence, she would join him. But Kéroualle, now the acknowledged *maîtresse en titre*, had effectively taken over Catherine's duties as queen.

In January 1674, Catherine organised the first Italian opera performance in England in honour of Mary Beatrice and her mother at Somerset House.[77] Catherine indulged her fondness for theatricals and commissioned John Crowne to stage the ballet *Calisto* in the theatre at Whitehall. The Duke of York's two daughters, Mary and Anne, both future queens, danced in the production in February 1675. Catherine also admired the tragedies of Dryden, and she held performances of his plays at Whitehall.[78] In January 1675, the Duchess of York gave birth to a daughter, christened Catherine Laura, in honour of queen Catherine and the duchess' mother.[79]

Hortense Mancini had arrived from the Continent, ostensibly to visit with her family. She was another niece of Louis XIV's old minister, Cardinal Mazarin, and a cousin of Mary Beatrice of Modena. Initially, Charles welcomed her as he would any noblewoman, allotting her apartments and a pension, and she set about establishing herself in London society. The rules of etiquette at court did not require the Duchess of York to meet the king's mistresses, but Mary Beatrice felt it was her duty to visit her cousin. Kéroualle felt insulted by this visit and complained. Ultimately, James took Mary Beatrice to see Louise, which insulted the queen.[80] During a ball a few days later, Mary Beatrice curtseyed to Catherine, and the queen failed to acknowledge her.[81]

By May, the high-spirited and captivating Mancini was the king's new mistress, much to Kéroualle's chagrin. The king kept the affair remarkably discreet, likely because Charles cared for Louise and did not want to threaten her position. Even Nell Gwyn, still in the company of Charles, found Mancini appalling. In early 1677, Hortense had an affair with the Prince of Monaco, which infuriated Charles. He ceased paying her allowance, but soon restored it.

Eventually, Charles ended his love affair with Mancini and Kéroualle returned to her position as principal mistress. Because of restrictions on the employment of Catholics at the end of 1672, Castlemaine lost her position as lady of the bedchamber to the queen[82] and, in the spring of 1676, she departed for France. Catherine stayed away from all the commotion at court. She visited the wife of John Evelyn at Sayes Court, Deptford, and took great pleasure in her independent life.

Near the end of September 1677, Luís de Vasconcelos e Sousa, sixth Count of Calheta, and third Count of Castelo Melhor arrived in London from Portugal. Previously the count had acted as the lead minister in her brother King Afonso's reign, but he had been forced into exile[83] when Pedro took the position as Regent. Catherine and the king warmly greeted him. He stayed with her at Somerset House, where he could mingle with the nobility and ministers of England. Evelyn wrote about him saying he was 'a very intelligent, illustrious gentleman'.[84] Castelo Melhor offered his services to Catherine to protect her during the palpable political and religious turmoil which now loomed on the horizon.[85]

Two parties had formed in the government. The Duke of York led the Catholic party, and the Duke of Monmouth headed the Protestant party. Monmouth had the backing of Shaftesbury and had high hopes of ascending the throne, recognising his uncle as the major obstacle to his aspirations. Shaftesbury continued to pressure the king to divorce Catherine. He urged Charles to admit he had married Monmouth's mother, Lucy Walter, his former mistress on the Continent while he was in exile.

Charles would have nothing to do with this scheme. He had never married Lucy Walter, and he would publicly declare it. In March, he wrote 'For the voiding of any dispute which may happen in time to come concerning the succession to the Crown, I do here declare in the presence of Almighty God, that I never gave nor made any contract of marriage, nor was married to any woman whatsoever, but to my present wife Queen Catherine now living'.[86] He could not have made it any clearer, yet he would be compelled to issue this statement three times over the next two years.

Besides this nonsense, his finances preoccupied Charles. He appealed to Louis XIV to triple his income from the Treaty of Dover. He needed the money because of spending restrictions imposed on him by parliament. To placate the Protestants, Charles agreed to marry his niece Princess Mary, the eldest daughter of the Duke of York, to his nephew, Prince William of Orange. In the fall, William arrived for the wedding. He had set his hopes on possibly inheriting the throne of England through his new wife.

Neither party was very keen on the match. Princess Mary dreaded the marriage and leaving England, the only home she ever knew. Mary was 17 and William was 27. Catherine did her best to comfort her. The marriage ceremony took place on 4 November, between 8 and 9 o'clock in the evening in Mary's apartments at St James' Palace. It was a small, private affair attended by family. After supper, Queen Catherine and the Duchess of York undressed the bride for the bedding ceremony.[87]

Four days after the wedding, the Duchess of York gave birth to a son. The birth diminished the prospects of William and Mary ascending the throne of England. Catherine's birthday ball had been moved forward ten days, allowing William and Mary to attend before they departed for Holland. They spared no expense for the festivities. Mary remained deeply depressed. Catherine tried to console her as she perfectly understood the circumstances of leaving home for a foreign court. William and Mary sailed on 21 November.

Chapter Five

The Popish Plot

The Popish Plot Begins

From the moment Catherine arrived in England she lived under a cloud of suspicion, simply for being a Catholic in a largely Protestant country, although the English were used to having their Stuart monarchs married to Catholic queens. Anne of Denmark, wife of James I, had converted to Catholicism, and Henrietta Maria, Catherine's mother-in-law, was notably aggressive in working to promote her religion in England. At the time of the Popish Plot, Catholics made up less than two per cent of the population.[1] However, it was not the masses who went to Mass. Those practicing the religion were concentrated among the highest echelons of society: the nobility and the Crown.

Besides the queen, the heir to the throne – the Duke of York and his wife – were Catholic, as was Kéroualle, Charles' *maîtresse en titre*, and many other members of parliament and lords of the realm. Since the alliance with France, bolstered by the Treaty of Dover in 1670, rumours and distrust emerged in anticipation that Charles would, at the very least, attempt to decrease restrictions on Catholics. As we have seen, parliament passed several acts of legislation reducing Catherine's household, limiting the ability of Catholics to work in the government, sit in parliament, and attend court.

Once the Duke of York went public with his conversion, England faced the prospect of a Catholic monarch for the first time in over a century. There were many in parliament who actively pursued legislation to alter the constitution in order to safeguard the realm from popery. These efforts included the exclusion of the Duke of York from ascending the throne, along with calls to extend penal legislation against Catholics and to distance the Crown from France.

Charles' outright rejection of proposals to divorce and marry a Protestant wife and his refusal to allow any measures limiting James' royal power were in effect a denial to reduce his own royal majesty by being dictated to in matters of succession and dynastic policy. If Charles surrendered to these measures, it would be a tacit admission that charges of 'popery and arbitrary government' had merit.[2] It is safe to say if the heir to the throne had not turned Catholic, the so-called 'Popish Plot' would never have gained credibility and gripped the nation.

The most perilous time in Catherine's life in England began on 13 August 1678. During Charles' habitual walk in St James' Park with his spaniels, a man approached him. Christopher Kirkby, who occasionally worked in the king's scientific laboratory, handed him a note and advised Charles he had information from a friend regarding something important. He requested an audience, hinting at evidence of a plot against the king, the Protestant religion and the English government.

Origins of the Plot

The origin of the Popish Plot came from a most unusual source. Titus Oates reportedly could only be described as ugly. It is said he had a broad face with his mouth in the middle, along with deep-set eyes, a bull neck, wobbling chins and a high raspy voice.[3] He had short bandy legs and long arms and had become skilled at mendacity at a very young age.[4] Yet he spoke with such conviction and charisma, he could easily fascinate his audience.

Born in 1649, Oates' father had a degree from Cambridge and worked as a rector in the Church of England. Oates began his education but would be expelled and obliged to attend another school. By the time he entered college at Cambridge, they labelled him a dunce and illiterate.[5] He fell into debt, was expelled, and took orders to become an Anglican priest. He officiated at several parishes, including acting as a curate to his father in Hastings. During his time there, he accused a schoolmaster of sodomy.[6]

Because of a lack of evidence against the man, they charged Oates with perjury. It would not be the first time. While in prison awaiting trial in Dover, he escaped, making his way to London where he obtained an appointment in the navy as chaplain aboard a ship sailing for Tangier. Within twelve months, they levelled charges of sodomy against him and dismissed him. The navy spared him of any punishment on account of being clergy.[7] Living in London, he found work several times but kept getting dismissed or accused of perjury and jailed.

By 1676, he was frequenting a club and meeting Catholics for the first time.[8] He got a position as a Protestant chaplain in the household of the Catholic Earl of Norwich, later the Duke of Norfolk. His father introduced him to an educator, rector and a man of letters named Dr Israel Tonge. Tonge was mentally unstable, and filled with paranoia and fear against the Jesuits.[9] Oates and Tonge had plans to write pamphlets on anti-Catholic and anti-Jesuit topics and formed a strategy for Oates to pretend to be a Catholic in order to uncover and expose plots, presumably for financial gain.

Oates entered the Catholic Church and enrolled in the Jesuit Royal College at Valladolid, Spain. While there, he hooked up with an old acquaintance and adventurer from London, Captain William Bedloe. Allegedly, the two men discussed the plot which would later unfold. Expelled after five months, Oates returned to London. At the end of 1677, he entered the Jesuit College of St Omer, where he lasted for six months before being asked to leave. He returned to London and renewed his association with Tonge.

Tonge urged Oates to write up a manuscript describing the machinations of the Jesuits, which he promptly produced in extravagant detail, outlining forty-three salient points. He claimed while employed by the Jesuits on the Continent, he uncovered a Europe-wide plot to return England to Rome. He alleged he attended a secret Jesuit meeting in April 1678 in London, where the discussion of genuine and specific plans took place. The plot encompassed the massacre of tens of thousands of Protestants with the help of an invading Catholic army, the burning of London, insurrection and uprisings in Scotland and Ireland and, most ominously, the assassination of King Charles II, replacing him with his Catholic brother, James, under the aegis of the Pope. The method of murder involved a shooting or stabbing of the king and in the event of failure, the queen's physician would poison Charles.

Slipped into the wainscotting of a gallery in the home of Sir Richard Barker, a former landlord of Dr Tonge,[10] Tonge claimed he stumbled upon this fantastical manuscript and presented the papers to his acquaintance, Christopher Kirkby. Kirkby considered the documentation so alarming, he felt compelled to warn the king what his friend had revealed. When he met the king during his walk in St James' Park, Charles shrugged off the worry for his personal safety and told Kirkby to tell the story to his personal staff member, William Chaffinch, and to bring his friend to Whitehall.

Dr Tonge arrived with a bundle of papers supporting Kirkby's statements. Charles intended to go to Windsor the next day, so he directed Tonge to leave the papers with the Lord Treasurer, Thomas Osborne, Earl of Danby. Danby reviewed the manuscript which revealed the hiring of two men, Thomas Pickering and John Grove, to shoot the king during one of his walks in St James' Park. Pickering was a Benedictine associated with the royal chapel at St James' Palace and a paid employee in the queen's service. Grove was a Jesuit lay brother.[11] The alleged conspiracy hinted at foreign involvement, including the king of France and his confessors, along with the encouragement of Don Juan of Austria.

It did not take long for the source of the information to be revealed as Titus Oates. In recognition of the seriousness of the situation, Danby went immediately to Windsor to see Charles, insisting they should disclose the information to the Privy Council, or at the very least, to the Duke of York. Charles made it clear he did not want his brother to be informed of the plot.

They searched for Grove and Pickering, but could not find them. Tonge stated the king's retreat to Windsor had altered their plans. Now the deed would take place at Windsor and Tonge specified the exact day of the murder. The day passed with not one plotter found. Danby once more insisted on telling the council, but Charles' scepticism of the plot led him to believe they should drop the matter as he did not want the idea gaining any publicity or traction.

The failure of the king to recognise their plot astonished Tonge and Oates but, undeterred, they manufactured more evidence. Father Bedingfield, the Duke of York's confessor, stopped by the post office to collect his mail and found five bizarre letters. Four were signed by Jesuits he knew personally and one he did not know. The letters caused alarm, and he immediately took them to the duke.

James went to the king, demanding an inquiry by the Privy Council. Contrary to his better judgement, Charles relented and summoned Tonge and Oates. Oates appeared before the king and council, exhibiting supreme confidence. Charles asked him did he know the handwriting of the mysterious letters. Yes, he knew the handwriting and named the authors. Additional letters of two of the designated writers had been seized and compared side by side with the confessor's missals. There was no resemblance between the handwriting of the seized letters and those from the post office.

One of the accused authors, standing before the council, exposed the fact that one of the pretend letters showed it came from St Omer and he had been in England at the time the letter was dated. All five of the letters, which supposedly were composed by five different people and came from different parts of Europe, contained the same errors in punctuation and orthography, and every one of them were written on paper bearing the same watermark. Oates explained they were written in a feigned hand.

To enhance the veracity of his accusations and give them more credibility, Oates disclosed further anecdotal details of London's geography, naming specific locations such as Somerset House, and charged some of the most prominent Catholics with being involved in the plot. He revealed he met personally with King Louis XIV's confessor, Père de la Chaise and with Don Juan of Austria and witnessed money paid to the queen's physician, Sir George Wakeman for poisoning the king. He claimed a Jesuit convention took place at the White Horse Tavern in the Strand on 24 April, where the plot came to fruition. In actuality, this habitual triennial convocation of the Jesuit order took place in St James' Palace. If the actual location of the meeting became public, the uproar against the Duke of York would have ruinous consequences.

The king asked Oates, what did Don Juan look like? Oates described him as tall, lean, and swarthy. Both Charles and James personally knew Don Juan from their time in exile and knew him to be short, plump and fair. The king asked Oates, where was Père de la Chaise living when Oates met him? Oates replied, he lived in the Jesuit House just by the Louvre in Paris. Charles' amusement became evident. There was no Jesuit house within a mile of the Louvre. Oates remained undeterred.[12]

The name of Edward Coleman arose in the discussion. Coleman worked as private secretary to Mary Beatrice, Duchess of York. If any of Oates' accusations had truth to them, Coleman would fit the bill. He personally conducted what could arguably be designated as an independent foreign policy, purportedly on behalf of the Duke of York. Coleman, in 1674, travelled to Brussels to meet with a cardinal[13] and actively corresponded with the confessors of King Louis XIV of France, Jean Ferrier and Père de la Chaise. In these letters, Coleman asked for money and aid to return England to Catholicism. Just how much the Duke of York knew about Coleman's efforts or if the information actually reached Louis XIV is speculative.[14]

Going further, Oates charged some of the most prominent Catholics with involvement in the plot. These included five leading peers and he specifically named Lord Arundel and Lord Belasyse. Charles knew these men as loyal friends of himself and his father and refused to hear any allegations against them. Oates backtracked, explaining the lords had no involvement in the plot but were only informed of it.

Charles' irritation erupted. Calling Oates a lying knave, the interview ended. The king saw right through these fabrications and initially denied a request for an investigation. The council recognised the dishonesty of Oates' story, but he had planted the seed of doubt. They must investigate on the off chance there was a kernel of truth to the plot. The Duke of York insisted on an examination of the charges as well.[15]

Operations went into motion. Most of the well-known Jesuits in London were rounded up and put in jail and their papers confiscated. They made exceptions for the chaplains of Catherine and the Catholic ambassadors. With a warrant issued for Coleman's arrest by the Privy Council, they searched Coleman's house and seized documents. He later surrendered and following an examination of his papers, the council committed him to Newgate.

The opponents of the king recognised a unique opportunity. The Earl of Shaftesbury in particular viewed the accusations as an opportunity for parliament to thwart any attempts by the Crown to introduce a French-style absolutist government, to compel the king to divorce his Catholic queen and to prevent Charles from being succeeded by his overtly Catholic brother.[16]

Dissatisfied with his reception by the council, Oates took it upon himself to make two depositions before the highly respected Westminster magistrate, Sir Edmund Berry Godfrey, on 6 September and 28 September. When Oates and Tonge testified before the Privy Council again, the list of allegations had grown from forty-three to eighty-one. The exposure of additional names of people allegedly involved in the plot reached as high as the offices of people in the employ of the queen and the Duchess of York, archbishops and others in government. They took more Jesuits into custody. On 29 September, the queen's physician, Sir George Wakeman, answered questions before the council.

Oates' allegations became even more plausible when they discovered Sir Edmund Berry Godfrey's body in October, run through by his own sword. Allegations emerged that the murder took place at another location with the corpse taken in a cart to Primrose Hill where it had been found in a ditch. To this day, the murder remains unsolved,[17] but the rumour mill went into overdrive. Suicide was mentioned and others believed the papists had killed Godfrey. Orders went out to search the house of every Catholic in England. Armed bands patrolled the streets at night and barricades were erected.[18]

Parliament empanelled a commission to look into the plot. The commission furnished Oates with a pension, lodgings in Whitehall and an armed bodyguard. Fanciful stories against Catholics abounded by many witnesses. A reward of 500 pounds, offered for the discovery of the murderers of Sir Edmund Berry Godfrey, yielded many informants. One man accused Samuel Atkins, a clerk in the office of Samuel Pepys who worked in the Admiralty, implicating the Duke of York by association.

Accusations against the Queen

Seeking to claim the 500 pound reward, Captain William Bedloe, Oates' acquaintance and conspirator from their days in Spain, came forward. He had been hanging around the queen's servants at Somerset House and claimed he had information on the murder of the magistrate. In his first version of the story, some men met Godfrey and told him they had details about some informers of the Popish Plot. Godfrey accompanied the men, who turned on Godfrey and murdered him.

Bedloe came forward to assist the magistrate and learned of his death. The men told Bedloe what had happened, and they took the corpse to the high altar of the queen's chapel at Somerset House, where it lay for several days while the men deliberated on what to do. Bedloe, corroborating Oates' testimony, mentioned Samuel Atkins as a murderer besides two Jesuits, the keeper of the queen's chapel and a servant of Lord Belasyse.

Under examination by the council, in the presence of the king, Bedloe's story shifted. Smothered by pillows, Godfrey's body was seen in the queen's backstairs where it lay for two days. Bedloe received an offer of 2000 guineas to take away the body. Some of the queen's people removed the corpse during the dark of night.

The king sent Bedloe with his son, the Duke of Monmouth, to Somerset House to identify the exact place where the body had been spotted. Bedloe's choice of location, which he labelled the 'backstairs', turned out to be a passage common to all the queen's servants, through which her meals were carried and where her footmen waited. Because of the public location and high visibility, it seemed likely there were witnesses. None came forward.

Conspirators in the streets fanned the flames against Catholics. That Catherine was living her retired life at Somerset House, her lack of being in the presence of the king, her foreignness, her religion, her chapels and priests, all worked against her. They even blamed her for the conversion of the Duke of York to Catholicism.[19] Realising these attacks directly implicated his wife, Charles feared for her safety. In order to show his commitment to her, he suggested she move from Somerset House into her old apartments at Whitehall, where she would be under his direct protection.

Mortified by these accusations, Catherine immediately sent a message to the House of Lords expressing her grief that such a crime could have taken place in her residence. She offered to do anything in her power to contribute to the discovery of the offenders. When the order came to search the palace, she willingly opened the doors and did everything possible to facilitate the process. The Lords were grateful for her confidence and cooperation and dispatched a message with their sincere thanks.[20]

Bedloe and Oates now engaged in an implacable competition to outdo each other in indicting the queen.[21] Before the House of Lords at the end of October, Oates began gently by suddenly remembering he had seen no letters to Jesuits from the queen, but he saw theirs acknowledging her favours. She provided them with 4000 pounds, although he could not say the money went directly to the plot. These accusations only hinted at Catherine's involvement for the moment. But clearly the scheme had advanced beyond the initial forty-three written charges and morphed into something more serious.

On 24 November, Oates testified before Henry Coventry, Secretary of State with a story about the queen plotting to poison the king. Four days later, before the House of Commons, he made the blatant statement: 'I, Titus Oates, do accuse Queen Catherine of conspiring the King's death and contriving how to compass it'.[22] His testimony now claimed in the previous July, he saw a letter in which Wakeman affirmed queen Catherine had given her consent to murder the king.

A Jesuit received a message from Sir Richard, or Sir Robert, from Somerset House in August, and Oates accompanied this brother. The Jesuit entered the queen's closet and Oates loitered in the anteroom. The door, conveniently left open, allowed Oates to eavesdrop on the conversation. He heard a female voice exclaim she could no longer suffer the indignity of the king's infidelities and was content with the murder of the king and the propagation of the Catholic faith.[23] Oates maintained Catherine fully comprehended the magnitude of the plot by her physician to poison her husband. The Jesuits left the closet and Oates entered, seeing no woman there but the queen. Oates had directly accused queen Catherine of being guilty of high treason.

Oates said he witnessed the Jesuits offering Wakeman 10,000 pounds for the deed, but the doctor refused, saying it was too much work for so little money. After offering 15,000 pounds, Wakeman accepted. The doctor agreed to prepare the poison with the queen herself administering it to the king. Oates also claimed to have witnessed part of the money being paid to Wakeman at a Jesuit meeting on 30 August 1678. Embellishing even further, Oates stated they promised Wakeman the additional reward of a post as physician-in-general in the army. And the aforementioned 4000 pound gift from Catherine to the Jesuits now became 5000 pounds, earmarked as payment for the king's murder and a down payment for Wakeman's services.[24]

These revelations disturbed the Privy Council. The next day they examined Oates, asking why he had not recognised Dr Wakeman when he first answered questions in September and why he kept information about Catherine and the doctor private for two months when the king's life clearly appeared in danger. Oates muddled his answer with something about wanting to keep the revelations private and disclose them directly to the king.

Compelled to admit he had never been in the queen's presence, he adamantly persisted in declaring he had seen her. What time of day did the meeting occur? Oates said just before High Mass, not a Sunday but some other solemn day. Were others in the room? Yes, he had heard others. Were the Duke of York and the Duke of Norfolk in consultation with the queen? Oates claimed they might have been.[25]

Charles could not abide these accusations against the queen and the royal physician. Considered the most accomplished Catholic doctor in the kingdom, Wakeman was a man of high integrity and stellar reputation.[26] Stalwart Royalists, the Wakeman family had unequivocally supported the Stuart monarchy for many years. Because of his excellent reputation, he received an appointment as physician-in-ordinary to Queen Catherine in 1670.[27]

Charles insisted on examining Oates himself. Oates vaguely mentioned he saw letters from Jesuit principals thanking Catherine for her favours and for her gift to the Jesuits of 5000 pounds for the general purposes of the society. Charles ordered Oates to be taken under guard to Somerset House to identify the room where he heard the queen speak. As he chaotically ran all around as if he was lost, it became laughably obvious he had never been to the palace before. He finally broke down, admitting he did not know the location. Charles had Oates confined to his apartments at Whitehall.

Bedloe miraculously produced corroborative testimony before the Privy Council. He witnessed an interview between Catherine, Lord Belasyse and two French priests in the gallery of the chapel at Somerset House, during which they exhorted her to countenance the death of the king. Catherine broke down into tears and agreed to Wakeman preparing the poison and affirmed her willingness to give it to Charles. But the council pointed out the grave inconsistencies in his testimony, forcing Bedloe to cave and be dismissed. The actions of the council signal while there may have been some credence for a plot in general, it was increasingly obvious Catherine had no part in it.

Oates and Bedloe repeated their statements before the Commons. The House went into an uproar and demanded the removal of Catherine and her household from Whitehall and from the king's protection. She must be sent to the Tower or if not, at least returned to Somerset House until the will of the people could be determined by parliament. They petitioned the House of Lords to join them in calling for the queen's removal from Whitehall, leaving Catherine in an exceedingly vulnerable position.

Oates and Bedloe took their accusations before the House of Lords, where their momentum collapsed. The Lords were extremely reluctant to take any steps against Sir George Wakeman. As devoted as he was to the Stuarts, the charges were highly offensive. The diarist, John Evelyn, knew Wakeman personally and said he was a 'worthy gentleman' and would have abhorred the deed of assassination. He commented the act of killing the king would have been breaking his Hippocratic oath and also his oath of loyalty to his monarch.[28]

Evelyn's thoughts on the entire situation echoed the thoughts of parliament and the people:

> The Queen's birthday. I never saw the Court more brave, nor the nation in more apprehension and consternation. Coleman and one Staly had now been tried, condemned, and executed. On this, Oates grew so presumptuous as to accuse the queen of intending to poison the king; which certainly that pious and virtuous lady abhorred the thoughts of, and Oates's circumstances made it utterly unlikely in my opinion. He probably thought to gratify some who would have been glad his Majesty should have married a fruitful lady; but the King was too kind a husband to let any of these make impression on him. However, diverse of the Popish peers were sent to the Tower, accused by Oates; and all the Roman Catholic lords were by a new Act forever excluded the Parliament; which was a mighty blow. The King's, Queen's, and Duke's servants, were banished, and a test to be taken by everybody who pretended to enjoy any office of public trust, and who would not be suspected of Popery.[29]

The Lords rightly refused to take any action against the queen based on uncorroborated statements of known perjurers. Catherine, no longer the woman she was when she arrived in England, endured the infidelities of the king and gained support because of her decorous and noble behaviour. She emerged as a character of outstanding fortitude, and her dignity and goodness were qualities that appealed to the English people.

Catherine's hostility to France and French influence was the nearest she came to taking a political stance, and in this she was more in tune with popular sentiment in England than her husband.[30] Despite her adherence to Catholicism, she had endeared herself to the people, so much so that when they accused her of plotting to kill the king, no one believed it.[31] Everyone knew how much she loved Charles. Many in the House of Lords knew Catherine personally and during the parliamentary debate, the queen had widespread support and they commended her virtues. From now on, no further actions were taken by the House of Lords and the Commons abandoned the matter.[32]

The Pressure Is Off Catherine but the Plot Continues

The Catholic Lords Arundel, Belasyse, Powis, Stafford and Petre went to the Tower. They put Coleman on trial, found him guilty and executed him on 3 December 1678.[33] Thousands of Catholics were driven from London. They made arrests with dreadful regularity, followed by trials, convictions and executions at Tyburn. Charles ordered Oates into even stricter confinement, but his popularity knew no bounds, compelling the king to release him.[34] He paraded around in Episcopal robes and gained frequent invitations to wine and dine with bishops, where he would sound off against the queen, the Duke and Duchess of York and many others.

Catherine's peril stimulated Charles into new displays of affection. The Plot created many problems for her and her Catholic household because of the public accusations of plotting to kill the king, promote Catholicism, and suppress Protestantism. Consequently, most of her English Catholic servants departed from her household.[35]

There were many who were loyal and looked out for her wellbeing, the most prominent being the king himself. She also relied on the advice of the exiled Portuguese Count of Castelo Melhor.[36] Letters were passing between Portugal and England. Melhor wrote to King Pedro: 'As to the king he has shown great affection towards the queen. Never before has he treated her with such kindness as now and I promise Your Majesty that Portugal is greatly indebted to this prince'.[37]

After parliament refused to give the accusations against Catherine credence, Charles wrote to Catherine's brother King Pedro to reassure him in January 1679:

> We doubt not but that your Highness hath already heard of the unhappy reflection that hath been lately raised against our dear consort the Queen, and do believe your Highness hath taken a sensible part with us in that indignation wherewith we have resented the same. We brought the matter (as soon as it was known) unto our Council Board, and the reception which there it had we are

> sure will not sound unpleasing to your Highness, because it gave satisfaction to us, and did let the Queen clearly see that all was done for her present vindication, which the time would permit. But this misfortune arising while the States of our kingdoms were assembled, who by their constitution may take cognisance of whatever happens of an extraordinary nature, they drew the inquiry before them. And even then, such of them as took but time to deliberate and to consider how the Queen hath lived, found motives to reject the complaint, and instead of favouring the accusation, the time was only spent magnifying her virtues....[38]

Catherine also wrote to her brother seeking his advice and help. The relentless pressure on Charles to remove all Catholics from his presence persisted. By 1 March, they compelled Charles to send his brother into exile to appease those who were calling for his exclusion from the throne. King Pedro promised to send an ambassador. In a letter to her brother dated 17 March 1679, Catherine says:

> ...You will by this time have learned the departure of the Duke not only from the court but from this Kingdom also, by decree of the King his brother. This was not expected, it being held indeed that the King would always uphold him, there being such manifest reasons, he being a Prince of notability, and having served him with great fidelity and competence; but the King fearing the fury of Parliament had seemingly closed his eyes to all this and taken a step so contrary to the affection he bears towards this Brother to whom he owes so much. Such decision evokes alarm that were others to support his attitudes they must suffer the same fate. In that which concerns me I am most sure of my Innocence of all those things which malicious reports do impugn against me; likewise, I am sure the King also doth hold me innocent of them, and all those who are fair-minded; but for the evil-minded there be no greater crime than innocence; my trust is that the Almighty will establish the Truth, 'tis to his hands I commend myself, desiring nothing save to conform to his will. See to it that Special Prayers and pious deeds are continued that it may help us in being heard.
>
> News comes that we may expect the Ambassador in a few days now. This Court be in such state of Turmoil I fear lest he be not received with that Acclaim I could desire.... from your unhappy, yet devoted & always faithful sister, Catherine.[39]

Although King Pedro showed filial concern for his sister, he failed to provide any serious assistance. He summoned the English agent, Francis Parry, from Lisbon who confirmed the declaration of the House of Commons that the queen consented to the establishment of the Roman Catholic religion and the death of the king and had petitioned for Catherine and her household to be removed from Whitehall. However, Parry explained, the Lords found the evidence inconclusive and would not agree to force Catherine out. King Charles declared his distress over the situation and his confidence in the queen's affection and loyalty.

This confirmed what King Pedro already knew, but it disturbed him and justifiably did so as the informers continued unpunished. He conferred with his council who expressed their deep concern for Catherine. The English had been remiss in their treatment of the Infanta, and the council determined Catherine must return immediately to Portugal. The severity of the situation led the government to send a new ambassador, Henrique de Sousa Tavares, Marquis de Arronches. Arronches was the Portuguese king's third choice for the position after plans to send two other noblemen fell through.[40] This assignment did not please Melhor, who believed Arronches was not trustworthy.[41]

Arronches arrived in April 1679 and confirmed Melhor's misgivings. Unfortunately, Arronches lacked any understanding of Catherine's situation. He demanded Catherine return to Portugal with him. Catherine refused, believing her place should be at the side of her husband. Making matters much worse, Arronches accused her of ingratitude to her brother, a lack of sisterly love and disloyalty to Portugal. This resulted in much acrimony between Catherine and the brother she adored. It was more than she could bear besides the hateful accusations of the plotters.

Arronches went even further in causing trouble. In December 1679, Catherine wrote again to her brother:

> Although the Marquis daily give me cause for affront, I have refrained from complaining so as not to worry you therewith, preferring to suffer these things rather than to give you acquaintance of them. Yet now am I compelled to inform you what new thing hath happened which hath affected me more on your account than my own. Having for more than a year been deprived of my former Equerry who was Catholic, the King was pleased to appoint for me a Frenchman, a faithful servant of his as likewise of the Duke my brother-in-law, and the most appropriate for my service in these times, being well disposed towards the interest of Portugal, & nephew to the Maréchal de Turenne, [her new master of the horse, nephew of the Marechal of Turenne, Louis Duras, second Earl of Feversham] but with little affection for the party toward which the Marquis leans. Yesterday the appointment was made with the full approval of the court, yet your Ambassador takes it upon himself being much offended thereby &

expressing himself to me in blunt terms against the [appointment of Feversham]. The Marquis in this manner not only brings discredit upon himself but also to some extent upon you which the more affects me in that he cuts a ridiculous figure in this court, which is a sign of the Hostility he bears against me, seeing to be at variance by taking part of my enemies, and according no credence to those who are loyal to me. This renders him odious & of little credit as your envoy which is a matter of grief to me that affairs of such grave purport it was hoped you should choose someone with greater talents. All this is mortifying to me, I beg you not to uphold him and if may be, that you bring some remedy thereto, it seeming to me sufficient all I suffer from the English, my only consolation being that I suffer on your behalf & for my mother country which I love so much; it is hard & new indeed for me that no Portuguese hath part in my disconsolations; I beseech you to effect a Remedy to all this in that I fear the Marquis shall proclaim my grievances have no mending & shall so misrepresent me to your eyes as to make my sorrow Everlasting……

Your affectionate Sister, Catherine.[42]

The Plot Dies Down

Hostility and suspicion persisted. Bedloe's testimony changed each time he came under examination. The amount of reward offered him to move the magistrate's corpse ranged from 2 guineas to 4000 pounds. One day Bedloe spied a man waiting outside the office of the council and pointed him out as one of the rogues seen beside Godfrey's body. This man was Miles Prance, a Catholic silversmith who occasionally worked for the queen.

They imprisoned Prance in Newgate and placed him in the unpleasant cell called 'Little Ease'. After a few days in this condition, he confessed.[43] He retracted. He confessed again and recanted. Eventually, Prance identified three men as the murderers of the magistrate named Green, Berry and Hill. Robert Green was a priest in Catherine's chapel, and Henry Berry worked as a porter at Somerset House.[44] Prance and Bedloe were the chief witnesses at their trial on 5 February 1679, where these three innocent men were convicted and later hanged at Tyburn.

After the Duke of York left for Brussels on 9 March 1679, a bill came before parliament requiring his exclusion from the throne. The opponents of the duke wanted Charles to confess he married his mistress, Lucy Walter, so the Duke of Monmouth could succeed him. Charles once again denied he had ever married anyone but Catherine.

Samuel Atkins established his alibi. He had been on board a ship at the time of the magistrate's murder and they released Atkins from prison. Parliament impeached Danby. In June, five Jesuits were convicted and hanged. The Whig leaders, such as Lord Shaftesbury, had gained outstanding success in the trials of the Popish Plot and were eager to pursue more 'plotters'. They realised if they could put Wakeman on trial and find him guilty, it would incriminate the queen.

The moment Wakeman heard of the charges he adamantly wanted to defend himself. He had already presented a resume of his life's work and loyalty to the House of Stuart, asking for reparations from parliament.[45] The trial took place at the Old Bailey on 18 July 1679, the Lord Chief Justice William Scroggs presiding.[46] Along with the physician, three Benedictine monks, William Marshal, William Rumley and James Corker faced arraignment.

The king's position was problematic. He had to pursue the charges to distance his government and the Crown from accusations of popery and protect his wife and others of importance. Wakeman's trial would implicate Catherine and, by extension, the king's own crown in the plot, creating a crisis.[47]

The ubiquitous Oates and Bedloe acted as the chief witnesses for the prosecution. Oates repeated his story of witnessing a document appointing Wakeman as physician-in-general for the army and a receipt for the 5000 pound down payment on the 15,000 owed to the doctor. He implied Queen Catherine knew of Wakeman's plan to poison her husband and place the Duke of York on the throne as revenge for Charles' unfaithfulness. In giving bonus testimony, he added they would kill King Charles' natural born son, the Duke of Monmouth. Bedloe swore he was on intimate terms with Wakeman.

Wakeman actively worked and argued in his own defence. He called witnesses and cross-examined those who gave evidence against him.[48] The preparation of Wakeman's case was given the highest priority by someone of authority, possibly on the orders of King Charles himself. The doctor had access to the records of parliamentary evidence, including the House of Lords Journal and other paperwork regarding the government's investigation into the plot.[49] Someone gave permission for the removal of the manuscript from the House. Whether this authority was the king or the council is a matter for speculation.[50]

In his inimitable way, Wakeman totally discredited the prosecution's evidence by establishing the letter Oates cited as proving him guilty was in reality a prescription by his assistant and not himself. The prescription had no notation at the bottom regarding the killing of the king.[51] Also, he forced Oates to admit he did not recognise Wakeman's handwriting. To be on intimate terms with a man like Bedloe was patently absurd for a man of his own position. Wakeman argued his family remained fiercely loyal to the Crown. During the Interregnum of Oliver Cromwell, they had imprisoned Wakeman for conspiring to restore the monarchy, and his brother Richard raised troops of cavalry for the king and for the king's father as well.

Lord Chief Justice Scroggs courageously stated his doubts about the truth of Oates' testimony. He commented harshly on the integrity of the evidence presented by the prosecution. The case went to the jury for deliberation. The jury asked if they could find the prisoners guilty of misprision of treason. Scroggs told them they could not, and the jury found the defendants not guilty.[52] It is said the king cried at the verdicts.[53]

A few days after the acquittal, Wakeman went to Windsor Castle to greet the king and queen and then promptly left England for Brussels. The physician would return to England in 1685 to testify at the perjury trial of Titus Oates in May, and after this he disappears from the record and we know nothing further of his career.[54] The outcome of Wakeman's trial did not end the Popish Plot, but it certainly turned the tide. Only two more Catholics went to trial, were found guilty and executed. Perhaps the most fortunate consequence of the trial was the queen's release from suspicion.

Charles' biographer, Ronald Hutton, ventures to determine why Charles so fiercely defended Catherine and his brother during this crisis, aside from the political reasons. Hutton says he had a strong sense of the sanctity of kingship. Charles inherited the throne because of his descent in blood, and because of this strongly rooted belief in hereditary monarchy, he may have been superstitious about tampering with this descent to anyone other than his brother, James. Hutton believes Charles sustained a strong sense of family, which was sharpened by his ten-year-long exile. His brother and his wife were precious to him, whatever their failings. It is evident Charles always strived to reward those who were loyal and obedient. He could rely upon Catherine and James to submit to his wishes in all matters except their faith, and for this, Charles willingly repaid them.[55]

Chapter Six

Last Years of Her Marriage, Charles' Death and Widowhood in England

The Last Years of Her Marriage

The unpopularity of Catholics resulted in Catherine being publicly insulted as she went to her chapel at Somerset House. From now on, she worshiped in the chapel at St James', because of its more private access.[1] Convinced of the futility of his mission, the Marquis of Arronches was persuaded to leave Catherine in peace, much to her relief. In the meantime, sporadic rumblings of the Popish Plot continued.

Titus Oates informed authorities that the house in Hammersmith, patronised by Catherine, harboured Jesuits and priests and was frequented by suspicious persons. The highly respected Cecily Cornwallis held the post of Abbess of Hammersmith, and she often entertained Catherine during her visits to the convent.[2] Much admired for her extraordinary learning, Cornwallis read and spoke Latin, Hebrew, Greek and other modern languages and was well versed in philosophy and mathematics. She regularly met with other intellectuals, foreigners and admirers.[3] During her examination by the Privy Council, Cornwallis swore she harboured no such obnoxious persons as suggested by Oates, and the council immediately acquitted her of any wrongdoing.[4]

In the summer after Wakeman's trial, Buss, the Duke of Monmouth's cook, brought additional charges before Lord Shaftesbury's committee concerning a servant of Catherine's confessor named Antonio. They arrested the man and committed him for trial. The Privy Council followed up this fresh charge by moving forward with bringing Catherine to trial. Charles vetoed the motion and went out of his way to show how deeply he cared for his wife.

Catherine settled down to a quiet life at Windsor while the king lived privately, walking in the park and fishing. They were as close as they had ever been. Lady Sunderland wrote to Henry Sidney to say Catherine 'is a mistress now, the passion her spouse has for her is so great'.[5] On 20 August 1680, Popish Plot informer, William Bedloe, died. On his deathbed he gave a deposition to Chief Justice

Francis North, swearing the Duke of York was guiltless of any evil intention toward the king. As for the queen, she had no knowledge of any design to kill the king.[6] For once, Bedloe spoke the truth.

In early September, Charles fell seriously ill and quickly recalled his brother from Brussels. By the time the Duke arrived, the king had recovered and much to James' annoyance, Charles ordered him back into exile, this time in Scotland. Shaftesbury once more brought an Exclusion Bill before Parliament, asking Charles to bar James from inheriting the throne. The bill passed the Commons and went to the House of Lords. Discussion of the bill included additional talk of divorcing Catherine so Charles could marry a Protestant.

Charles recalled James to England and personally visited the peers, asking them to vote against it, and Shaftesbury's motion duly suffered defeat. Charles went directly to Catherine to tell her the news and slept in her chamber after dinner, something he usually did in the apartments of Kéroualle. The constant stress and feelings of guilt about the political pressure on the king seriously undermined Catherine's health. For the next four months, she suffered chills and fever, rendering her very weak. She wrote to her brother praising Charles for his esteem, his proof of his love and his generosity.

By November, they had imprisoned five Catholic Lords in the Tower, including the nearly 70-year-old Lord Stafford. Stafford went on trial with the accusations against him mirroring those against Catherine, namely plotting to kill the king and bring Catholicism to England. Catherine attended the trial with her ladies, eagerly following the proceedings from a private box in Westminster Hall. Catherine's name arose during the testimony.[7] They found Stafford guilty and sentenced him to a traitor's death, which the king commuted to beheading. Another Catholic Lord died in captivity, and they eventually released the other three.

On 25 December 1680, Sir John Reresby attended a dinner hosted by the Bishop of Ely. Also present was Titus Oates, who pontificated before the guests, insulting the queen, the Duke of York, and even the now deceased queen mother. Reresby quickly realised what a fool he was and, unable to take much more, proceeded to openly castigate Oates in front of the guests. Oates left the table in a huff.[8]

In 1681, new accusations put Catherine and the Duke of York in danger. An Irishman and employee of Kéroualle named Edward Fitzharris wrote a pamphlet bringing the succession into question and committing libel by accusing Catherine and James of conspiring to kill the king. He declared the Portuguese ambassador, Francisco de Melo Manoel da Câmara,[9] informed him of Catherine's involvement in a design for poisoning the king.[10] Charles forbid the questioning of his wife and brother and determined to make an example of Fitzharris. He ordered the indictment of the man in common law for treason for the publishing of the pamphlet.

All this trouble caused Catherine to become withdrawn. In Newmarket, during the month of the Fitzharris trial, one of Catherine's dressers reported that when the other ladies of the court went out riding, Catherine remained in solitude and retired for most of the day at her devotions and reading. She also abstained from playing cards, something so unusual it was remarked upon.[11]

Catherine and Charles travelled to Windsor and then moved on to Oxford, where parliament opened on 21 March with Shaftesbury determined to call the queen and the Duke of York for questioning in the trial of Fitzharris. Charles opened parliament in state and witnessed the debate of the Exclusion Bill and the proceedings of Fitzharris' trial. Shaftesbury presented the king with a note asking him to name the Duke of Monmouth as heir to the throne. Charles said he loved his son, but nothing would make him alter the law of succession against his brother because that would go against the law and the dictates of his conscience.

There was considerable debate when the Commons called for the exclusion of James from the throne. George Savile, Earl of Halifax, argued if they deprived James of the throne, they could manipulate the law to deny the hereditary right of the nobility to pass on their estates to their own heirs. Halifax then introduced a scheme for limiting the prerogatives of a Catholic monarch.[12]

Charles countered with an unusual offer. James would become king in name only but be proclaimed unfit to rule. A regency would be declared to govern the country, with James' daughter, Mary, and her husband, William of Orange, named as joint protectors of the realm. Although James would bear the title of king, he would be banished from his dominions during his lifetime. This offer failed to satisfy the Commons, and they introduced a new Exclusion Bill omitting the name of Charles' successor, something the king could not countenance.[13]

During the discussion regarding the case of Fitzharris, Shaftesbury argued his trial should take place in parliament while the Lords argued a jury of his peers should try him. The discussion ran for six days, leading to an impasse regarding the succession and Fitzharris' trial. Charles ordered the Black Rod to summon the Commons into the Lord's chamber where he appeared before both Houses in full regalia, crown and robes. He sat on the throne and announced parliament dissolved and declared Fitzharris would stand trial in civil court.

The king and queen went to Newmarket in May, and they attended the launch of the *Britannia* at Chatham. Kéroualle, called to testify at Fitzharris' trial in June, defended herself well. Following a guilty verdict, they executed Fitzharris at Tyburn. Shortly after his execution, six Irish witnesses, five of whom were Protestant, came forward and gave evidence against Shaftesbury, revealing he was responsible for the false accusations against Catherine and the Duke of York. They arrested Shaftesbury on the charge of high treason and imprisoned him in the Tower.

Kéroualle, feeling unwell, sought permission from Charles to go to France and take the waters at Bourbon. Charles readily agreed and she departed. On 1 April, the king signed a treaty with Louis XIV in which the French king agreed to pay him a subsidy of 400,000 pounds, freeing Charles from the need to seek authorisation for expenses from parliament. On 2 July he arrived in London where the king and his council seized all of Shaftesbury's documents. By the end of the day, he greeted Catherine at Windsor. Exonerated, she could breathe a sigh of relief at last. Kéroualle returned that same month. In August, they arrested Titus Oates for sedition, fined him 100,000 pounds and threw him into prison.

In early 1682, the king and queen received the Moroccan ambassador in the Banqueting House. The ambassador presented gifts, including lions and ostriches.[14] Later, Kéroualle entertained the Moroccans with a banquet in her chambers. Her involvement with Fitzharris had displeased Charles and she made her best endeavour to get back into his good graces. Catherine did not attend the meal, remaining quietly at Somerset House.

Catherine would appear at court upon Charles' command, and they enjoyed each other's company during the summer. She wrote to her brother of her happiness and gratitude for her husband's defence of her during the Plot.[15] While travelling to Newcastle in September, they received a grand welcome from an enthusiastic crowd in Cambridge. Catherine and Charles enjoyed a newfound popularity. They spent their evenings together playing basset, and Catherine took many long walks at all hours of the day and night. Catherine continued her patronage and visited high-ranking ladies.[16]

With grand celebration, the Duke of York returned to England, ostensibly for a brief visit. James persuaded his brother to allow him to stay and bring his wife and daughter, Anne, home. Following this, James' outlook for inheriting the throne looked more conclusive. Calm returned to England and trade flourished.

The king and queen travelled throughout the country for pleasure. Charles began a program of improving some of his royal palaces. Windsor received a complete, resplendent refurbishing. Sir Christopher Wren designed a new palace for construction in Winchester. Charles laid the cornerstone of the palace and supervised the work while living with Catherine in modest lodgings. He brought Nell Gwyn to town in order to enjoy her company.

Based on the designs for the palace at Winchester, it is believed Charles wanted to imitate his cousin Louis XIV's great home of Versailles. And there was a noteworthy aspect to the design of the palace. While English palaces normally were built with a chapel designed for joint royal worship and accessible from both the king and the queen's apartments, this was not the case at Winchester. There was no plan for a communal chapel, but instead two separate chapels, one in the king's and one in the queen's apartments. It seems Charles was no longer apologising for Catherine's Catholicism and recognising that the king and queen could worship apart as members of equally legitimate Churches.[17]

The Earl of Shaftesbury died in Holland in early 1683, the place he had escaped to the previous November. In April, Catherine admonished Charles at Windsor.

She protested that his mistresses dominated him while they humiliated her. Charles immediately went to Kéroualle's apartments and complained about the incident to a gathering there.[18]

They uncovered another assassination plot, dubbed the Rye House plot, named for Rye House near Hoddesdon, Hertfordshire on the way to the horseracing town of Newmarket. A certain Captain Richard Rumbold and many others planned to waylay the king and his brother in March on their way back from the races. The plan involved putting a cart across the road the men traversed on their way, blocking their coach where they would be ambushed and shot. They planned to conceal 100 men on the grounds, leaving little chance of escape. Following the conclusion of the deed, they would declare the Duke of Monmouth king.

In a strange twist of fate, a fire broke out in the town centre of Newmarket and quickly spread, cancelling the races. Charles and James departed for London earlier than expected and foiled the plot. By June, one plotter, named Keeling, revealed the Duke of Monmouth as one of the main conspirators and a grand jury implicated Monmouth in the plot. Exasperated with his eldest son's behaviour, Charles planned to make an example of him, but Catherine interceded for the duke to save his life. Monmouth swore he had no part in the assassination plans, but revealed his involvement in a conspiracy to create uprisings. He later recanted this confession. Incensed, Charles exiled his son from court. The king told Monmouth the queen's entreaties had gained his pardon, and she alone was to thank for it.[19]

Catherine took part in the preparations for the marriage of Princess Anne, daughter of the Duke of York, to Prince George of Denmark. She greeted the prince upon his arrival in England and they celebrated a modest wedding at St James' Palace on 28 July 1683. Afterwards, the king and queen were guests of honour at a wedding banquet and they remained at St James' until they bedded the couple.[20]

Catherine's brother, the deposed King Afonso, died in September 1683. The English court went into mourning and Catherine spent many hours in prayer. The only entertainment she allowed herself was card-playing. Charles would often visit her chambers and they talked for hours. The queen's birthday party in November would be the grandest of them all and turned out to be the last such celebration at Whitehall. The fireworks in front of the palace were dazzling, with rockets shot out of forts and castles. Charles and Catherine's coats of arms filled the sky in molten gold. Afterwards, everyone danced in their finest outfits during the evening ball.

The winter was so cold, the Thames froze over. Charles and Catherine attended a market held on the ice and enjoyed themselves immensely. He resumed his liaison with Kéroualle. She had been allowed to remain in Catherine's household with the stipulation that she not attend the queen in person. In the spring of 1684, Kéroualle insinuated herself among Catherine's maids and waited on her during dinner. Her tactics and behaviour were mean and heavy-handed. She laughed at the queen and Catherine broke down in tears in public. Kéroualle must have viewed Catherine as a threat.[21]

During the rest of the year, Catherine and Charles relaxed and enjoyed each other's company. They took trips to Winchester, Windsor and Newmarket, walked in St James' Park and played games in the evening. In September, Catherine was in residence at Windsor where she enjoyed one of her favourite pastimes, a picnic in the sun in which all her servants treated her.[22] Charles spent time in his laboratory conducting scientific and chemical experiments, and passed the time with his spaniels and tame foxes and the birds in his aviaries. In May, the king and queen came to London for the birth of Princess Anne's first child. She gave birth to a stillborn baby on 12 May.[23]

Charles' Death and Deathbed Conversion to Catholicism

In early 1685, Charles had a sore leg, forcing him to shorten his long walks in the park. On the evening of 1 February, he was seen in the company of his former and current mistresses, Castlemaine, Hortense Mancini and Kéroualle. He felt lethargic and distracted, unable to eat. After spending the night groaning and restless, he looked pale and ill in the morning. At 8 o'clock, while his barber prepared to shave him, the king collapsed. The doctor bled him, and Catherine flew to his side, with the Duke and Duchess of York arriving soon after.

It would be the first of many gruesome treatments given the king. The imminent death of Charles seemed a harsh reality to Catherine and she spoke to Mary Beatrice, asking her to inform the duke to look to the king's immortal soul. Catherine then fainted and they carried her away to her chambers. An hour would pass before the duchess spoke to James as the doctors put Charles to bed and gave him purgatives. He remained stoic over the next two days as he underwent countless horrific medical procedures.

Catherine stayed with her husband at his bedside as much as she could, feeling faint and queasy herself. At one point, when he regained consciousness, he asked for his wife who had gone to her rooms. She sent word, asking the king to excuse her absence and begged his forgiveness if she had ever offended him. Charles replied, 'Alas! Poor woman! She begs my pardon! I beg hers with all my heart'.[24]

When Catherine could come to him, she stayed nearby and Charles tried to console her. Also attending the king were the Archbishop of Canterbury and the bishops of London, Durham, and Bath and Wells, Thomas Ken. Bishop Ken read the prayers for the sick and dying, asking the king if he repented of his sins and prepared to receive holy communion. Charles replied he repented of his sins, but there would be time enough for taking communion.

Ronald Hutton, Charles' biographer, states many people took credit for the king's deathbed conversion and the narratives changed as time passed. There is no doubt the king converted to the Catholic faith and Hutton says Charles did not initiate the idea. Those who claimed credit in the history books include the French ambassador Barillon, Kéroualle, the Duchess of York, an English priest named Benedict Gibbon, Queen Catherine, and the king's brother. The Duke of York did obtain Charles' consent for the conversion.[25]

They made a search for a priest. The laws barring Catholics had decimated the number of Portuguese priests in Catherine's chapel, and those remaining spoke no English. Father Huddleston, another of Catherine's priests and the king's companion since the days of the English Civil Wars, was in her chambers, having been summoned from Somerset House. The Count of Castelo Melhor, who had not left the queen's side since she first fainted, appealed to Huddleston and he agreed to go to the king. They gave him a Protestant cassock to wear and one of the queen's friars went to fetch the Holy Sacrament from St James' Chapel.[26]

James cleared the bedchamber of everyone except the earls of Bath and Feversham, two Protestants, both of whom Charles and James implicitly trusted. Huddleston arrived by a private door. He heard Charles' confession, absolved the king of his sins, and Charles received Holy Communion. The priest left through the same door he entered and the others, puzzled by their expulsion, returned to the chamber. They noticed Charles refused the Anglican sacraments following the incident. After this, the king rallied a little and his thoughts turned to his family. He expressed his love for his wife and brother and commended to James' financial care his mistresses Kéroualle and Nell Gwyn along with all of his natural born sons with the exception of the Duke of Monmouth.[27] His daughters were not mentioned.[28]

Catherine, on her knees at midnight, begged the king to forgive her. He replied there was nothing to forgive, and on the contrary, it was he who had offended her many times and therefore in need of her forgiveness. On the morning of 6 February, he had a long conversation with his brother, who knelt by his side and kissed his hand. After giving James the keys to his cabinet, he thanked him for being the best of brothers. King Charles II died just before noon.[29]

Widowhood in England during the Reign of James II

Mary Beatrice was the first to console the queen.[30] The Privy Council called on Catherine to offer condolences, followed by James, who made the first of many formal visits. During these visits, James remained on his knees, even though his status as king allowed him to be seated.[31] Catherine ordered her chamber to be lined with black cloth with the windows shut and with only candlelight, making the room sombre and funereal. Dressed in mourning, she received letters from heads of state and from her brother, and visits from ambassadors and envoys from all over Europe. She arranged to have Masses sung in Lisbon on the anniversary of Charles' death for as long as she lived.[32]

They proclaimed James king shortly after Charles' death. The former king's remains were taken discreetly to Westminster Abbey at night on 14 February to avoid burying him in accordance with either Catholic or Protestant rites. Catherine remained at Whitehall for two months, moving back to Somerset House in April. She appointed Louis Duras, Earl of Feversham, to oversee her household. A French Huguenot, he had immigrated to England in 1663 and served as master of the horse and lord chamberlain to Catherine. Charles had trusted him implicitly, having served as one of the king's lords of the bedchamber. Rumours ran rampant that Feversham and Catherine were lovers but she would never have affairs.

The accession of James II to the throne gave Catherine considerable security. The Catholic faith now had official recognition, with Catholics and Protestants enjoying the same rights, allowing Catherine to practise her faith publicly. On 7 April, Catherine paid her first formal call on the new queen. During this visit, she presented the chapel of St James' and the adjoining friary to Mary Beatrice, after having recently spent 5000 pounds for renovations. Both women attended to their devotions together in public in St James' Chapel. They crowned James and Mary Beatrice on 23 April. Catherine was eager to maintain a good relationship with the king and queen and they frequently visited her at Somerset House.

All of her Portuguese priests from St James' chapel retired with her to Somerset House. Catherine's apartments at Whitehall were now in the hands of the new queen.[33] Kéroualle sailed for France in August, and Titus Oates, accused of perjury and defamation, was found guilty. There was no death penalty for perjury, so they sentenced him to be pilloried and whipped on the route from Newgate to Tyburn every year.

Catherine ordered an elaborate marble bust of Charles II.[34] Depressed, restless and unhappy, life was quiet for two years. She spent hours in prayer in her chapel and took long walks for exercise in her gardens and in St James' Park as her physician's prescribed. She would sometimes drive into the country, leave her coach and walk. In the evenings she played basset, ombre or quadrille or listened to her musicians.[35] After a year, she recovered from her grief and resumed interest in her household affairs. She firmly resolved to maintain her recent weight loss through diet and exercise.[36]

Catherine's restlessness led her on a search for more comfortable surroundings, and she sought a country residence for some time. She inquired about purchasing Chatsworth from the Earl of Devonshire and considered building her own home, visiting Knowle and Euston, neither of which were entirely satisfactory. After taking a lease on Euston Hall for 400 pounds a month, her hunt continued.[37]

She finally settled on a residence in Hammersmith near the convent she patronised. From the Auditor's Memoranda in the Land Revenue documents kept at the Public Record Office, there are many details regarding Catherine's establishment at Hammersmith. In a note dated 6 September 1686, she instructed her treasurer 'to pay unto Ralph Box [the current owner] for a Fine for his house near Hammersmith hired for our service the sum of one hundred and twenty-five pounds'. The rent paid was sixty pounds per annum.

Catherine's attraction to the existing house is demonstrated by the accounts of the queen's disbursements, sparing no expense to enhance its beauty. Among the buildings mentioned in the Auditor Memoranda are: The Old House, the Great House, the Chapel, the Friary, the Dairy, the Banqueting House, an Orangery and the Billiard Table Room. The gardens and the greenhouse are consistently referred to with its Italian marble cistern. There was a birdcage and a record of wages paid for the employment of a 'keeper of the pheasants'.

She took possession immediately and hired two gardeners. Alterations to the house and the gardens included the rebuilding of the wharf or landing stage for her barge and the planting of elm trees. They took chimneys down and levelled the ground where the stables were located. Workers reinforced the wall in the Old House next to the Thames, painted the dairy, put in a drain and altered some windows. She acquired a carved pedestal used for a table stand in the greenhouse.[38]

Certain adjacent property was also rented, with records of several pounds being paid per year to various owners. She needed the extra space to accommodate her staff and the entire complex must have resembled a miniature colony. The four acres included carefully laid out walls and buildings.[39] Catherine was living in the house by 5 April 1687, and for the rest of her time in England she alternated between living in Somerset House, this idyllic manor and Euston Hall.

Catherine left England in 1692 but the establishment at Hammersmith continued until Michaelmas, 1706 when the last rent payment arrived, and her porter received his final wages. The house was described in 1705–6, around the time of the queen's death, as 'magnificent enough to entertain Queen Katherine, now Queen Dowager, where she kept her Palace in Summertime'.[40] The owner of the 'Dowager's House' tore it down in 1808 to build a new house on the property.[41]

James, Duke of Monmouth, rose up against James, something the king expected. Catherine's chamberlain, Lord Feversham, took troops to put down the rebellion. The army chased down the duke and engaged him in battle at Sedgemoor, with Feversham victorious. They captured 500 of Monmouth's men and eventually apprehended the duke as he tried to escape. Monmouth wrote to Catherine asking her to intercede with the king on his behalf, in memory of king Charles.[42] He stated others had coerced him into making a bid for the crown.

Catherine went to Whitehall to plead the duke's case and implore the king to pardon him. He had crossed a line with his rebellion, and King James could no longer save him. Catherine convinced the king to meet with the duke, something he previously refused to do. But nothing was gained by the audience. Found guilty of treason, they executed Monmouth on Tower Hill on 15 July 1685.

In the fall, Catherine fell ill with groaning and perspiring for several hours at a time, writing to Pedro she was in great pain. At one point, she believed she would die. Queen Mary Beatrice stayed with her during her illness. She attributed her recovery to the oil from the lamp of the Immaculate Conception of the Virgin Mary from the chapel at the palace of Vila Viçosa, the same cure used for her quinsy when she was 3 years old.[43] Once she recovered she maintained a small, dignified court at Somerset House with regular state visits from King James. John Evelyn sent his daughter to kiss Catherine's hand. Catherine played cards with Lord Feversham keeping the bank for the players.

The Count of Castelo Melhor was recalled to Portugal and this brought back fond memories for Catherine, leading her to contemplate returning to her motherland. In order to make this happen, she needed two things. Ships to make the voyage and permission from her brother the king. Nostalgic for her family, the sunshine, the gardens and healthy breezes, she quietly began a letter-writing campaign to Pedro, asking to return as her marriage treaty permitted, without telling King James of her plans.

Pedro's first wife had died in 1683 and he had committed to marry Maria Sophia Elisabeth of Neuberg. A proxy marriage took place in July 1687. Maria Sophia's father, Philip William, Elector Palatine, contacted Catherine for help with his daughter's travel arrangements to Portugal. Catherine got King James' permission for an English convoy to sail with the princess to Lisbon, and they scheduled the ships to stop at Portsmouth along the way. She could not ignore this opportunity. Catherine wanted to accompany the convoy to Portugal for the wedding, but Pedro withheld his permission and the ships sailed without her.

The couple were married in Lisbon on 12 August 1687. Letters from Catherine continued to arrive in Portugal in the hope she could obtain her brother's permission to return in the future, or in case she needed his protection. Preparations began for her journey home.

Shortly after Charles' death, James granted Catherine an annual annuity of 6000 pounds for life. She continued to receive the queen mother's dowry of 18,000 pounds along with Post Office revenues of over 19,000 pounds and another charge on the Exchequer of 10,000 pounds along with other dower-lands and annuities. This amounted to roughly 50,000 pounds per annum.

Catherine set to work in reckoning her income and realised there was a shortfall. It soon became clear her Lord Treasurer, Henry Hyde, second Earl of Clarendon, formerly Lord Cornbury, besides his 50 pound annual salary, had taken other rights, profits, privileges and advantages belonging to his office to the tune of 36,000 pounds.[44] She now believed Clarendon had not always managed her revenue as he should and took measures to reclaim her money.

With the advice of her chancellor and keeper of her seal, George Savile, now Marquess of Halifax, she sued Clarendon in January 1688. This lawsuit was against her better judgement, but she needed the funds for her journey. The case would continue for many months. If she left England without settling the debt, she would never see the money. The Portuguese court was poor and she knew she had to be self-sufficient once there. Mary Beatrice took Catherine's side as she knew this could happen to her. James took a middle course but was ashamed Catherine had pressed the matter to the extent she did.[45]

Eventually, Pedro gave her permission to come to Portugal and he agreed to send an ambassador. Catherine's decision to leave England disappointed King James, for he truly believed she was happy and took it personally. But he agreed to provide the ships necessary to carry her household goods and staff. She awaited Pedro's ambassador to accompany her and inquired for Pedro's advice regarding various arrangements. Her primary concern focused on where she would live once in Portugal, believing a farm or country house would be conducive to her health. The idea of the dowager queen returning delighted the people of Portugal.[46]

Once word came that the Count of Ponteval was on his way, King James went to Chatham to choose the appropriate ships for the crossing the English Channel. But all these plans were disrupted when Catherine developed a painful growth on her breast and her physicians forbade her to travel. It took some time to recover from the illness, but she improved. While she recuperated, Catherine worried about her unsettled lawsuit against Clarendon. A good portion of the debt had already been paid, but there was still an outstanding balance. She decided to remain in England and see the lawsuit through, and they intercepted the Portuguese ambassador.

Since the beginning of his reign, King James had begun enacting measures which alarmed parliament and the people. He allowed Catholics to obtain offices in the government and the military. He attempted to lessen the penal laws against Catholics and replaced the professors and administration of the universities with Catholics. While these actions created anxiety, the people were willing to put up with them, as long as James' heir was his Protestant daughter, Mary, and her husband William of Orange.

All this changed in the fall of 1687 when it was confirmed Mary Beatrice was expecting a child who would undoubtedly be raised as a Catholic. Catherine suffered some kind of ailment, making her hand so stiff she could hardly hold a pen, but she could write to her brother expressing her joy.[47] Gossip began almost immediately, much of it induced by James' daughter, Princess Anne, that the queen was not really pregnant. In early June, James requested Catherine witness the birth of his child. He wanted no controversy over the delivery of the heir to the throne. She and James had always agreed to work for the legitimate, hereditary Stuart succession.[48]

Catherine received a summons when Mary Beatrice's labour began and she arrived at a quarter past nine on 10 June 1688, and greeted the queen in her bed. She then posted herself in a chair under a canopy of state beside the chimney-piece clock along with many other witnesses, staying for the entire birth.[49] To his parents' great joy, a prince was born and baptised James Francis Edward. Even with all the precautions taken by the king, rumours circulated that the queen had delivered a stillborn son and a substitute had been borne into the bedchamber hidden in a warming pan. The notion of a Catholic heir to the throne was hard to bear for James' Protestant daughter Anne, her sister Mary and her husband, and for the English people.

Catherine agreed to serve as godmother to the child. The rumours about the child not being the real prince astounded the king. He called a special meeting of the Privy Council on 22 October. Attending were the entire council, dowager queen Catherine, the Archbishop of Canterbury, all the bishops who were in town, judges, eminent lawyers, the Lord Mayor of London, aldermen and sheriffs and all those who attended the birth of James Francis Edward, Prince of Wales.[50]

Catherine swore before the council she witnessed the birth of the boy and signed an affidavit. Other ladies who had witnessed the birth testified in great detail about the delivery of the baby. James wanted no questions to arise over the legitimacy of his son. But it was too late. Seven Protestant English nobles sent an invitation to Prince William of Orange to come to England to establish order and protect the Anglican Church. William and Mary had significant doubts about the legitimacy of James' son and truly believed the English people never wanted a Catholic king.

William arrived with an army in early November. Knowing the invasion was inevitable, James went through the motions of raising his own army, intending to engage William in battle. He never followed through. He sent Mary Beatrice and his son into France with a promise to follow her. As he tried to make his escape, they captured him and brought him back to London. Upon arriving, he visited Catherine at Somerset House to give her his reassurances. During the invasion, Catherine remained silent. She sympathised with James but did not want to offend William. William and Mary were proclaimed joint sovereigns on 12 February 1689.

The powers that be eventually allowed James to make his way to his wife in France. As he left, he visited Catherine on 18 December 1688, and they would never see each other again. Feversham acted as an intermediary between James and the new king, delivering a letter from the deposed king to William which so infuriated him, he threw Feversham in prison. After James withdrew to Rochester on 20 December, William visited Catherine at Somerset House, where he found her sitting idle. William asked Catherine why she was not playing her usual game of basset. She replied she had not played basset since he had sent her chamberlain to the Tower as he always kept the bank. William released Lord Feversham and restored him to Catherine's service.[51]

Catherine Orchestrates Her Return to Portugal

James made his way to France, leaving Catherine as the only remaining Catholic member of the royal family. The people, and the new king and queen regarded her with suspicion. King William had appropriated the dowry of Mary Beatrice and Catherine feared the same would happen to her. William was accommodating and would remain kind and just in his treatment of Catherine, but the queen appeared to harbour a petty jealous dislike for the dowager queen. Catherine made her official visit to Whitehall on 24 March 1689, to pay her respects to the new monarchs.

The coronation took place on 11 April in Westminster Abbey and Catherine declined to attend, hoping to keep a low profile because of the peril of being a Catholic in England. She awaited the outcome of her lawsuit and Pedro suggested she come home. She very much wanted to leave but the confused state of affairs in England created disarray and she could not make her case for the needed ships until things calmed down. William and Louis XIV were impeding her return, with Louis denying her passage through France twice.[52]

Those who continued to support the restoration of James to the English throne were known as Jacobites and their first rebellion took place in May 1689. The nervous government discussed curtailing certain clauses of Catherine's marriage settlement. The House of Commons passed a bill against Papists. It did not pass the House of Lords, but Catherine's entire staff of Catholic servants was reduced to eighteen.[53] The House of Lords stated:

> … that Her Majesty had for many years made such moderate use of the said articles [of her marriage treaty], that there had not been any just occasion of complaint: that it was evident in the time of King James, when Her Majesty might have been encouraged to entertain more Persons of her own religion, that most of her servants … were continued, and other received into her family though Protestants….[54]

The situation became frightening enough for Catherine that she threatened to move outside of London to a smaller house. She followed through and took a lease on a humble residence in Islington, which she called her 'retreat'.[55] In letters to her brother, she tells him she lived in the house of an apothecary where she could walk among the trees. The property consisted of a small cottage, with two others, one on the right hand and one on the left, which could more properly be called closets than houses.

There were her apartments with those of her servants being in cupboards or alcoves. She had six or seven women and three or four men to wait on her.[56] In poor health, she took medicines and experimented with her diet. For six months, she travelled to London to go to chapel to hear one or two Masses, this being all she

1. Wedding of King John I of the House of Avis of Portugal and Philippa of Lancaster. King John negotiated the first treaty of commerce with England in 1386 and founded the House of Braganza when he endowed his illegitimate son, Afonso, with the title of Duke of Braganza. (Chronique d'Angleterre (Volume III). S. Netherlands [Bruges], late 15th century. Source: Royal 14 E. IV, f.284, British Library)

2. Treaty of Windsor, 1386. (Public domain from Wikimedia Commons)

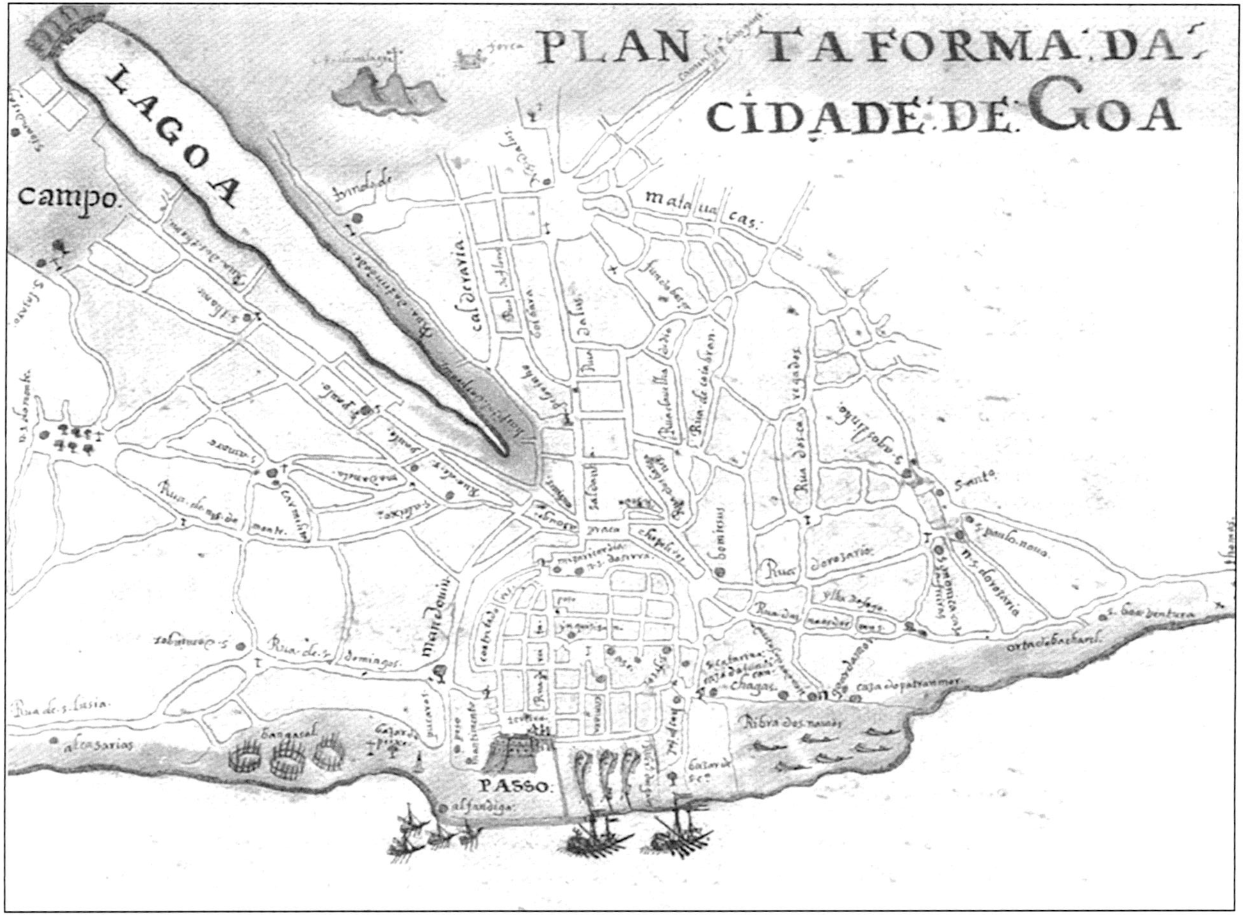

3. A map of Portuguese Goa on the western coast of India in *Livro das Plantaformas das Foralezas da India* made by the Portuguese cartographer Manual Godinho de Herédia in 1620. (Public domain from Wikimedia Commons)

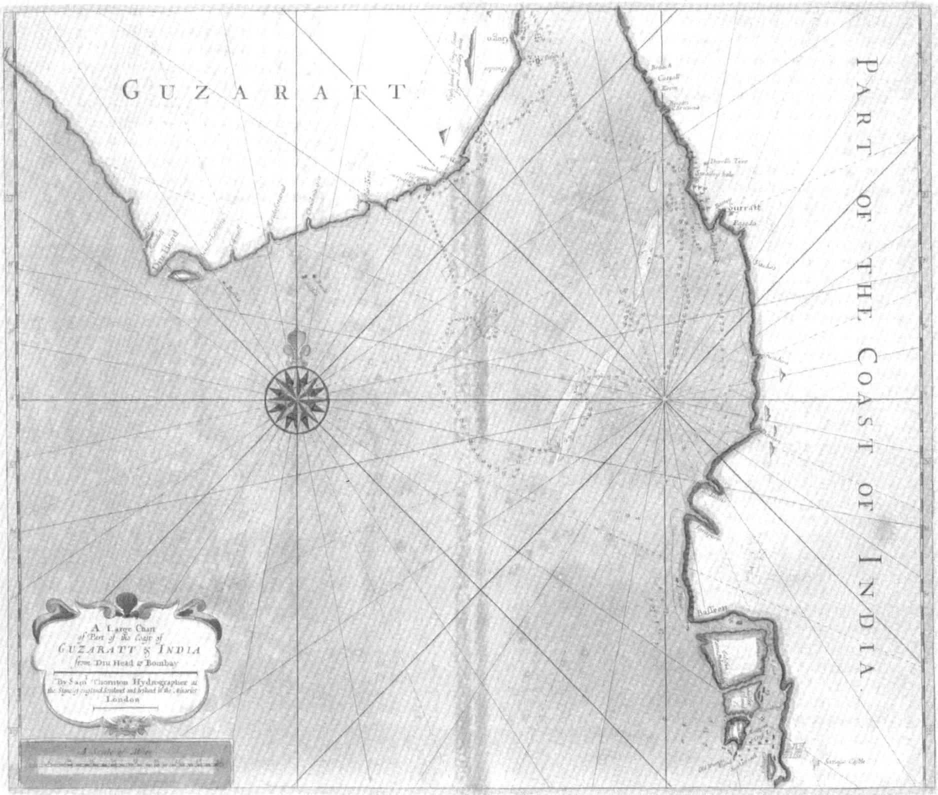

Above: **4.** A large chart of part of the coast of Guzaratt [Gujarat] and India from Diu Head to Bombay in the early eighteenth century by Samuel Thornton, cartographer. (New York Public Library; public domain image from the Look and Learn website)

Right: **5.** King John IV of Portugal, father of Catherine of Braganza. Engraving by Hendrik Hondius. (Rijksmuseum; public domain image from the Look and Learn website)

Left: **6.** Luisa de Guzmán, queen consort of Portugal and mother of Catherine of Braganza, attributed to José de Avelar Revelo. (Public domain from Wikiwand.com)

Below: **7.** Episodes from the Portuguese Restoration of Independence in which Philip IV of Spain was overthrown from the Portuguese throne, thus ending the Iberian Union, and John, 8th Duke of Braganza is made king of Portugal. (Public domain from Biblioteca Nacional de Portugal)

8. The Ducal Palace of Vila Viçosa with the statue of King John IV of Portugal and the royal chapel on the right. (Jack Moreh from Freerange Stock)

9. The monastery of the Holy Sacrament (Santíssimo Sacramento) located at Rua do Sacramento a Alcântara, nos. 43 to 51, was founded by a deed of donation made in Evora, on 20 October 1605, by the Counts of Vimioso D. Luís de Portugal and D. Joana de Castro and Mendonça. Intended for the nuns of the Order of St Dominic (Dominican), this convent is a possible contender for where Catherine of Braganza received her education. (Public domain from website of the Santíssimo Sacramento)

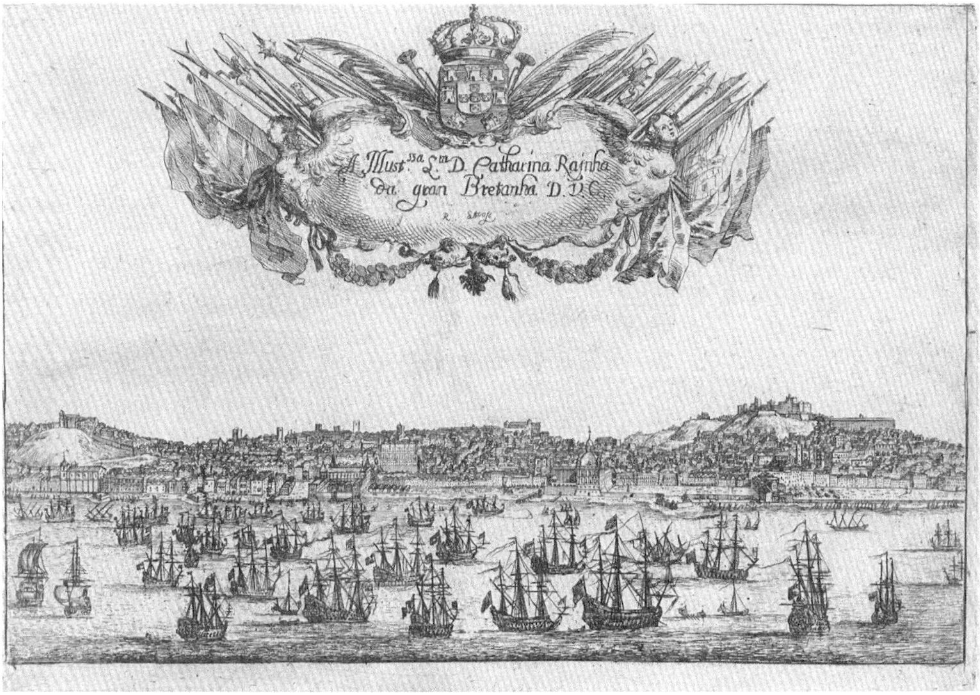

10. View of Lisbon from the Tagus River in 1662 by the Dutch artist, Dirck Stoop. (Rijksmuseum; public domain image from the Look and Learn website)

Above left: **11.** Possible contender as the marriage negotiation portrait of Catherine of Braganza sent to King Charles II of England. By or after Dirck Stoop. (Author holds written permission for use of this image. © National Portrait Gallery, London)

Above right: **12.** Charles Stuart, King Charles II of England in 1653 by Philippe de Champaigne. (Cleveland Museum of Art; public domain image from the Look and Learn website)

13. Embarkation of Queen Catherine of Braganza from Lisbon in 1662 by Dirck Stoop. The ship *Royal Charles* can be seen labelled to the right. (Rijksmuseum; public domain image from the Look and Learn website)

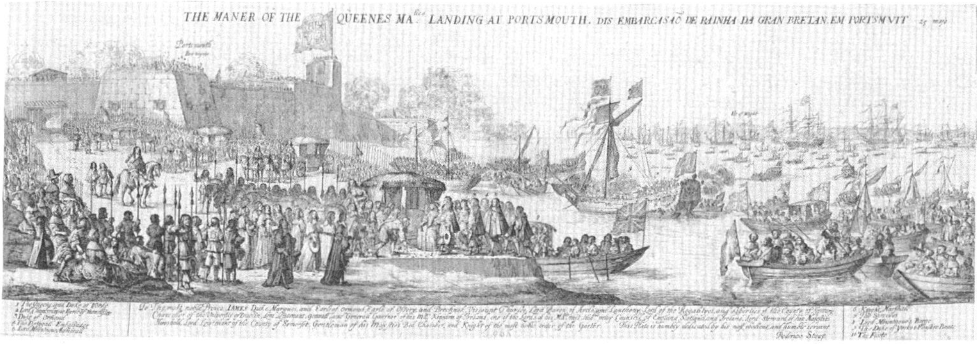

14. Arrival of Queen Catherine of Braganza in Portsmouth, England, in 1662 by Dirck Stoop. (Rijksmuseum; public domain image from the Look and Learn website)

15. In lieu of a coronation, they celebrated a triumph — the *Aqua Triumphalis* on the River Thames — at the arrival in London of King Charles II and Queen Catherine of Braganza. Image by Dirck Stoop, 1662. (Rijksmuseum; public domain image from the Look and Learn website)

16. Portrait of Queen Catherine of Braganza and King Charles II of England by an unknown artist. (Public domain from Wikimedia Commons)

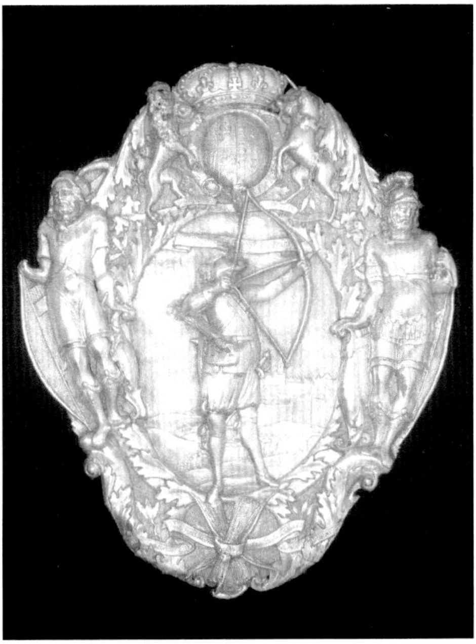

Above left: **17.** Catherine of Braganza (1638–1705), queen consort as wife of King Charles II of England. Portrait by Peter Lely, oil on canvas, c.1665. (Ian Dagnall Computing/Alamy Stock Photo)

Above right: **18.** The Catherine of Braganza Shield which is very generously on permanent loan to the Victoria and Albert Museum by the Royal Toxophilite Society. (Image © Victoria and Albert Museum, London)

Above left: **19.** Portrait of Barbara Villiers, Duchess of Cleveland. One of the major mistresses of King Charles II, Cleveland was a thorn in the side of Catherine for many years. (BTEU/RKMLGE/Alamy Stock Photo)

Above right: **20.** Portrait of Louise de Kéroualle, Duchess of Portsmouth in a landscape, 1678, by Gerard Valck. Louise, as principal mistress of King Charles II, eventually took over the duties of queen, leaving Catherine free to live an independent life in her palace of Somerset House. (Rijksmuseum; public domain image from the Look and Learn website)

Below: **21.** A drawing of Old Somerset House by Jan Kip, 1722. (Public domain from Wikimedia Commons)

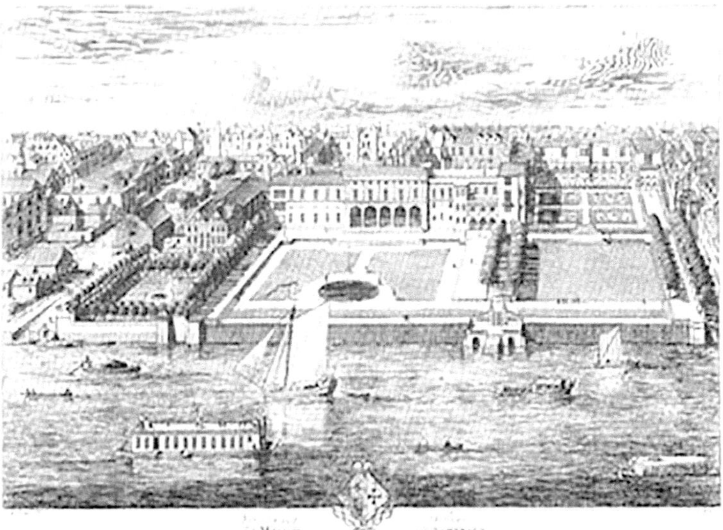

Left: **22.** Catherine of Braganza, queen consort of England, c.1679, in an engraving by Abraham de Blois. (Rijksmuseum; public domain image from the Look and Learn website)

Below: **23.** Titus Oates standing in the pillory surrounded by medallions of people executed as a result of his lies during the Popish Plot in an etching with engraving, 1678. (Wellcome Collection; public domain image from the Look and Learn website)

Right: **24.** King Pedro II of Portugal, brother of Catherine of Braganza. (Grafik aus dem Klebeband Nr 1 der Fürstlich Waldeckschen Hofbibliothek Arolsen, Motiv: König Peter II von Portugal, from the University of Heidelberg Library; public domain)

Below: **25.** The façade of the chapel of Bemposta Palace, the home built by Catherine in Lisbon, Portugal. (Attributed to Rick Morais; public domain image from Wikimedia Commons)

Left: **26.** Catherine of Braganza in an engraving by S. Freeman published in *Portraits of Illustrious Personages of Great Britain,* UK, 1830. (Classic Image/ Alamy Stock Photo)

Below: **27.** View of the Jerónimos Monastery in Lisbon in 1662. Engraving by Dirck Stoop. Catherine was initially buried here in the church following her funeral. (Rijksmuseum; public domain image from the Look and Learn website)

28. Monastery of St Vincent de Fora, the mausoleum of the Braganza kings in Lisbon. Catherine's remains were transferred here along with other members of her family in the nineteenth century. (Attributed to Brian Snelson; public domain image from Wikimedia Commons)

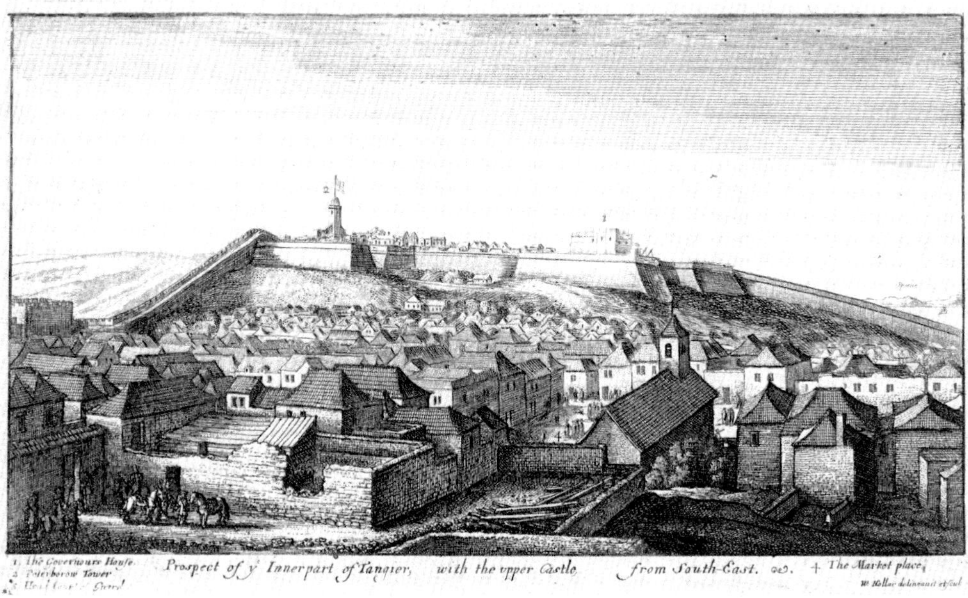

29. Prospect of the inner part of Tangier, with the upper castle, from the south-east. Engraving by Wenceslaus Hollar, published in London in 1673. (Folger Shakespeare Library; public domain image from the Look and Learn website)

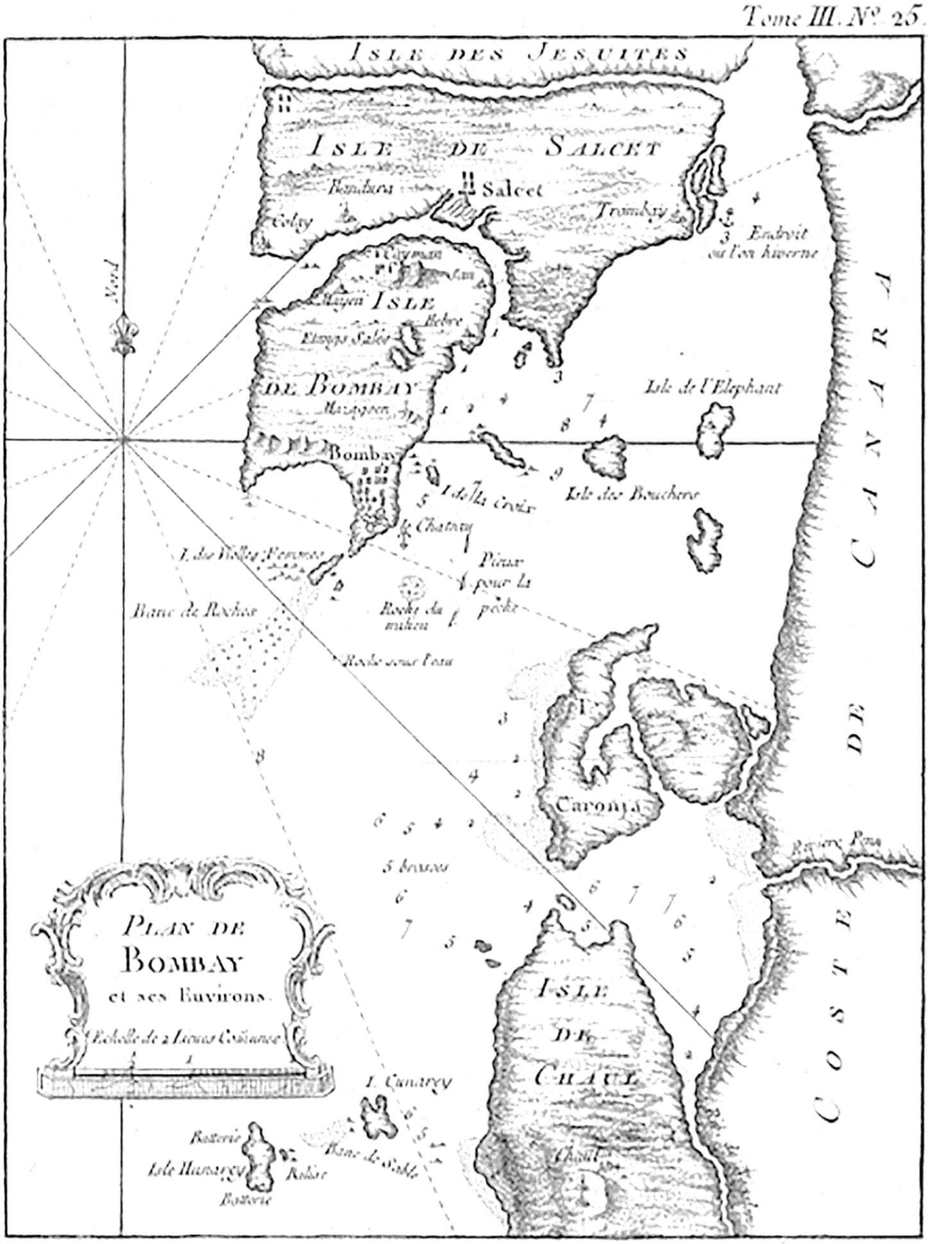

30. Map of Bombay or Mumbai, India, c.1764, by Jacques-Nicolas Bellin. (Public domain from Wikimedia Commons)

Above: **31.** Red Chinese lacquer cabinet from the eighteenth century. (Public domain image from the Metropolitan Museum of Art, New York open access program)

Right: **32.** Fine china teapot. (Public domain image from The Graphics Fairy website)

33. Chair of walnut and stained beech, the cresting carved with a crown supported by cherubs. The seat and the back panel are made of woven rattan cane. (© Victoria and Albert Museum, London)

could manage with the state of the Catholic Church being so dire.[57] In October, she returned to Somerset House where not long after she was informed that the palace would be searched.

The Earl of Shrewsbury had information regarding arms and treasonable papers hidden in the lodgings of one of Catherine's servants and he had a warrant to search for Popish priests allegedly hiding there. This greatly alarmed Catherine, but they found nothing. Her letters to her brother are now pitifully pleading for him to send one of his own ships for her. But the waters were being patrolled by all the European nations at war, and he could not risk Catherine's life or the ship.

In March 1690, the deposed king, James, landed with a French invasion force in Ireland and King William prepared to meet him. Lord Nottingham delivered a message from William saying he had information that there were secret meetings at Somerset House and requested that Catherine leave town and move to somewhere at least ten or twelve miles from London such as Windsor or Audley End. It appalled Catherine that the king was asking her to leave her primary residence. William had no power whatsoever to interfere with her place of residence based on the terms of her marriage treaty.[58]

Her response to Nottingham stated she just needed ships to quit King William's territories altogether. If William wanted her to leave, he should provide the transportation. She had no intention of leaving her house, which belonged to her by treaty. The next day, she dispatched Feversham and Lord Halifax to William to press her case. Nottingham arrived the next evening and told her she could stay. In April, many people flocked to Catherine's chapel to worship as it was the only remaining working Catholic chapel in England.

King William left for Ireland to deal in person with the forces sent by Louis XIV with James II to regain his throne. Queen Mary had full authority to rule in William's absence. Shortly before his departure, Mary ordered prayers be said in all the churches of England for her husband's success in the Irish campaign. The Savoy Chapel, attached to Somerset House and under Catherine's jurisdiction, was used by her Protestant servants to worship. Because of an unexplained omission, the chaplain failed to say Mary's prayers.

An unknown person informed Queen Mary of the error and she had the chaplain arrested and brought before the Privy Council. It is unclear if Catherine ordered the prayers not be read or if it was just an oversight. The chaplain declared that the Lord Chamberlain, Feversham, ordered the prayers to be omitted, fearing if he did read them Catherine would stop all further services in the chapel. This explanation only increased Queen Mary's anger.

Feversham met with the queen personally and took the entire blame for the incident,[59] saying Catherine knew nothing about it and begging the queen's pardon. Mary persisted in believing Catherine had ordered the prayers not be read, and scolded Feversham, refusing to pardon him because the matter concerned the king.

She continued to hold a grudge and was ready for a fight the next time Catherine came to court. But Catherine knew better than to engage with the queen and the next time she attended, she only stayed for a short time and hardly spoke while she was there.[60]

This unfortunate incident appears to have rekindled Catherine's desire to leave England, her patience exhausted. Fed up with being in a Protestant country, she wanted to go home, but continued to get resistance from the English regime and from her brother. She planned to go to Hamburg in Germany, but many talked her out of this. French ships were patrolling the coast so she could not go to the Continent. She raised the idea of a trip to Bath, but the queen refused to provide her with an escort. Catherine threatened to return to her 'retreat' in Islington, but the queen's ministers persuaded Mary to not even answer the request until they knew the outcome of affairs in Ireland. Catherine had always been kind and courteous to Queen Mary, even when she was a child, and could not fathom the queen's antagonism.

King William claimed victory at the Battle of the Boyne on 1 July 1690. Six days later, Catherine called on Queen Mary to take ceremonious leave before she left London for her house in Hammersmith. Mary demanded Catherine close the Catholic chapel at Somerset House, something they had never asked her to do before.[61] Catherine sent Lady Arlington to the queen after news arrived of the victory at the Battle of the Boyne with her compliments and congratulations on William's escape from death after being wounded.[62]

During the summer, she lived in Hammersmith before moving on to Windsor. She stayed there for a while, but it brought on memories of her time there with Charles. She continued her letter-writing campaign to her brother, begging for ships. His replies were non-existent but eventually a Portuguese envoy informed her Pedro had suffered an attack of erysipelas. By now rumours were rampant that Catherine intended to poison Queen Mary, and she went back to Somerset House. William would return from Ireland soon, and Catherine intended to embark on an aggressive campaign to lobby him for ships to take her home.

Catherine dispatched Manuel Dias as a special agent in secret to her brother, urging action in the matter of her return to Portugal.[63] Now that England was at peace, ships could surely be spared. More letters flew between England and Portugal and by early 1692, Catherine had the long sought for permission from Pedro to return. Preparations for moving her entire household were set in motion.

Chapter Seven

Return to Sunny Portugal

The Journey Home

Finally, in January 1692, King William III agreed Catherine could depart England and provided her with a promise of ships for her cargo and an escort to Dieppe, a port on the northern coast of Normandy. Somerset House came alive with preparations for her journey, along with 120 of her servants. Her brother had cautioned her not to bring more servants than necessary. Catherine dedicated 10,000 pounds of her annual income to maintaining Somerset House and her remaining English staff after her departure.[1]

Principal maids who accompanied her to Portugal were the Countess of Fingall and her daughters, along with Lady Tuke. Part of her entourage included Sandys as first gentleman, her assistant physician Dr Street, seven ladies, four of them Portuguese and three English, and several Englishmen in positions of lesser importance. On 30 March 1692, heavy carriages traversed through the open gates of Somerset House on their way to Dover. More coaches and persons of quality from court who came to honour her upon her departure followed them.[2] The Tower of London gave its standard salute.

The cavalcade travelled as far as Rochester where she spent the night. The following day the party arrived in Dover. Lord Feversham, in charge of providing sea transport for the contents of Catherine's entourage, had engaged and mobilised three yachts. The *Friend's Adventure*, the *Dover of Denmark* and the *Anne*[3] had their decks cleared, and the cargo holds emptied in order to take on the carriages, the horses, suitcases, and furniture and bedding, along with the dowager queen and her staff. Everything was ready by 5 April.

King William was in Holland and it was up to the queen to issue the orders and provide the escort before the yachts could sail. The entire party stayed in Dover Castle as ten days passed. A permit was issued for the ships to sail, but no escort arrived. On 18 April, on the orders of Queen Mary, Lord Nottingham instructed the Commissioners of the Admiralty to appoint some men-of-war to attend the dowager queen on her passage. Finally, in early May, the English warships appeared, and the entire fleet finally reached Dieppe.[4]

Her arrival in France was greeted with the proper courtesy owed to a dowager queen. King Louis XIV sent a special envoy to present his welcomes and an invitation to visit Versailles. He provided an escort of honour and a fresh relay of horses to accompany her to the palace, although the French king was engaged at the siege of Namur. She accepted the escort, but because of her desire to travel privately through France, she refused the invitation to appear at Versailles.[5] She made her way to Rouen, where she took a brief rest.

Catherine spent some of her time in Rouen with the English nuns at the Covent of the Poor Clares. After the Dissolution of the Monasteries during the reign of Henry VIII, the only outlet for recusant English women to enter religious life involved leaving the country to join a community overseas, leading to the establishment of convents like the Poor Clares. We have already seen Catherine's association with the Institute of Blessed Virgin Mary, founded by Mary Ward and the origin of the convent Catherine helped establish at Hammersmith in England. In 1607, Mary Ward founded a community of English nuns of the Order of St Clare at Gravelines in the Spanish Netherlands, now in France. The Gravelines convent had daughter houses in Aire, Dunkirk and in Rouen, founded in 1644.[6]

The Chronicles of the English Poor Clares of Rouen (volume 1) have an entry recalling Catherine's visit. It is worth quoting the entire text as she discussed with the nuns the death-bed conversion to the Catholic faith of King Charles II.

> On Ascension Day (1692) Charles II's widow Catherine of Braganza, in Rouen on her way back to Portugal, heard Mass in the Poor Clares' church and spent the following Sunday [May 18] with them, giving much pleasure through her gracious demeanour, accepting 'a Collation….of sweetmeats, cream, oranges, biscakes, chiscakes, fresh butter and white wine and sugar…' and, 'Amongst other things that she said to Mother Abbess, she told her with much sensibility that many would not believe that the King her husband dyed a Catholick, which certainly he did. Some of our Sisters spoke to Madam Crane about it, because she was actually with the Queen when he fell sick and was eye-witness to all that passed at his death, and she affirmed that he died a true Catholick and that no man could die with more repentance than he did nor pray with more fervour, which the very Protestants themselves took notice of. They asked her also about many things which they had heard of him, as of his giving his ring to the Duchess of Portsmouth, [Kéroualle] &c. but she assured us "twas all false…"'.[7]

Following her relaxing visit in Rouen, Catherine moved on to St Germain-en-Laye, the home of her brother-in-law, the exiled James II, his wife Queen Mary Beatrice, and their children. James was away and James Francis Edward, the little Prince of Wales, whose birth she had witnessed, greeted her. She spent two hours in deep, private conversation with Mary Beatrice.[8] She also visited with her old friend, the Italian painter Benedetto Gennari, who was living in St Germain. Because she had left many of her paintings in Somerset House, she wanted a new artwork to take to Portugal, giving Gennari a commission to paint the Virgin Mary for her.[9]

She arrived in Moulins exhausted from her journey and wrote to her brother, describing the courtesy of Louis XIV's reception. She took the waters at Bourbon for three months, which refreshed her. The lengthy respite permitted her to continue to Lyon, travelling at a much more leisurely pace than previously. It was not just the poor travelling conditions that slowed her journey. Catherine relished the ability to live freely in a Catholic country that welcomed her with reverence.[10] Her brother wrote to her, inquiring about her plans. He proposed a path for her entrance into Portugal, which would permit him to make the proper arrangements.

She left Lyon on 23 September, making her way to Avignon, where she lodged in the Papal Palace for a week. The next stop was Bayonne. She dispatched her messenger, Father Manuel Dias, to Madrid to inform the Portuguese envoy, Joseph of Faria, of her itinerary with the expectation the envoy could receive her at the Spanish border. On 1 November, she entered Bayonne in State and the Duke of Grammont welcomed her with a religious ceremony.

Grammont escorted her to Irun, just across the French border in Basque country and she presented the duke with a jewel, valued at ten thousand écus. After this, the cheerful procession became subdued. Joseph of Faria awaited Catherine and immediately they observed the ubiquitous Portuguese court etiquette. Rain fell as they departed on 7 November on the road to Guipuzcoa. During the ride, Catherine felt a pain in her arm and hand, signalling the development of a serious case of erysipelas.[11] She refused treatment by a Spanish doctor and she only had an apothecary in her company.

King Pedro had issued orders for Catherine to be lodged in any city as if she were the king of Portugal himself, making meticulous plans for her arrival and reception. Pedro nominated Catherine's nemesis and England's former ambassador, the Marquis of Arronches, as her keeper. Arronches' grandson accompanied him, along with the Seneschal Prince of Ligne; Anthony of Noronha, Count of Vila Verde; Alphonse de Sousa, Count of Calheta; and Joseph Meneses and his son, among others. The rest of the Portuguese entourage consisted of twelve gentlemen, six pages, and thirty servants along with many common people employed in royal household administration.[12]

As soon as her arrival became known, these noblemen made the trip from Lisbon to Almeida, on the border between Spain and Portugal, in only seventeen days. At Coimbra, Dr Anthony Mendes, who served as a physician of King Pedro's chamber, joined them. This was a stroke of luck. Joseph of Faria had sent notice of Catherine's illness and lack of physicians. Arronches and Anthony Mendes presented themselves to Catherine to offer their services.

At Mata Puelos, the men found Catherine in pain and Dr Mendes proceeded with the recommended treatment of applying leeches. Fifteen days later, Catherine was well enough to continue her journey. They prepared a bed in a carriage for her and she made the trek over the Castilian plateau.[13]

The Spanish received her with every honour, as if she were the king of Portugal. An envoy from the king of Spain arrived, offering to pay all of her expenses for the journey through the country. Catherine declined the offer, her animosity toward the Spanish still intact. At the Portuguese border, the Viscount of Barbacena, commanding a troop of uniformed soldiers, greeted her with waving flags and an impressive display of artillery.

As soon as she was a half mile inside Portugal, the Marquis of Távora, Anthony Louis and his son, the Count of St John, came forward. The marquis was the first in line to kiss Catherine's hand, followed by other noblemen. After the brief ceremony, everyone entered Almeida where they accommodated the dowager queen in the home of John Dantas of Cunha. Many people from the surrounding area joined in the festivities.

The Road to Lisbon

At the beginning of 1693, Catherine, the Marquis of Távora and the rest of the entourage departed for the upcoming twenty day procession to Lisbon. As the heavy carriages made their way through Beira Alta, they rolled up and down the steep slopes, all while enduring the severities of winter. At Pinhel, Catherine's old English teacher, Richard Russell, now Bishop of Viseu, came to wait on her.

They climbed the mountain of Celorico and passed by Gouveia, where they stayed for a day to rest the animals. From there they went to Oliveira do Conde and Santa Comba Dão, where the dowager queen stayed in the home of the baron. To this day, there is a stone above the entranceway and a portrait in one room marking her visit there.[14] Next she arrived in Vacariça and the mountain range of Buçaco, where the cavalcade experienced great fear as the road skirted the cliffs. She entered Coimbra with great pomp on 8 January. Under superbly ornamented triumphal arches, the Bishop, the Dean and all the University's professors greeted her with honours.

Catherine and her entire entourage were housed in the bishop's Episcopal Palace. They stayed for three days and every afternoon celebrations of fireworks and bullfights honoured her. Catherine, still recovering from her illness, could not attend every activity. Because of the importance she placed in her faith, she visited the Chapel of the Holy Queen and viewed the relics.[15] Everyone remarked on her kindness. King Pedro issued a decree pardoning every prisoner serving up to three years.

The departure from Coimbra saw them taking the king's prescribed route through Condeixa, Pombal, Leiria and Alcobaça, where they lodged in various religious places or mansions. When they reached the Monastery of Batalha, Catherine went on foot to sprinkle holy water on the graves of her ancestors. The monastery remains one of the most important Gothic sites in Portugal. Constructed in celebration of the victory of the pivotal Battle of Aljubarrota, King John I and Queen Philippa, among others, have tombs there.

Next her route took her to Caldas da Rainha, Alcoentre and Vila Franca de Xira. Taking a shortcut, the procession passed through Via Longa and arrived at Povoa of St Andrião, where they awaited King Pedro. After a delay, a message arrived instructing Catherine to meet him in the Square of Lumiar, a neighbourhood in the northern sector of Lisbon. King Pedro left the Palace of Corte-Real in the morning to meet Catherine. They had not seen each other in over thirty years.[16]

The two carriages of Catherine and Pedro drew up parallel to each other and a carpet was put down between them. Pedro left his carriage with several courtiers to walk over to Catherine. While they felt much joy in seeing each other, strict Portuguese etiquette frowned upon any overt display of emotion. After exchanging formal salutes, Catherine entered the king's carriage and sat to his right, an impressive honour, as the procession made its way to Alcântara where Catherine would stay. Along the route, at Campo Grande, the Duke of Cadaval waited at the head of an army, to receive the dowager queen of England.

Pedro's wife, Maria Sophia of Neuburg, greeted Catherine at the top of the stairs of the Palace of Alcântara. They exchanged salutes, and both displayed obvious emotion and happiness, in blatant disregard of the obligatory etiquette. Catherine was tired, so the king called off the public reception to allow her to rest. Finally, home in her beloved, sunny Portugal, Catherine could bask in the love of the people. She could now freely worship publicly as a Catholic, put aside the strain and anxiety she had experienced since the death of her husband, and live life to her own satisfaction.[17]

A Home of Her Own

The Palace of Alcântara, Catherine's first home upon her return, was originally the private residence of a wealthy Italian. Philip II of Spain purchased the property and Catherine's father and two brothers, kings Afonso and Pedro, lived there at various times. Afonso proclaimed his majority there in 1662 and Pedro would die there in 1706.[18]

The court celebrated Catherine's return with many days of celebration and ceremonies. Slowly, the festivities ended and Catherine could finally settle down to some kind of regular life. Her sister-in-law became an intimate friend.[19] The two women agreed to not allow intrigue or jealousy to interfere with their relationship and abandoned the annoying court etiquette when they were together.

At first, Catherine could not seem to find a place where she was content and could settle down. She moved around, inhabiting various places. She stayed in the Palace of Alcântara for some time but the location did not suit her health so she moved to the Quinta on the estate of the Conde of Redondo in Santa Marta.[20] From there she moved to the Palace of the Conde of Soure at Bairro Alto and it was during her stay in this location she drew up her will, on 14 February 1699. At the end of the same month, she left for Vila Viçosa to visit the home of her childhood. They welcomed her procession with festivals as she made her way across the countryside. But she found the atmosphere much too warm and in May returned to the fresh, pleasant breezes of the Tagus River in Lisbon, travelling through Evora where she made a state entry.

Her next residence was the Palace of the Conde of Aveiras in Belem. This isolated mansion was very near a Dominican monastery which she would frequently visit. She decided to construct her own home for her health and to have a place where she could take her exercise and live privately. She bought the property of the daughter of her chief accountant, Louis Pereira of Barros. This daughter had married Plácido Castanheira of Moura and the property was the Campos of Bemposta. She also purchased the farms and gardens of several surrounding owners to enlarge the size of her property. The area from Estefânia to the actual Palace of Bemposta would all be owned by Catherine.[21]

Construction of the palace began in 1699. The architecture would be austere and grandiose with a beautiful chapel, Our Lady of Conception. In this chapel, Catherine accumulated and displayed precious works of art, some of which she brought from England and some which she acquired in Portugal. Prominently displayed there was *The Virgin, the Child and the Saints*, painted by Hans Holbein the Elder (now in the Museo Nacional de Arte Antiga in Lisbon).[22]

The Great Earthquake of 1755 damaged the Palace of Bemposta, but there are still some fragments from her time visible today. One can see the coat of arms of England over the main doorway and in the chapel, there is a loge or royal enclosure facing the high altar where Catherine sat and worshiped. Until the proclamation of the Portuguese Republic, the chapel of the Palace of Bemposta belonged to the Braganza family.[23]

Catherine remained at the house of the Count of Aveiras during construction of her new palace. Her beloved sister-in-law, Maria Sophia, died in August 1699. By this time, most of her English ladies had succumbed to boredom and returned to England. Catherine took the saved wages and paid them to her Portuguese servants, all widows and ladies of the first nobility. Only a few English servants in minor positions remained. Catherine now relied increasingly on the dedication of her Portuguese servants, compelling her to return to her Portuguese roots.[24]

When she eventually moved into the unfinished palace of Bemposta in April 1702, it was not a lively Portuguese court but the small home of an ailing widow on a farm on the outskirts of Lisbon. She received a few visitors from time to time, but mostly she lived a secluded and retired life. John Colbatch, a chaplain in Lisbon from 1688 to 1705, wrote about this time in Catherine's life in *An Account of the Court of Portugal, Under the Reign of the Present King Dom Pedro II...*, published in 1700.

Colbatch states:

> But tho' her Majesty be herself the same, her outward Circumstances are somewhat alter'd, since her leaving England; her Court is lessen'd almost to a private family, those few Persons that waited on her from hence, being, for the most part, either dismiss'd with their Salaries continued to them, or excused their Attendance; there is now no Noise, nor Ostentation of Grandeur about her House, but all things are quiet and still, except it be on days of Ceremony, when Persons of Quality will be coming to express the great Veneration they have for her; then, indeed, her court is as great, and full, as the Nobility of the Country can make it.[25]

The War of the Spanish Succession

Events leading up to the outbreak of the War of the Spanish Succession commenced in 1700 with the death of King Carlos II of Spain. This conflict would have a profound effect on Catherine's life, interrupting her solitary existence at Bemposta. King Carlos had no qualified heirs of his own, starting an expected scramble for power. He had two sisters, Maria Theresa who married Louis XIV of France, and Margaret Theresa who married the Hapsburg emperor, Leopold I.

Both these women's descendants had a claim to the Spanish throne. In his will, Carlos II named Philip, Duke of Anjou, grandson of Louis XIV as his successor. This was unacceptable to Leopold, and he declared war.[26] It dismayed Catherine when her brother the king sided with the Spanish and defended the rights of the French claimant, Philip of Anjou.[27] England, the Low Countries and Austria formed a Grand Alliance against France, and this uneasy state of affairs lasted about two years.

During her time at Bemposta, Catherine received many English visitors and maintained contact with those she knew in England. On certain occasions she missed her adopted nation. She was always eager to get news from England or from her brother-in-law, James, or his wife Mary Beatrice. She remained loyal to the Catholic James until his death in September 1701, when she ordered her house in Portugal to adopt rigorous mourning and asked her servants in Somerset House in England to do the same.

In 1702, John Methuen, the British envoy, arrived at the court of Lisbon. He received a warm welcome and Catherine was on excellent terms with him and his son, Paul. She would tell Paul Methuen she had already forgiven the English for their faults.[28] Both men were on a determined mission to persuade the Portuguese king to switch to the Grand Alliance in the War of the Spanish Succession.

King Pedro remained cautious. Breaking with France had its perils, and he urgently sought reassurance the Alliance had the power and the will to win the war.[29] After a few aborted naval battles, King Pedro was still not ready to switch sides. But it was increasingly clear the Portuguese merchantmen were at risk on the high seas, and Pedro could not maintain a benevolent neutrality for much longer.[30] The English writer, Jonathan Swift, mentions King Pedro received intelligence that Philip V of Spain intended to renew the Spanish claim to the Kingdom of Portugal.[31]

In the fall of 1702, John Methuen tried to force the issue. He presented King Pedro with territorial concessions in Estremadura and Galicia, along with generous cash subsidies and supplies for troops on campaign for active support of the Grand Alliance. They resubmitted this offer in December with the territorial concessions unobtrusively omitted as they were obviously undeliverable. The French tried to preserve their partnership with Portugal, but their effort failed. Pedro used this rivalry for his support to his best advantage and eventually, the Portuguese agreed to join with the Grand Alliance.[32]

John and Paul Methuen helped to negotiate the treaties bearing their name. Some historians mention Catherine aided in the discussions of this alliance. It is possible she had Methuen's ear and expressed her opinion. But there is no hard historical evidence regarding this.[33] What is certain is that Portugal's entry into the Grand Alliance with England pleased Catherine. She had always made it clear she supported her adopted country in all things. They had brought her up to believe England alone saved Portugal from being swallowed up by Spain. If there was a choice between allying with France or with England, she would always choose England and support English policy.[34]

This treaty appealed to the Portuguese government because of the proposals for improved and expanded British trade and because of the opportunity it offered to redress the political preponderance of Castile in the Iberian Peninsula.[35] The Methuen Treaty confirmed Portugal's ties with England. The first treaty, ratified in May 1703, sealed the Anglo-Portuguese political and military alliance.

The second treaty of December was purely commercial. Portugal allowed English woollens to enter the country on the same basis as before the recent new sumptuary laws, and England permitted Portuguese wines be taxed at a rate only one-third of that applied to wines from France.[36] These exceptional trade privileges would have far-reaching consequences for Portugal,[37] with both treaties drawing Portugal even further into England's orbit.[38]

The treaty between Portugal and the Grand Alliance was signed in Lisbon on 16 May 1703, and ratified in London on 14 July. The military terms of the Methuen Treaty established a resolute alliance between Portugal, England, Austria and Holland. Terms also stipulated that Archduke Charles, son of Holy Roman Emperor Leopold I, be declared King Carlos III of Spain and subsequently come to Lisbon to press his claim to the throne by force of arms.

Following his arrival, King Pedro would declare war on King Philip V and provide an army of 15,000 men with an additional 13,000 auxiliaries, all paid for with Allied subsidies and supplies. The other parties of the alliance would supply 12,000 troops for the campaign, along with a cruising squadron of 12 ships. Portugal consented to serve as a base for allied operations, and the maritime services of the Allied Powers guaranteed the territorial integrity of Portugal. All this remained dependent on the archduke succeeding in his claim to the throne of Madrid.[39]

They crowned Archduke Charles, King Carlos III in Vienna on 12 September 1703. Within a few days, he departed for England and from there, he sailed to Portugal where he arrived in Lisbon on 4 March 1704. He had brought with him 4000 British and Dutch troops, who were greeted with the requisite amount of suitable pomp and celebration. Shortly after his arrival, Catherine became ill again with erysipelas. Carlos expressed a desire to pay his respects to Catherine as dowager queen of Great Britain, but the simple life and reduced staff of the Palace of Bemposta were woefully inadequate to accommodate an official visit of such momentous import. Decorum demanded there be members of the nobility present for such a ceremony.[40]

The Secretary of State summoned all high dignitaries, officials of the King's House, and the nobility to appear. Catherine gathered together all the important ladies of the court. Carlos III arrived in his carriage at Bemposta and entered the queen's chamber, escorted by the Prince of Liechtenstein, who offered him a seat in a black velvet chair placed at a respectful distance from Catherine's bed. Catherine received him with great courtesy, assisted by her lady-in-waiting, Inês Antónia of Távora. The day was not perfect by any means, but Portuguese etiquette had been respectfully observed and everyone seemed gratified by the proceedings, remarking on Catherine's prudent and virtuous behaviour.[41]

Catherine Becomes Regent of Portugal

During his absence in prosecuting the war, King Pedro turned the reins of government over to Catherine. With his son being too young to rule, Pedro trusted

Catherine's abilities and judgement. Before he left Lisbon, to assist the Council of State, he named the Duke of Cadaval and his son James, the Marquis of Cascais; the Marquis de Niza; the Grand Inquisitor Father Joseph of Lencastre; the Archbishops of Lisbon and Braga; the Counts of Val de Reys and the Sarzedas; Garcia of Melo; Francisco of Sousa; the Secretary of State Anthony Pereira of Silva; the Bishop of Elvas; Tomás of Almeida; and the Secretary Roque Monteiro Paím.[42]

Catherine took this well-deserved opportunity to prove to the English they had underestimated her. While Catherine may not have had the political savvy of a Cardinal Mazarin, she proved worthy of the challenge of running the government, issuing orders, demonstrating she expected deference and conformity. She dismissed two Portuguese colonels for failing to report to their regiments, making it clear she had no intention of tolerating disobedience.

Because of her diligence, they increased recruiting, remounted cavalry, and facilitated the movement of troops. She established magazines of food for men and forage for the animals, drawing attention to a phase of the war previously overlooked.[43] In her dealings with the Council of State, she heeded their advice but did not hesitate to take an independent viewpoint when circumstances required.[44]

All of this set her up for blame and disapproval. The men on the council resented being led by a woman, and they viewed her as being tainted by her obvious loyalty to England. The promised subsidies from the Grand Alliance partners failed to arrive. These obstacles led to a course of passive resistance by the men on the council. Catherine stood her ground and persisted in executing her vision for making the campaign a success.[45]

She acted with uncommon determination in the conflict between the Papal Nuncio, Miguel Angelo Conti, later Pope Innocent XIII, and the Company of the Jesuits Portuguese delegation. She would always be protective of the Company, remembering how they backed her father's bid for the throne. This order of priests assisted her with religious advice, and she regarded them as defenders of the faith. She was indignant with Monsignor Conti's subpoena, issued in the name of the Holy See, demanding the Jesuits satisfy the obligatory payment of tax revenue from their churches.[46] She promptly notified the Nuncio 'that he should not enter the Palace nor be admitted by his Lecturer [the Duke of Cadaval] to discuss any matter', focusing on the duke her anger resulting from the implied attack from the Vatican on her protégées.[47]

In March 1704, King Philip V of Spain implemented his plan of attack by taking his troops to the Portuguese border. The Spanish army of 40,000, under the command of the Duke of Berwick, attacked the garrison of Salvatierra, which fell in May. The French Bourbon strategy was to take Lisbon and generate a pincer movement on three sides.[48] Besides Salvatierra, they captured Segura and Castelo Branco and were preparing a manoeuvre to join the forces of the Prince of Tilly in the Alentejo.[49]

With the capture of a few cities, the entire province of Alentejo was ultimately in the possession of Spain, placing Lisbon under direct and serious threat. Fortunately for the city, supplies were running low and the terrain encumbered the troops, which forced the Spanish royal army into a defensive footing. King Philip returned to Madrid in July and the Allies made use of this respite to regroup. Several naval battles ensued, and the Allies took Gibraltar, a loss that seriously wounded Spanish prestige.

The Allies planned to use Portugal as the base for an invasion of Spain in the next campaign. By the spring of 1704, the entire commitment of troops in Portugal amounted to 20,300 foot and 700 horse. The commander of the English troops was the Duke of Schömberg, second son of the Schömberg who had executed the War of the Restoration for Catherine's mother, Queen Luisa. The Portuguese commanders were the Count of Galveias and the Marquis of Minas, and the early campaigns were purely defensive.

For the fall campaign, Schömberg was recalled to England and replaced by Henri de Massue, second Marquis de Ruvigny, Earl of Galway. They made Minas supreme commander. The Marshal de Tessé replaced the commander of the Spanish troops and his first task was to recover Gibraltar. However, all efforts failed to recapture the port.[50] Subsequently, resistance to the Allies would collapse for whole provinces of the Spanish monarchy because of inadequate means of defence, whereas Allied resistance to the Bourbons often succeeded because they took care to garrison and equip places they had overrun.[51]

The winter weather hampered Allied military efforts at the border, so King Pedro returned to Lisbon on 17 November 1704 and took back the reins of government. He was gravely ill and depressed because of the unfavourable campaign, his body numb with a strange malady, possibly a stroke, and he suffered from an extreme and irresistible drowsiness. Neither the gravity of his affairs nor the advice of his ministers prevented him from sleeping during the Council of State.

Pedro's health suffered further complications, manifesting as a severe sore throat, which significantly impeded his ability to swallow. In the first days of the New Year, his distress was so great the doctors despaired of his life. He received extreme unction on 3 January, and again named Catherine the kingdom's Regent.[52]

Catherine, also unwell, fulfilled the role entrusted to her. Conscientious and meticulous in every action, she dedicated herself to the service of the nation. The country geared up for the next campaign. During two conferences of the Council of State, Catherine set in motion the national bureaucracy, crucial in arranging for the acquisition of supplies and the movement of the troops. The military build-up and intensity were reminiscent of the Restoration campaigns after her father ascended to the throne.[53]

Catherine's energy deeply impressed the English party in Portugal. The English ambassador informed London the war progressed with vigour because the dowager queen enforced her decisions and those taking the orders complied. Catherine's forcefulness reduced the enthusiasm of those who backed the French in the conflict.

The personal animosities continued at court. Several high-ranking ministers became agents for King Louis XIV to limit Catherine's actions because they sympathised with the French cause as well as being traitorous and corrupt. The Duke of Cadaval, who presided over the Council of State, was the worst offender. He became recriminatory of Catherine.

This critical lack of support, along with the delay in funds from the Allies, hindered Catherine from fulfilling her intentions to her maximum ability. Despite the dissent and lack of money, the spring campaign of 1705 was brilliant and successful. The Count of Galveias, governor of arms at Alentejo, conquered Valença of Alcântara and Albuquerque, two significant Spanish strongholds and the Marquis of Minas, governor of arms at Beira, recovered Salvatierra from the enemy.[54]

The drought and heat forced the Portuguese army to withdraw and wait for more favourable weather before any further engagements but Catherine remained active in Lisbon. She compelled the English ambassador to take responsibility for the late payment of the subsidies which the Allied treaty required. Her difficulties with the Council of State increased. The men refused to attend periodic meetings and then insisted Portuguese officers should have precedence over English officers of equal rank.

Catherine gave in to this last demand to pacify the councillors. But the English ambassador objected, complaining the extravagance, injustice and inconvenience of such a resolution could only have been suggested by those who wished to cause a fracture between Portugal and England. Catherine held her ground despite the consequences,[55] knowing that backing down would create more difficulties than she could manage with the Council of State.

In October, the Marquis of Minas replaced the aged Count of Galveias as governor of arms at Alentejo, and led the fall campaign. The troops besieged Badajoz with the English company of the Earl of Galway. During an attack of the stronghold on 11 October, Galway lost his right arm after being struck by a cannon ball and they took him to Elvas for treatment. Days later, the Marshal of Tessé lifted the siege before the Portuguese could prevent it from falling.[56] The cold and rain concluded the failure of the siege, and the Portuguese army departed for winter quarters. They talked of plans to attack Madrid in the spring.[57]

Catherine could now take a rest. But on 31 December, she suffered a violent attack of colic.[58] They summoned King Pedro to the Palace of Bemposta, but his sister's suffering, and his own, made the visit unbearable.[59] He called a Council of State to complete the documents transferring the regency from Catherine back to himself,[60] and at 9 o'clock in the evening, he retired to Alcântara, ordering the Council of State to stay at Bemposta to handle affairs in the event Catherine died.

As she lay on her deathbed in violent agony, she declared to her English doctor that they had falsely accused her of trying to introduce the Catholic faith in England, insisting she had never desired additional advantages for those who shared her faith, beyond those embedded in the Articles of Marriage. Never having been a defender of French interests in Portugal, she was heartbroken over any support for France from her brother's court and feared the harm it might bring to England.[61]

Death and Burial

Catherine died at 10 o'clock in the evening[62] and they read her will (see Appendix III). Breaking the five seals of the document, the Secretary of State declared the testament consisted of three pages and verified there was no flaw in letter, risk or line, and every word was coherent. The English ambassador in Lisbon, present during the reading, later examined the official translation of the testament into English. They would ratify the will in London on 1 April 1706. Princess Louise, daughter of Queen Mary Beatrice, upon hearing the news of Catherine's death, asked her mother if there were any grounds for the reported partiality of the late queen for Lord Feversham. Mary Beatrice replied, 'none'.[63]

Due to austerity and accumulation of her revenue, Catherine had amassed a substantial fortune. Early on, after her return home, she had established an annual convoy of ships between Portugal and England to ensure she received her allowances due from London. She named her brother the king as first executor of her will and the Count of Chesterfield, the Count of Feversham, Sir Richard Bellings, Sir Estevan Fox and Father Manuel Dias as executors in Great Britain.[64]

After the reading of the testament, the council made plans for her burial. In the will, she stipulated they should bury her next to her brother, Teodósio, in the church of Saint Mary of the Jerónimos Monastery at Belem in Lisbon. She further stated my 'Brother (now with God), and in case his Bones shall be carried to the Convent of St Vincent without this city (as the King Dom João the Fourth, my Lord and Father, ordered by his Will) it is my will that mine shall likewise be carried and buried in the Great Chapel of the same Convent'.[65]

The council agreed they would give Catherine a funeral with the same pomp and grandeur as if she was the reigning sovereign of Portugal.[66] On 3 January 1706, the Catholic vigil service, *Do corpo presente*, was performed at Bemposta in the presence of Catherine's remains. Anthony of Saldanha, the Bishop of Portalegre, officiated, assisted by the Bishops of Algarve, Maranhão, Bonn and Hiponia, all of whom intoned the liturgies.[67]

The funeral took place in the afternoon. King Pedro did not attend upon the advice of his councillors. Catherine's nephews, the princes John, Francis and Anthony, were present at the Palace of Bemposta and sprinkled holy water on Catherine's body. They lifted the body onto an open bier, according to the Portuguese custom. Manuel de Vasconcelos de Sousa performed the duties of chief groom of the chamber in the absence of his brother, the Count of Castelo Melhor, Catherine's devoted servant and friend. De Sousa lifted the pall covering her remains, leaving her face visible.[68]

The Marquis of Marialva, the Count of Sarzedas, the Count of Atalaia, the Count of S. Vincente, the Count of Vila Verde, the Count of Alvor, the Count of Falveias and Francis de Sousa, all members of the Council of State, lifted the coffin and placed it on the litter[69] which was taken in state to the church at Belem. This monastery was on the same spot where Vasco da Gama had sailed on his greatest voyage of discovery, the passage to the Indies. The entire court and Catherine's faithful retinue accompanied the grandees.

They draped the route to Belem in black. As the procession made its way to the church, it passed the streets of St Antony of Capuchos, St Joseph, Anunciada, Rossio and Esperança, going slowly between rows of priests and monks from all the orders of the kingdom with their eyes downcast. Many weeping people joined the procession to get one last glimpse of their beloved princess.

At the church of Saint Mary, the members of the council removed the coffin from the litter and delivered it to the Brotherhood of Misericordia, according to the customary practice of the Portuguese kings.[70] They buried Catherine in the church next to Teodósio as she requested. Tribunals were suspended throughout the country for eight days, while the entire country grieved Catherine's death. The court observed mourning for a year.

In 1855, King Ferdinand II of Portugal *jure uxoris*, Regent for his son King Pedro V, ordered the construction of a Pantheon of the House of Braganza in the Convent of St Vincent de Fora and the bones of the Braganza monarchs and their families were moved to the convent, including Catherine's. From 1932 to 1934, they completed cleaning and restoration work on the graves, bringing order to the huddle of coffins, graves and crowns clustered there. Catherine's remains now lie in a modest white marble drawer with the inscription 'Rainha de Inglaterra D. Catharina 1638–1705'.[71]

Chapter Eight

The Legacy of Catherine's Marriage

The Fate of the Cash Portion of Catherine's Portuguese Dowry

Item V of the Articles of Marriage of 1661 required Portugal to pay England two million cruzados for Catherine's dower portion. The cruzado was a gold coin issued by Afonso V (1438–1481) who attempted to organise a crusade against the Turks in retaliation for the fall of Constantinople in 1453. It had a value of 400 réis. The name comes from the Portuguese word *cruzado,* which means cross, referring to the cross of the patron saint of Portugal, St George, which appeared on the reverse of the coin.

King John II (1477–1495) introduced a new silver coin called the cruzado at a value of 324 *real branco*. John III (1521-1557) fixed its value to 400 réis and Pedro II (1683–1706), Catherine's brother, increased its value to 480 réis. Catherine's father, King John IV (1640–1656) also minted the cruzado with a value equal to 750 réis.[1]

It is nearly impossible to convert the value of a cruzado in 1661 to English pounds. While doing research, various authors and historians have estimated the contemporary value to be 300,000 pounds, 330,000 pounds, 350,000 pounds, 353,000 pounds, and 500,000 pounds.[2] According to the currency conversion chart on The National Archives website, this would translate to between 37.5 million pounds to 52.5 million pounds in value of today's currency.[3] This was a lot of money and explains Charles' keen interest in negotiating the Portuguese marriage. Whatever its equivalent in English money, it was to date the largest dowry ever offered to any English monarch.[4]

So, what happened to the two million cruzados?

The Portuguese disputed every penny of the dowry, primarily because of the poverty of the nation. The Portuguese Council of State considered the first half of the dowry, one million cruzados, as reimbursement for the help in the defence of Portugal by the English. In reality, the cost of this defence to the English amounted to over one million cruzados. The wording of Item V of the Articles of Marriage of

1661 may have read as it did because the English did not want this made public, or perhaps Charles wanted to have the money to spend at his own discretion.[5]

The first payment of one half of the dowry sailed to England with Catherine of Braganza and did not amount to one million cruzados. After the conversion of the assets, there was a net of 176,500 pounds (18.5 million pounds in today's money). According to the Treasury records, 100,000 cruzados were used to cover the expense of Sandwich's mission to transport Catherine to England. Portugal made no further payments on the dowry until after the Treaty of Lisbon brought peace between Portugal and Spain in 1668. At that point, England put pressure on the Portuguese government to collect the balance.[6]

Sir Robert Southwell, English envoy to Portugal since 1666, came to an agreement for the second half of Queen Catherine's dowry in 1668. He negotiated an allocation of the half custom on future imports of English goods into all Portuguese ports as payment toward the remaining balance of the dowry. He also got an assignment of a portion of the annual donative [donation] raised in Brazil to cover the cost of the marriage of Catherine to Charles.[7]

Portugal perennially argued they had overvalued the cruzado in their previous sterling payments and also further declared a variety of deductions, allowing them to claim a reduction of the second one million cruzados to 669,093.They arranged for payments to resume in 1670. In 1672, Francis Parry, England's representative in Portugal, petitioned the Regent, Prince Pedro, for payment of the queen's portion.[8] More devaluations in the value of the Portuguese cruzado reduced the value of the dower even further. Upon the death of King Charles II in 1685, there was still 24,000 pounds remaining on the debt. When Charles Fanshawe travelled to Portugal to collect the final debt, 11,000 pounds or 85,000 cruzados went toward paying for his ambassadorial mission.[9]

The Port of Tangier under the English

As we witnessed during the marriage negotiations, Charles II and his council believed Tangier would be a valuable commercial asset to England. The Lord Chancellor, Edward Hyde, Earl of Clarendon, felt so strongly about it, he insisted they turn the port over to an English garrison even before Catherine left Lisbon and Item II of the Articles of Marriage specifically spelled out this requirement. England commissioned Edward Montagu, first Earl of Sandwich, to take control of Tangier, which he did in October 1661. Fernando de Menezes, governor of the port by hereditary right, refused to hand over the city to the English despite Queen Luisa's command to do so, claiming it would be an insult to his ancestors. Queen Luisa supplanted Menezes and replaced him with a more deferential ruler, Luis de Almeida.[10]

Ultimately, Sandwich marched into Tangier at the head of his regiment, and during a charming ceremony received from Luis de Almeida the insignia of his office. These included the keys to the city, a horse and saddle, bridle and silver spurs, a scimitar and a lance.[11] He administered the evacuation of the Portuguese from the port and awaited the English garrison.[12] After delivering Tangier to the new governor, the Earl of Peterborough, Sandwich sailed for Lisbon to escort Catherine to England. From the beginning, Tangier drained English manpower and cash, just as it did for the Portuguese dating back from the time they conquered it during the reign of Afonso V in 1471.

The trouble was immediately apparent as the Venetian ambassador in Spain, Giovanni Cornaro, wrote to the Doge and Senate:

> The English garrison at Tangier, having made a sortie and engaged with Galian, the leader of the Africans, has suffered serious losses, six hundred English being left on the field. The Moors appeared on the field with firearms, and in wonderfully good order. Here they have rejoiced at the news, seeing that at the beginning of this new possession the English may not be without loss and trouble. This leader of the Moors is in high esteem, strength and valour. He has correspondence with the Spaniards. He has offered them harness and horses at very low prices, on condition that they do not send over succour from the Spanish shore to the opposite party with whom he is engaged in hostilities. Madrid, 7 June 1662.[13]

By 1680, the English government used revenue appropriated from Ireland to pay for the maintenance of the port. The costs had become prohibitive, and the English concluded they could put the Irish revenues to better use for other considerations. Tangier had proven of little value for trade. Difficult to defend, the port suffered repeated attacks by the Spanish and the Moors[14] and ongoing blockades by the Berbers and Barbary corsairs. In August 1683, Charles made the tough decision to evacuate the inhabitants and demolish the town. They kept the preparations for the expedition secret, but at the last minute, in July 1684, the Portuguese ambassador in London received notification of the mission.

He informed the Count of Castelo Melhor who wrote up a memorandum to Catherine's brother Pedro, Prince Regent, containing every argument for not destroying Tangier and leaving it intact. He maintained Portugal could defend the port with seasoned troops, and had the ability to take immediate possession of the town, thus sparing Charles' government the expense and trouble of the demolition. There is evidence this effort by Castelo Melhor may have been at the behest of Queen Catherine herself.

George Legge, first Baron Dartmouth, appointed admiral on 2 August 1683, received orders to level the fortifications and destroy the mole, ruin the harbour and recall the garrison and the colonists to England. He arrived in Tangier on 14 September. The *Colonial Office Papers, Tangier* contain a memo he wrote dated 19 October:

> The Address of the Portuguese to His Majesty [Pedro, Prince Regent for his brother King Afonso VI] I hope will in some measure satisfy her Majesty [Queen Catherine] (if it be possible) besides the fathers of the Church here have written a letter to her Majesty (as they tell me) in behalf of Dr Ken and I, so that we are yet both in hopes of not being thrown quite out of her Majesty's favour.[15]

Apparently, the queen had never forgotten Tangier was her own gift to England. Because of her influence with the king, the Portuguese priests in Tangier had received many privileges. Lord Dartmouth's memorandum undoubtedly shows Catherine's disapproval of the abandonment of Tangier, and this led to Castelo Melhor's last ditch effort to save the port.[16]

In the end, the arguments had no effect on Pedro or King Charles, leaving Dartmouth to carry out his orders with the operation being completed on 6 February 1684. The English acknowledged the decision to abandon Tangier as being sensible.[17] The garrison regiment, the second Regiment of Foot, was renamed by King Charles 'our dearest consort, the Queen's Regiment', which exists to this day as the Queen's Royal Regiment.

The Port of Bombay Is Ceded to the English

While Tangier proved easy for the English to gain from the Portuguese, Bombay was another matter entirely. One of the more obscure outposts of the Portuguese Casa da India, it comprised a cluster of inconsequential islets off the western Gujarat coast of India. Under the control of the Portuguese since 1534, it consisted of a few rural estates in the hands of private individuals and religious corporations. The English sought an outpost in the area and viewed Bombay as an asset. It had a strategic position, a good harbour and a great deal of commercial potential.[18]

The confusion about Bombay lay in its geography because it was made up of seven islands amid an expanse of salt flats. The monsoon season created a dividing flood, but during the dry season at low tide, the islands were united. Eventually, they reclaimed the islands and the salt flats and it became one complete entity.[19] But that would be far in the future and at the time of the Articles of Marriage Between

His Majesty and the Lady Infanta of Portugal in 1661, no definitive map of the area existed and no one knew exactly what part of the site would be ceded to the English.

The secret clause of the Articles of Marriage specified Bombay for use by the British in defence of Portugal's other Indian settlements. With the marriage of Charles II and Catherine of Braganza, Lisbon believed they got a firm commitment from the English to defend Portuguese interests in Asia, even providing and sending soldiers and to engage in the fight.[20] After the ratification of the Marriage Treaty, the new incoming viceroy, Antonio de Melo e Castro, travelled to Goa, the headquarters of the Portuguese Indian Empire, in a ship from the English squadron sent to India by Charles II and commanded by James Ley, third Earl of Marlborough.

Upon his arrival, Melo e Castro's orders were to turn over Bombay to the representatives of King Charles II. When he reached India, he found Cochin and Cannanore, two Portuguese fortresses on the Malabar Coast of southern India, under siege by the Dutch. Considering the understanding of the Portuguese regarding the Articles of Marriage, he appealed to the English for military support. But the local English authorities declined to give any help. Besides this state of affairs, Melo e Castro discovered the Portuguese in India entirely opposed ceding Bombay, primarily for commercial and political reasons. The viceroy would make his own opinion known when he wrote, '… I foresee the great trouble that from this neighbourhood will result to the Portuguese, and that India will be lost on the same day on which the English nation is settled in Bombay'.[21]

Melo e Castro refused to relinquish anything to the English. He stated he received no specific orders from Goa. He argued about what exactly they would surrender to the British. Just the Island of Bombay? Or all of the islands? He dismissed the Letters Patent from King Charles II as not being lawful proof of the transfer. Exasperated, Marlborough left the area, returning to England and leaving 400 of his men near the area on a deserted island where a good many of them died while awaiting further orders.[22]

The confusion and consternation caused by the viceroy's refusal to turn over any territory seriously compromised the Anglo-Portuguese alliance. King Charles demanded the punishment of the viceroy, reparations for expenses incurred for sending troops to occupy the island and the immediate cession of the territory, utterly surprising the Portuguese. The viceroy contended the Portuguese Crown should purchase Bombay back from the English without delay.

Charles probably would have considered this a possibility but was well aware the war with Spain drained the Portuguese treasury and they dropped the idea.[23] Lisbon sent firm orders for Melo e Castro to comply with the Articles of Marriage, and he grudgingly relinquished control to the English governor in February 1665. England now had its coveted foothold on the western coast of India.

The Acquisition of the Port of Bombay by the English East India Company

There were many transformations and iterations of names for the English East India Company, the merchant trading company originally founded by the Merchant Adventurers during the reign of Queen Elizabeth I of England. For our purposes, to reduce confusion, we will call it the English East India Company or simply the Company. Author Nick Robins calls the East India Company 'the corporation that changed the world' and Bombay would play a crucial role in the Company's history.

When the Company first directed its ships to the western coast of India, its primary purpose was to exploit trade links in the area. The English East India Company established its main factory on the north westerly coast of Gujarat at Surat, the only adequate harbour not previously controlled by the Portuguese or the Dutch.[24] Ships from the Gujarat sailed to Java and Sumatra to exchange cottons for spices and pepper, and called at the ports of the Red Sea and Persian Gulf. In these early beginnings, they never intended to expand India's internal trade, and they certainly gave no credence to the idea of gaining a political toehold on the subcontinent.

William Hawkins, in command of the ship *Hector*, arrived to investigate the potential of Surat in 1608. He was the first commander of an English East India Company vessel to set foot on the coast of India, and he understood the significance of Surat as the principal port of the Mughal Empire.[25] Despite some troublesome issues with the Portuguese and Mughal officials in charge of the Gujarati ports, the English initiated trade just north of Surat at Swalley Hole. By 1611, commodities from England were arriving in India and calicos and indigo, a blue dye obtained from various plants, were purchased. There were discussions about establishing a factory in Surat for the Company.[26]

But the English left the area after failing to get permission from the Mughals to trade. Over the next couple of years, the Company fought off the Portuguese while continuing to seek a license to trade from the Mughal emperor. By 1613, a factor of the Company, Thomas Aldworth, persuaded them to leave goods and factors in Surat with the expectation of English broadcloth creating a brisk trade.[27] Aldworth was mistaken because the sale of English tweed never captured the market for human apparel in the warm and humid climate. However, trade in indigo dye and in several varieties of cloth manufactured from Indian cotton flourished. Trade in these items prospered in Indonesia and increased in popularity in England as well.

In 1614, after a falling out between the Mughal emperor and the Portuguese, the English filled the vacuum. The activity at Surat flourished,[28] and affordable cottons and indigo flooded the market. In 1626, raiders made their first visit to Bombay intent on dislodging the Portuguese, burning down the warehouses, the friary, the fort and many mansions along with two frigates. The English surveyed the harbour, finding it excellent. For a short time, they contemplated the possibility of occupying it, but they soon deemed it to be too challenging.[29]

Depredations, plundering and entanglements ruled the day until they brokered the Convention of Goa in 1635. This treaty provided the Company factors of Surat with access to the Estado da India's ring of ports extending all the way to Macau, the Portuguese colony in China.[30] Once they made peace with Portugal, the Company could look into procuring Bombay. The Company's factors started tactful diplomatic negotiations in Persia and Surat, promoting this possibility in 1640 and again in 1653-4.[31]

The Crown of England, from the very beginning, always favoured the monopoly of the English East India Company. Periodically, the Company required a revision or confirmation of their charter and found it essential to call on the Crown for financial, political and diplomatic support. The English Civil Wars, lasting from 1642 to 1651, reduced the size and frequency of shipping to the East, and the factors of the Company in Asia found themselves on their own. This forced them to search for new markets in Bengal and to consider increasing commerce with Burma. Some even resorted to building smaller vessels more suited to inter-port trade in the Arabian Sea and the Bay of Bengal.[32]

To exercise this new class of shipping in relative safety, the factors of Surat once again brought up the idea of obtaining a secure and fortifiable harbour from the Portuguese. During the Protectorate of Oliver Cromwell, while negotiating with Portugal for a treaty of commerce in 1654, the Surat factors proposed the inclusion of a harbour such as Bombay, Diu or Bassein, where they built most of the Company vessels.

Their appeal to Cromwell met with no success.[33] During these lean times, it reduced the Surat factors to a handful. They invested in the trade of saltpetre for which Cromwell was grateful, but the market for silk in England declined as the Puritans had no inclination to wear such a luxurious and costly fabric.[34] In 1657, the Company ended up liquidating its prior reiteration and created a new charter which became the foundation of a joint stock company and presaged the future of the English East India Company. The charter included a grant allowing the Company to fortify and colonise any of its establishments with the ability to transport settlers, supplies and ammunition.[35]

The Restoration of the Stuart monarchy greatly benefited the English East India Company. The position of the Company needed to be redefined and details worked out regarding the building of fortresses, and rules of conduct created in relation to the Indians and the Free Traders in the area.[36] Following the restoration of Charles II in May 1660, the directors of the Company enthusiastically voted to give His Majesty three thousand pounds of silver plate. Charles renewed Cromwell's charter for the Company with one in his own name and in 1662, the Company gave the king a ten thousand pound loan. They voted for further loans amounting to one hundred and fifty thousand pounds, and additional charters were awarded with even greater privileges.[37]

The English East India Company had mentioned the idea of acquiring Bombay in 1660 directly with the Portuguese ambassador, a few months before the Stuart Restoration, but he rejected the proposition. The Company made another attempt during the summer with the Portuguese king, while Francisco de Melo, the Portuguese ambassador negotiated for a marriage with the king's sister Catherine and king Charles II. As part of Catherine's dowry, Melo offered the cession of Tangier and Bombay, commercial privileges and complete liberty of conscience for English merchants.[38]

The ratification of the Articles of Marriage between His Majesty and the Lady Infanta in England on June 23, 1661, included a secret clause specifying the use of Bombay by the British for the defence of Portugal's other Indian settlements and implied a British defence against the encroachment of the Dutch. This burden applied only to the English crown and not the English East India Company. The Company was not actively looking to gain more territory. Because of the amiable relations between Charles and the Company, the king accepted the obligations attached to Bombay in supporting the Portuguese in the East. But the Company was not yet willing to shoulder the burden of actually occupying the place.[39]

This attitude is obvious according to the minutes of the Company. The notes disclose the Lord Chancellor, the Earl of Clarendon made an offer to the Company to consider whether it would be to their advantage to dispatch men and shipping at their own expense to possess, maintain and fortify Bombay, to undertake part of the mission jointly with the king, or leave it wholly to His Majesty. The Company gave the idea sufficient consideration and concluded it would not be to their advantage to act on the offer. They thanked the Lord Chancellor and left the matter to the king's goodwill and pleasure. Ultimately, they paid for the manning and victualling of four ships sent by the king to take possession of Bombay and for lading them back again.[40]

When England finally gained control of Bombay, the port lay within the Company's territories, but they had no jurisdiction over it.[41] The area was prone to infection, disease and death. There were internal disputes, a shortage of funds, mutinies, revolts and attacks or the threat of attacks from four separate but occasionally collusive enemies: England, the English East India Company, the Dutch and the Portuguese.[42]

The Portuguese took pleasure in exploiting the friction in the area between the king of England's men and those of the Company, with the Jesuits complicating the situation even further. There was a scarcity of funds to fortify the island against enemies and pirates, and a dire shortage of manpower.[43] Trade in the islands did not thrive, making the cost of the upkeep of Bombay much greater than the income actually realised from commercial endeavors.[44]

The Portuguese remained in the area, using the ports of Thana and Karanja to collect customs and taxes, levying as much as ten to twelve per cent in duty on merchandise and provisions.[45] The Company disputed the Portuguese claims to these two cities and intensely objected to paying the taxes. In addition, complicating matters further, friction existed within the Company itself between the factors at Surat and those in Bombay.[46]

By 1667, it was abundantly clear to His Majesty's government Bombay was a senseless drain on the Crown's treasury. The Portuguese detected an opening and had hopes of buying it back. When the Company got wind of this, they quickly seized the moment, viewing it as the long-awaited, fortunate opportunity to gain Bombay for themselves. King Charles agreed to sell Bombay to the English East India Company for a loan of fifty thousand pounds at six per cent interest and rent of ten pounds per annum, which the Company paid in gold to the Crown until 1730.[47] The possession of Bombay changed hands in London, with the transaction handled personally by the Company's directors in May 1668.[48]

Letters Patent issued by the king created the directors of the Company custodians 'in free and common socage' of all British India. The actual volume of land only amounted to about twenty square miles of mostly water, but it made the Company a sovereign power in Asia.[49] This was a remarkably historic moment. The English East India Company gained their first substantial possession and responsibility, inconspicuously beginning the process which would one day transform the British presence in India into what Mahatma Gandhi referred to as 'the most powerful secret corporation the world has ever known'.[50]

Word of the transfer did not reach the factors in Bombay until a passing ship brought the news in September. It surprised the local men of the Company in Bombay but they were also pleased. According to the Charter, the Company could collect all revenues of Bombay, which at the time amounted to two thousand eight hundred and thirty-three pounds per annum, as well as make laws and enforce them. Bombay had a deputy governor who answered to Surat. They recognised anyone born on the island as a natural subject of Great Britain and guaranteed the free exercise of their religion. The Company aspired to establish an English colony and expand trade, and discussions began for the port of Bombay to become a centre of shipbuilding for the Company.[51]

When the Company took over the port, it had an unhealthy climate, negligible trade and limited access to the mainland. In the beginning, it appeared the costs of fortifying and garrisoning Bombay against the marauding fleets of the Dutch and the Indian pirates would never be recouped. However, Company men such as Sir George Oxenden and Gerald Aungier, the first and second Governors of Bombay, knew the area well and possessed the ability to positively assess the port's potential for commerce and exploitation. A man could build his own house on British soil and the Company allowed employees to stay after their term of service expired. Outsiders could take up residence and promote their own businesses, as long as they did not compete with the Company.

Company administrators actively sought to increase the number of residents, even exporting English women to the colony. Over three years, Bombay's population increased exponentially, and it grew into a flourishing colony, with the people demanding the establishment of judicial, fiscal and administrative institutions.[52] Gerald Aungier, considered the founding father of Bombay, served as governor from 1669 to 1677.[53]

Aungier was the first of the Company's servants to try his hand at creating and administering civilian government. During the 1670s, he regulated the existing magistrate's court and set up a Supreme Court of Judicature. He established a mint and, for security, constructed a chain of Martello towers, which had the effect of intimidating the Dutch and pirates in the area. These improvements and reforms made Bombay more attractive and planters, weavers, merchants and moneylenders arrived while commerce and trade prospered.

The importance of Surat for the Presidency of the Company in India declined, although it still kept its supremacy as a factory.[54] Aungier wrote to the Directors of the Company in London on 3 February 1671: 'And for that it hath unfortunately happened that for two years together your President [in India] hath been hindered from going to Bombay to his own trouble and no small detriment to your Island, we have thought it our duty upon serious consideration of your affairs to offer you our humble advice, that it now seems consistent with your interest to settle your chief Government on your Island Bombay, and to that end you would please to order your President to reside there constantly, except extraordinary emergencies may require his repair to Surat or elsewhere'.[55]

Aungier's attempts to move the Company headquarters from Surat to Bombay were unsuccessful. In 1672, he transferred his personal office to Bombay to devote his energies to building and improving the city.[56] It was not until 1687 that orders came from the Company in London declaring Bombay would take the place of Surat as their headquarters on the west coast of India. John Child, who had authority over all the Company's establishments in India, moved to Bombay Castle, transforming the city into the Presidency and downgrading Surat to a mere Agency of the Company.[57]

A few years later, the Bombay Presidency became the seat of administration of all British forts and depots in India. By 1686, the Company waged war with the Mughals. In 1689, the Company definitively decided it must become a nation in India, otherwise they would always be interlopers only fit to trade.[58] By the mid-eighteenth century, Bombay achieved undisputed commercial supremacy on the west coast of India.[59] Although Bombay was already established, 'the infant settlement would take most of the eighteenth century to emerge from its canopy of coconut palms, bravely front the Arabian Sea, and declare itself the Gateway to India'.[60]

The English East India Company and the Trade of Merchandise from Asia

In the words of Portuguese historian Malyn Newitt, the worldwide reach of the Portuguese Empire led to a vast expansion of markets and the acceleration of the economies of the rest of Europe. Portugal operated as the doorway through which the European Continent received the ideas, cultures and tastes of the rest of the world. Portuguese merchants provided the Continent with American and Asian foodstuffs, medicines, drugs, cotton textiles, Chinoiseries, exotic cultural artifacts, luxury items such as diamonds, fine furniture, *objets d'art* and new fashions in everything from cooking to hairstyles, the use of hammocks and the wearing of pyjamas.[61] During the seventeenth century, these items transformed the taste and material culture of Europe.

The former Portuguese colony of Bombay emerged as a bustling Indian port in the hands of the Directors of the English East India Company. The Articles of Marriage of 1661 confirmed the privileges of the English merchant community and the Methuen treaties of 1703 authenticated England's position as the dominant trade partner of Portugal. Portugal became the principal supplier of wines to Britain while they removed all tariffs against English woollens.[62] The English manufacturers produced light woollen and worsted textiles which were in demand in the Brazilian market, and these were re-exported to Brazil via Portugal.[63]

Beginning in the early 1600s, the English East India Company factory in Surat found the money-making product of the Indian trade to be the vast quantities of various types of cloth made by highly skilled handloom weavers. These artisans decorated cloth on the loom and some had gold or silver threads woven into them. The supreme achievement of the Indian weavers was the mastery of colour-fast dyeing techniques and the attractive designs and colour combinations produced by hand-painting and wood-blocking.[64]

The Company exported napkins and tablecloths, bed sheets and soft furnishings, and underwear, gowns and dress fabrics. They sold cotton yarn by the end of the 1660s. These items soon became essential in every respectable household, while new words emerged and entered the English lexicon. Chintz, calico, taffeta, muslin, gingham, and cashmere soon replaced the time-honoured linen normally found in English cupboards.[65]

The lower classes adopted these less expensive fabrics and they used them for carpets and quilts and to clothe children. Contemporary writers expressed amazement in how far and fast chintz and calicoes rose in popularity, eventually making their way into aristocratic and royal circles.[66] Catherine and King Charles were never seen wearing their gowns made of Indian cotton cloth but it is recorded that in 1684, the king employed an Indian gown-maker named Robert Croft and a Mrs Mandove was the Indian gown-maker to the queen.[67]

Besides these fabrics, pearls, porcelain, folding fans and monkeys, silks, rugs and perfumes were already well known in Europe. With Catherine's arrival in England, curiosity about all things Portuguese intensified. The items she brought with her were an interesting amalgamation of designs, materials and customs which were divergent in origin but well blended through generations of use in Portugal. This foreign influence, in conjunction with the increase in trade inaugurated by the English East India Company from Bombay, altered the shape of a chair leg, promoted the use of woven cane, made fashionable the drinking of tea in Chinese porcelain and enhanced the lives of the English.[68]

To simplify life and reduce the accumulation of material goods, the puritanical Protectorate of Oliver Cromwell deprived the English of entertainments, beauty, and design. One observable example of this was the angular and spare construction of chairs. Chairs manufactured during the Protectorate were wooden, usually oak, and of a square design with little comfort or decoration. With the restoration of the Stuart Monarchy, they would replace the ordinary Cromwellian style with more opulent and magnificent decoration.

Built along the same lines as the Cromwellian chair, they constructed the frame of the Restoration-style chair from French walnut. The legs and back were given a spiral twist, sometimes called the 'Portuguese twist', an effect manufactured by a creative new device called a poppet or lathe-head.[69] Another important innovation was the use of cane in the construction of chairs.

Following the reconstitution of the English East India Company after the Restoration, bundles of cane appeared in shipments to England. Cane was native to the Malay Peninsula, China, India and Ceylon and had been known in Portugal for decades. Also called rattan palm, it was any of the various climbing palms of the genus *Calamus* or allied genera. The tough stems of these palms were woven and used for wickerwork.

The seats and the slightly concave, square backs of the newly designed chairs had cane of narrow strips woven into a wide coarse mesh. These chairs would be strong and comfortable, yet lightweight and easily moved around a room. They were sold by the dozens, especially in London to households having to burn their chairs after an attack of the Great Plague in 1665, and after the Great Fire of London in 1666 destroyed homes and furniture.

One could see the Restoration chairs in halls and bedrooms and used for sitting around the newly introduced gate-leg tables for eating, drinking, gambling and playing games.[70] During the 1670s they became increasingly popular, not only with the aristocracy and gentry, but among merchants and tradespeople. Less expensive than upholstered chairs, they manufactured them in enormous quantities in London from the 1680s onwards for export and home consumption.[71] The use of cane would last until the turn of the century and eventually be utilised to make daybeds, stools, tabletops and screens.

Among the many items Catherine brought with her from Portugal were her lacquerware cabinets. Shortly after the English East India Company took over Bombay, the Company observed the unprecedented surge in the trade of lacquerware.[72] With Catherine's introduction at court and the viewing of her cabinets by many visitors, 'much Indo-Portuguese furniture, of ebony and blackwood, richly carved and with twisted columns, was imported'.[73]

Courtiers admired the Japanese lacquer cabinets which adorned Catherine's apartments at Hampton Court. Variously called 'Chinese', 'Japanese' or 'Indian', the cabinets would take on the name of the country, the district or the port from which they shipped. The cabinets played an essential role in seventeenth-century decor, having single or double doors which fastened shut with a sliding bolt and concealing the curiosities or rarities of the owner in various niches and drawers.

Most of these lacquerware cabinets were black on which artists painted, in colour or in gold, native scenes symbolic of their surroundings. Sometimes, the lacquer would be a warm brown, red, olive green or a deep plum colour called aubergine. The cabinets came in various shapes and sizes, displayed on the floor or raised on a stand.[74] Lacquerware was also used to make screens and tables. Restoration chairs made from woods other than walnut would be painted black by artisans to simulate the ebony hue of the lacquer cabinets. Occasionally, they lacquered the chairs red or green and covered them with small imitation Chinese figures.[75]

It is often stated Catherine introduced marmalade into England. This is not true, but quince marmalade arrived in England via Portuguese trade, followed shortly thereafter by the same product from Spain and Italy. The earliest possible record available for the arrival in an English port of quince marmalade dates from 10 March 1495, which would have been during the years of the celebrated Portuguese exploration of a route to the Indies.[76] The name of the shipper and his ship and the value of the ship's cargo are listed so they could collect duties on the merchandise.

In Portugal, the local dialect went through a transformation as the Mozarabic word for quince, *malmâlo,* became *marmelo*, the modern Portuguese word for the fruit. A version of the term marmalade appears in many other languages, even though the actual preserve may have been produced from fruits other than quince. The form of quince preserves made in the late Middle Ages gained the name marmalade and the recipe went through a critical change. Initially made with quince boiled in honey, the fruit was later boiled in sugar.[77] In the sixteenth century, they said it was the Moors of North Africa who taught the Portuguese to appreciate marmalade, so it seems Arab food customs and recipes were the original source of Portuguese marmalade.[78]

Following the arrival of the quince preserves in England, it was not long before English travellers to the Mediterranean brought back recipes, with English cooks making marmalade from home-grown quinces and imported sugar.[79] During the reign of King Henry VIII, they considered marmalade a very special gift. Nearly all the cookbooks from the time of Queen Elizabeth I into the future contain recipes for marmalade. Marmalades and other jellies, often perfumed and decorated with gold leaf, became one of the best loved sweetmeats of the Elizabethan banquet.[80]

Historical evidence exists showing marmalades consumed by the English during the Tudor and Stuart eras for therapeutic reasons, with recipes appearing in household books and dispensatories of the period. Besides quince pastes, various confections and jellies prepared using other fruits would become known as marmalades. By the seventeenth century, marmalade came in various flavours such as grape, redcurrant, plum, citron, cherry, and apricot. Samuel Pepys mentions marmalade in his diary. In the entries dated 2 and 4 November 1663, he writes that his wife Elizabeth is cooking the preserve.[81]

Confectioners soon realised stiff marmalade paste made from pippins and apricots worked well as modelling material for making decorative features like knots, jumbals (small thin cakes) and artificial fruits. Originally Tudor banqueting conceits, they were readily available in confectioner's shops and remained popular into the late eighteenth century.[82] Eventually, marmalade would be the name exclusively given to the favourite British breakfast preserve made from oranges or lemons.

Tea and Porcelain

Initially, China reluctantly allowed trade with Europeans. The Portuguese were the first Europeans to maintain continuous and direct commercial relations with Chinese merchants[83] establishing a settlement on the peninsula of Macau on or around 1557. They developed a regular trade from there and would ship mainly porcelain and silks to Europe via the Cape of Good Hope. Those Europeans who found their way to China would come into contact with tea, a drink the Chinese called *cha*.

One of these men was a Portuguese Dominican friar from Evora named Gaspar da Cruz (1520–1570) During his sojourn, he spent some time on Lampacau, an island to the east of Macau. Upon his return to Lisbon in the mid-1560s, he wrote *A Treatise on the Things of China* [*tratado das cousas da China*] in which he explains that when people come to any man's house of quality, they are offered a porcelain cup in a fine basket with a kind of tea, red in colour and considered somewhat bitter and medicinal. Tea was offered to anyone the Chinese respected, even if they were strangers.[84]

By the second decade of the seventeenth century, European travellers to Asia were incorporating tea into their lifestyles and diets. Tea had not caught on in Europe just yet and the emphasis of trade to Europe continued to be in silk and spices. Eventually, certain friars and general employees would send small quantities of tea to their favourite relatives, friends and patrons in cities like Amsterdam, Paris and Lisbon.

In the beginning, European shipments of tea were very small. By 1637, the Dutch observed tea's increasing popularity back home and began shipping jars of the commodity with nearly every ship. Within fifteen years they imported tea in moderate amounts and offered it in shops of elite retailers in Paris, London and Holland, opening the European tea market. These early shipments usually contained old and ruined tea leaves and were costly, but despite this, the Dutch earned good profits.[85]

The first printed advertisement for tea in England appeared on the front page of *Mercurius Politicus*, dated 23–30 September 1658, during the time of the Protectorate under Oliver Cromwell's son, Richard.[86] We find an entry in the diary of Samuel Pepys dated 25 September 1660, a few months after King Charles II's restoration. He says, 'And afterwards did send for a Cupp of Tee (a China drink), of which I had never drank before.[87] Charles II's new government, looking for ways to make up an increasingly burdensome lack of cash, was granted excise duties on certain beverages served in coffee houses. This included tea.[88]

Still contingent on the success of the more lucrative commerce in woven fabrics, tea made its way to England in the second half of the seventeenth century, typically through the trading posts of the English East India Company instead of directly from China.[89] On 10 September 1664, the Company messaged Bantam with an order for 100 pounds of the best tea.[90] The Company kept a few odd lots of tea leaves for themselves and they mention in the minutes of the Committee Meetings of 1666 that they served tea to the members. In 1670, one of the English East India Company Directors gave a silver teapot to the Company. After this, the Company arranged for regular shipments of tea leaves for sale.

Meanwhile, in Holland, tea briskly rose in popularity where the people drank it for medicinal purposes. In the 1680s, Dutch medical writers encouraged a debate about tea's properties. The discussion gathered momentum when they translated a summary of the excellent properties of tea, written by Steven Blankaart in 1686, and circulated it in manuscript form among scientific circles in London.[91] Tea appealed to different social interests, all of whom offered different interpretations of its advantages and downsides. The variety of these discourses broadened the market for tea and created a demand for the product.[92]

The tea trade became progressively more substantial for the English East India Company. The Chinese Imperial Government formally allowed foreigners and Europeans to trade at Guangzhou beginning in 1684. From that point forward, commercial involvement in China by European companies and the English East India Company in particular grew exponentially, driven by European demand for tea.[93] Tea first appeared on the 'List of Investments' required of vessels heading to China in the late 1680s.

Large ships sailing from Bombay to Amoy in China had instructions to purchase as much fresh tea as possible. They brought moderate quantities of tea leaves to London by two ships returning from Bombay in 1689 and 1690. In January 1694, the *Dorothy* sailed with orders to purchase fabrics, porcelain, lacquerware and live birds along with as much fresh tea as possible in air-tight containers, making this the first ship to set out from London with specific, official Company instructions to buy tea in China.[94]

They established regular trade in 1699, when the Company purchased 13,082 pounds of tea leaves.[95] Tea arrived from Bantam, Macau, Surat, Bombay and from Britain's earliest trading post on the Chinese mainland, Amoy.[96] Drinking the beverage was still considered a luxury and too expensive for the masses, but it had become an established feature of elite and aristocratic social and domestic life in England.[97]

The early British tea experience began with diverse customs among three distinct groups of people: virtuosi, merchants and aristocratic women and their maids of honour. For these groups, the primary path through which tea came to be known was the consequence of European contacts, especially with the Dutch and the Portuguese. The virtuosi consisted of natural philosophers, men of science, and doctors of medicine. This group's interest in tea revolved around its physiological effects and therapeutic benefits. The second group were merchants and men of commerce who viewed tea as an exotic commodity whose sale could bring them profits. The last group consisted of the elite female court culture surrounding Queen Catherine of Braganza, for whom tea was an exotic and expensive luxury.[98]

Stimulated by the interest shown at the royal court, and by wealthy merchants and medical authorities, the upper echelons of society would appropriate the demand for tea. This class of people could afford to pay the high price initially demanded by the purveyors of tea. Two stories are often repeated about how tea permeated upper society, both of which are most likely apocryphal or at the very least, jumbled and confused.

The first story relates to Queen Catherine of Braganza and her maids of honour, and the second involves the wives of two courtiers acting as ambassadors for King Charles II. The difficulty with both tales is the lack of historical evidence validating either of them, and they originated long after the events allegedly occurred. For example, according to royal hagiography, Queen Catherine established patronage for the oriental taste and ritual of drinking tea for pleasure. The trouble is the idea of Catherine introducing the social drinking of tea in England was first written about in the mid-nineteenth century by the historian, Agnes Strickland (1796–1874). Strickland offers absolutely no historical evidence to support this claim.[99]

The second tale revolves around the wives of two statesmen at Charles II's court. In this version, Henry Bennet, first Earl of Arlington and secretary of state, and Thomas Butler, sixth Earl of Ossory, introduced tea to England in 1666, following their return to London from a diplomatic mission to The Hague. The men allegedly brought back a chest of tea purchased in Holland and their wives engaged in the drinking of it to increase their popularity and sociability at court. Lady Arlington and Lady Ossory were sisters, daughters of Lodewyck van Nassau, Heer van Beverweerd, the illegitimate son of Prince Maurice of Orange and cousin of William of Orange, the future King William III of England.

The root of this story is an essay written by the philanthropist Jonas Hanway in 1756, lecturing about the pernicious effects of tea-drinking. The historical record shows Arlington and Ossory made no diplomatic mission in 1666 but did travel there in 1674. In 1756, Samuel Johnson (1709–1784), the English literary critic, biographer and writer, authoritatively points out that Hanway's story could not be true because, as we have seen, they had taxed tea in England since 1660.[100] Despite these inconsistencies, there is enough evidence to conclude tea socializing was prevalent and fashionable among women at court and in other aristocratic circles in the late seventeenth century.[101]

The consumption of tea was conspicuously about presentation and spectacle, both of the tea itself and the accoutrements used to drink it. For some decades, tea would remain a fashionable drink for the rich, but by the end of the century one could find tea being sold with milk in the streets.[102] In the early 1770s, tea developed into a mainstay of both international commerce and domestic taxation and an everyday ritual in the lives of the polite and middle classes.[103]

Tea drinking in the early eighteenth century invoked the use of another import from China: porcelain. They initially manufactured the equipment employed in tea drinking, such as teapots, kettles, jugs and sugar bowls, in silver or other metals. Because they served tea hot, many considered metal incompatible as it could easily conduct heat and burn the lips. Locally made pottery could not withstand the thermal shock of hot beverages. When people drank tea from British earthenware pottery, even when it was glazed, the dishes would physically degrade, causing cracks and crazing.[104] Despite the thinness and fragility of porcelain, they valued its resistance to hot liquids. The story of tea in England is also the story of porcelain.

The first imports of porcelain to Europe and to England predate tea. Historical record says Vasco da Gama returned to Portugal with porcelain for King Manuel I. The king placed orders for more porcelain from Francisco de Almeida and Afonso de Albuquerque, the viceroys in India. In 1513, King Manuel presented his wife, Queen Maria, with expensive gifts of porcelain. Although the exact date for the beginning of the porcelain trade cannot be determined, records in Portugal show that by as early as 1522, the king decreed those ships returning from India could transport porcelain ware up to one third of the total goods carried.[105]

As early as 1513, Portuguese traders were established in China and by 1536, a factory existed on the site of the Portuguese colony of Macau. Shortly after 1521, the Chinese emperor banned trade with foreigners but despite this prohibition, commerce continued to persist in areas such as Macau. In exchange for gold, spices, ivory, precious stones brought from Ceylon, amber from Timor and other European articles, the foreign merchants received varnishes, tea, silk, lacquer and Chinese porcelain ware. The Portuguese sent these items to their possessions in India and from there, transported them in carracks to Europe. These pieces were fascinating, exotic novelties and became popular with kings, nobles and clergymen in Portugal, Spain, France, England, Italy and the Holy Roman Empire.[106]

In Lisbon, around 1550, there were six shops in one street selling Chinese porcelain.[107] There is some historical evidence showing that by the time of the reign of King Philip I [Philip II of Spain], they manufactured porcelain in Portugal.[108] Portuguese *faience* was undoubtedly the first to imitate Chinese porcelain and also the first to be imitated by the Chinese.[109]

In 1563, Frei Bartholomeu dos Martires, the Portuguese Archbishop of Braga, presumptuously told Pope Pius IV he should set a good example for other prelates and princes by substituting Chinese porcelain for costly silverware in table services. Martires declared the beauty of blue and white Ming porcelain surpassed that of sapphires and alabaster. Its washability and cheapness offset the fragility of porcelain. In addition, it was plentiful and available in the Lisbon market.[110]

By 1580, an abundant variety of porcelain ware was for sale in Lisbon. Forty years later, one could find seventeen porcelain merchants with most of them centred primarily in the Terreiro do Paço in the heart of Lisbon. Chinaware invaded the home market and competed well with coarser Portuguese ware made in the potteries of Caldas, Aveiro and Panasqueira.[111]

The Portuguese royal porcelain collection surpassed all others. Following the restoration of the Portuguese monarchy, as King John IV sought recognition of independence from the countries at war with Spain, Catherine's mother, Queen Luisa sent, among other gifts, a quantity of porcelain of middle and small sizes, to the queen of France. To Queen Christina of Sweden, she shipped two japanned desks inside of which were gloves, furs, earrings and objects made of porcelain.[112]

The Portuguese experienced trouble in their overseas factories with the Chinese, English and Dutch in the early seventeenth century. Eventually, the settlement of Macau declined and most European trade originated in Canton, where all orders were placed for porcelain destined for Portugal and Portuguese India by the eighteenth century. Porcelain was widely known in Europe by the mid-fifteenth century. Sino-Indian trade flourished until 1750 when the Chinese founded a factory at Calicut which they later rented to the Portuguese.[113]

The market for Chinese porcelain, like that of tea, was vested in the hands of the English East India Company. Porcelain's imperviousness to water damage made it a complementary cargo in the ships of the Company. Chinoiserie, the taste for Chinese ornamentation in the eighteenth century, would come to be associated especially with the aesthetic of elite women and their domestic spaces in the home.[114] They used the colourful porcelain pieces imported to Europe and England in the ritual of drinking tea and for display in lacquerware cabinets.

The apocryphal stories about Queen Catherine of Braganza and the noble ladies of the court establish an aristocratic and royal context for the hospitality of tea drinking. The marketing departments of the tea companies swiftly seized this narrative and used it to intensify demand and sales. These tales also show the important association of tea with elite female circles in England in the 1680s and 1690s. Queen Catherine's taste for tea was notable enough for poets to praise her for it in verse.

The courtier Edmund Waller, a tea enthusiast himself,[115] posthumously published a poem in 1690 about Catherine's love of tea. The actual date he authored the poem is unknown, but it is believed to have been in the early 1680s. Waller wrote the verse in honour of Catherine's birthday as an encomium, honouring her for her taste in tea:

Venus her myrtle, Phoebus has his Bays;
Tea both excels, which she vouchsafes to praise.
The best of Queens, the best of Herbs we owe
To that bold Nation which the way did shew
To the fair Region, where the Sun does rise;
Whose rich Productions we so justly prize.
The Muses Friend, Tea, does our fancy aid;
Repress those Vapours, which the head invade:
And keeps that Palace of The Soul serene,
Fit on her Birthday to salute the Queen.[116]

Waller's poem serves to praise the queen through her poetic association with tea and the trade with the East Indies. The poet connects the explorers of Portugal, 'that bold Nation' with the eastern trade routes opened to China, which stimulated the trade in many luxuries, 'rich Productions we so justly prize'. Waller speaks of tea as the pre-eminent prize of the explorer's voyages, 'The Muses Friend'. In addition, the poet praises the healthful benefits of tea, such as encouraging tranquillity.[117]

Catherine of Braganza's tea drinking habit established both the queen's fashionable oriental taste and tea's privileged exclusivity.[118] Besides tea, Catherine's opposition to French interests and her introductions and contributions to English taste, in music, in costume, design and interior decorating all show her substantial contribution to the cosmopolitan character of the English court in the late seventeenth century,[119] all of which extended and enhanced her artistic and cultural patronage and her agency in practicing the duties of queenship. Within a century of the Articles of Marriage between his Majesty and the Lady Infanta of Portugal, tea and sugar and lacquerware cabinets had become necessities in England, washable porcelain and cotton cloth were seen everywhere, and the design of English chairs had been transformed. The English East India Company found itself in control of many square miles of Asia. The remarkable and abundant international trade derived from the Articles of Marriage would be the basis upon which eighteenth-century England established an Empire; in part, the legacy of Catherine of Braganza.

Epilogue

Catherine of Braganza, England's only Portuguese queen consort of England, Scotland and Ireland considered herself thoroughly Portuguese. The daughter of a mere duke in the year of her birth, she came from a country that had only recently won independence from Spain and was not yet recognised by other nations. Despite these obstacles, she made a spectacular marriage.

Her sheltered upbringing left her woefully unprepared for the complex politics and frivolousness of the Restoration Stuart court. It is not surprising that in her adopted country, she put up with a lot of suffering, which her Roman Catholic education taught her to expect. But her greatest sorrow would be her inability to provide King Charles II of England with a legitimate heir.

Occasionally, she displayed a temper. Despite this, Catherine had a genuine, kind, forgiving, selfless, patient and loyal personality. There was no grasping or overweening ambition on her part and, after an initial attempt early in her marriage, she rarely inserted herself in any overt way into government policymaking or legislation, although she took an active, clandestine interest in the support of her religion and displayed an anti-French stance. She learned to live with Charles' infidelities and have a good relationship with his mistresses, endearing herself to her husband. Catherine could practise the elements of early modern queenship to the best of her ability, despite drawbacks and limitations.

The economic and political relationship between England and Portugal was long-standing, having originated in the Middle Ages and figured largely in Catherine's life and marriage. Another component integral to Catherine's life is the significance of the great Portuguese explorers and the establishment of the country's trading empire. Catherine's dowry included the ports of Tangier and Bombay and trading privileges with Brazil along with other ports of call within this empire. These concessions, along with an enormous amount of cash, attracted Charles II to consider a marriage with the newly restored royal house of Portugal. England had formed a trading empire of its own during the reign of Queen Elizabeth I, but the acquisition of Bombay allowed the merchants of the English East India Company to gain the traction needed in the East Indies to exponentially expand its trade and grow into the one of the first worldwide corporations.

Catherine was one of only a handful of queen consorts who returned to her country of origin as a widow. She would rule in her own right as regent for her brother, just as her mother did before her. She would end her life there and to this day, Catherine remains revered and beloved in Portugal. Catherine's loyalty to her husband, England, Portugal and her family, and the Catholic Church is without dispute.

Acknowledgements

Writing this book has been a labour of love for me and there are many people who have been an immense help. For their encouragement and positivity, I would like to give thanks to Alison Weir, Dr Linda Porter, Mike Dooley, Keira Morgan, Dr Kimberly Shutte, Sharon Bennet Connolly, Rozsa Gaston and my sisters here in Denver [you know who you are]. I could not have done it without you.

I am deeply indebted to Daniel Costa for his translation services. His work was instrumental in unlocking the secrets of Catherine's early life and her time in Portugal as dowager queen and regent. I am grateful for the research help of Søren Kruse, Christine Morgan (those bloody footnotes!), and Danica Monteiro and the British Historical Society of Lisbon.

Artistic help was provided by Barbara Barnhardt and her partner John Kjos in designing the mock-up of a possible book cover. And I have to thank all my beta-readers: Patty Eilers, Roberto Gonzales and Christine Shaeffer along with others. Thanks to you all.

Cast of Characters

The Portuguese

Fernando I, King of Portugal – Reigned from 1367–1383. His death created a succession crisis that eventually led to the establishment of the House of Aviz on the throne.

John I, King of Portugal – Illegitimate half-brother of King Fernando I of Portugal and Grand-Master of the Military Order of Aviz. After the death of his brother, John politically and militarily established himself on the throne, founding the House of Aviz dynasty of Portuguese kings. John I had a natural born son, Afonso, who was the founder of the House of Braganza.

Philippa of Lancaster, Queen Consort of Portugal – English wife of King John I. The couple had several brilliant and successful children who would be known as the 'illustrious generation'.

Duarte (Edward), King of Portugal – Eldest son of John I and Philippa of Lancaster, he ruled after the death of his father.

Pedro, Regent of Portugal – Second son of John I and Philippa of Lancaster, he was the brother of King Duarte and served as Regent for Duarte's son, King Afonso V of Portugal, and would become a patron of many Portuguese explorers and traders.

Afonso V, King of Portugal – son of King Duarte.

Henry the Navigator, Duke of Viseu – Son of John I and Philippa of Lancaster. He would become known as the patron of many Portuguese explorers and traders.

Fernando, Prince of Portugal – Son of John I and Philippa of Lancaster. After becoming a prisoner of war in Morocco, he tragically died there in captivity.

Afonso I, Duke of Braganza – Natural born son of John I, later legitimised. The first Duke of Braganza, Catherine was his descendant.

John II, King of Portugal – Son of King Afonso V, he would act as co-ruler with his father and become a visionary of Portuguese exploration, especially to India.

Manuel I, King of Portugal – Brother-in-law of King John II and as his successor, would continue Portuguese exploration and found the Estado of India.

Vasco da Gama, Portuguese explorer – Found it was possible and profitable to sail directly from Europe to India.

Afonso de Albuquerque, Viceroy of the Estado of India – Founder of Goa and the colony of Bombay in India.

Sebastian, King of Portugal – Grandson of King John III and the last monarch of the House of Aviz. He died in a blaze of glory at the Battle of Ksar el-Kabir in August 1578. He had no immediate successors and after a short rule of his elderly uncle, King Philip II of Spain strong-armed his way onto the throne of Portugal as King Philip I. This led to the Iberian Union which lasted until the restoration of the House of Braganza in 1640.

Philip II, King of Spain – Also King Philip I of Portugal, his family would rule the united monarchies of Spain and Portugal until the restoration of the House of Braganza on the throne of Portugal in 1640.

Francisco de Melo, fourth Count of Tentugal, third Marquis of Ferreira – Godfather of Catherine of Braganza, he was a member of the Council of State and of War and one of the ministers of Dispatch, as well as butler to the Duchess of Braganza, Catherine's mother. He would serve as Marshal when they acclaimed Catherine's father King of Portugal.

John IV, King of Portugal and eighth Duke of Braganza – Catherine's father. When the Portuguese monarchy was restored, he became King John IV of Portugal, the first monarch of the House of Braganza.

Queen Luisa Maria Francisca de Guzmán y Sandoval – Catherine's mother. She served as regent for her son, Afonso VI, until he declared his majority and ruled in his own right. Queen Luisa lobbied for an English marriage for Catherine from the very beginning.

Teodósio – Catherine's eldest beloved brother who died before his father.

Joanna, Princess of Beira – Catherine's sister who died at the age of 18.

Afonso VI – Catherine's brother who became king of Portugal upon the death of their father. After displaying erratic behaviour, he was deposed and replaced by the regency of his brother, Pedro, and kept prisoner until his death.

Pedro II, King of Portugal – Catherine's brother who became regent for their brother, Afonso VI, following his deposition. Upon Afonso's death, he became King Pedro II. Catherine would serve as regent for him during the War of the Spanish Succession.

Maria Francisca Elizabeth of Savoy, Queen of Portugal – Sister-in-law to Catherine of Braganza. She first married Catherine's brother, King Afonso VI, who was deposed. She had her marriage annulled so she could wed Catherine's brother King Pedro II. She died in 1683.

Maria Sophia of Neuberg, Queen of Portugal – Sister-in-law to Catherine of Braganza. She was the second wife of King Pedro II.

Gaspar de Guzmán y Pimentel, first Duke of Sanlúcar, third Count of Olivares, GE, KOA, known as the Count-Duke of Olivares – The royal favourite of King Philip IV of Spain, he served as prime minister from 1621 to 1643. He over-exerted Spain in foreign affairs and created conditions in Portugal leading to the restoration of the Portuguese monarchy and the Braganza dynasty.

Francisco de Melo e Torres – Ambassador to England from Portugal, he was the first Marquis of Sande, governor of Olivença, and artillery general of Alentejo during the Restoration Wars. He negotiated the Articles of Marriage between his Majesty and the Lady Infanta of Portugal in 1661. His sister, Mary Drago of Portugal, Countess of Penalva served Catherine of Braganza for many years. He was a member of the Council of State and War. In 1666, he negotiated the marriage of King Afonso VI and Maria Francisca Elizabeth of Savoy and was assassinated on the night of 7 December 1667.

Father Domingos do Rosário —— Née Daniel O'Daly, Father Domingos was an Irishman born in 1595; he died in Lisbon on 20 June 1662. He was the confessor to Queen Luisa, who employed him as an *ambassador extraordinaire*, giving him an important role in Portuguese politics and diplomacy and in the negotiations for Catherine's marriage to King Charles II.

António de Sousa de Macedo – Secretary of the Portuguese embassy, remained in England during the first English Civil War and acted as Charles I's agent for the procurement of guns and ammunition. Possibly the first person to mention the marriage of Catherine of Braganza to King Charles II of England.

The Stuarts

Charles Stuart, King Charles I of England – Father of King Charles II of England. He believed in the divine right of kings and tried to rule England without Parliament. He was unsuccessful, found guilty of treason and executed in January 1649.

Henrietta Maria, Queen Consort of England – Wife of King Charles I, mother of King Charles II and James II of England and mother-in-law to Catherine of Braganza.

Charles Stuart, King Charles II of England – Catherine's husband. During civil disturbances in the reign of Charles I, he went into exile on the Continent. Later restored to the throne of England in 1660, he searched for a wife and found one in Portugal – Catherine of Braganza, the daughter of the newly minted King John IV.

James Stuart, King James II of England and Duke of York – Brother of King Charles II. He was Duke of York and became King James II of England upon the death of his brother. He converted to Catholicism in 1673, creating a crisis in the succession to the English throne. He abdicated or was deposed depending on who is telling the story, by William of Orange and James' own daughter, Mary, in the Glorious Revolution of 1688. James went into exile in France.

Anne Hyde, Duchess of York – Daughter of Edward Hyde, first Earl of Clarendon and Lord Chancellor of England during the reign of King Charles II, and first wife of Charles' brother, James.

Mary Beatrice d'Este of Modena, Queen Consort of England and Duchess of York – Second wife of James Stuart. She gave birth to a healthy son, James Francis Edward Stuart, with many witnesses, including Catherine of Braganza. However, her stepdaughters Mary and Anne spread rumours the child was not hers and may have been smuggled into the delivery room in a 'warming pan'. The controversy led to the Glorious Revolution of 1688, with William of Orange invading England. William and his wife Mary were declared joint Sovereigns of England.

Henriette Anne Stuart, Duchess of Orleans – Younger sister of King Charles II of England, who referred to her by his pet name of 'Minette'. She married Philip, Duke of Orleans, brother of King Louis XIV of France and was known as 'Madame' in France. The Secret Treaty of Dover in 1670 was negotiated between Minette, King Louis XIV and Charles II.

Mary II, Queen Regnant of England – Daughter of James Stuart and Anne Hyde, born when they were Duke and Duchess of York. She married her cousin William, Prince of Orange, and he brought an invasion force to England during the Glorious Revolution in 1688 to depose Mary's father, King James II.

William III, King of England and Prince of Orange – Nephew of King Charles II and James II, he was married to James' eldest daughter by Anne Hyde, Mary Stuart. He invaded England in 1688 during the Glorious Revolution. After ousting James II, he ruled with his wife as joint sovereign until her death in 1694 and as sole sovereign until his death in 1702.

Anne Stuart, Queen Regnant of England – Daughter of James Stuart and Anne Hyde when they were Duke and Duchess of York. Anne married Prince George of Denmark and would have seventeen pregnancies, with no surviving children. She conspired to have her half-brother, James Frances Edward Stuart, barred from the throne so she and her sister could reign in England. She became queen regnant upon the death of William III in 1702.

The French and the English

Louis XIV, King of France – Cousin of King Charles II and James II of England.

Cardinal Richelieu – Chief minister of France during the reign of King Louis XIII. He was instrumental in unsuccessful negotiations to marry Catherine of Braganza to King Louis XIV.

Cardinal Mazarin – Chief minister of France during the early reign of King Louis XIV and instrumental in unsuccessful negotiations to marry Catherine of Braganza to King Louis XIV.

General George Monck – Respected general of English troops during the Republic of Oliver Cromwell, after the execution of King Charles I. He brokered the restoration of the Stuart monarchy in 1660, bringing King Charles II to the throne.

Oliver Cromwell, Lord Protector of the Commonwealth of England, Scotland and Ireland – Cromwell ruled England after the execution of King Charles I. He worked to establish significant commerce and trade policies and treaties with Portugal.

Edward Montagu, first Earl of Sandwich – Sandwich escorted Catherine from Lisbon to Portsmouth for her marriage and negotiated the Treaty of Lisbon in 1668 which ended the Restoration War between Spain and Portugal.

Edward Hyde, first Earl of Clarendon – Lord Chancellor to King Charles II.

Henry Hyde, second Earl of Clarendon – Son of Edward Hyde, Catherine appointed him as her lord treasurer. She later learned he had embezzled some of her money and she sued him to get it back.

Samuel Pepys – Diarist during the early years of the reign of King Charles II. He has many insights into the court of the king.

John Evelyn – Diarist during the reign of King Charles II.

Anthony Ashley Cooper, first Earl of Shaftesbury – Prominent English politician who served as Lord President of the council, among other offices, during the reign of King Charles II. He politically manipulated the exploits of the known perjurer, Titus Oates, during the height of the Popish Plot in an effort to force King Charles II to abandon his brother James as his successor to the throne and to divorce Catherine of Braganza in order to marry a Protestant princess.

Appendix One

Complete Text of the Articles of Marriage between his Majesty and the Lady Infanta of Portugal, 1661

Articles of Marriage between his Majesty and the Lady Infanta of Portugal, 1661

It being upon mature deliberation mutually and fully agreed between their Majesties, Charles, by the grace of God, King of Great Britain, France, and Ireland, Defender of the Faith, etc. and Alphonso, by the same grace of God, King of Portugal and Algarve, etc. that the King of Great Britain shall, with all possible speed as such an affair can be transacted in, many and take to wise the most Excellent Princess Dona Catherina Infanta of Portugal; for a more firm and durable peace and alliance between the two Crowns, and for the good of both nations, which are henceforward to take each other's interest to heart no less than their own, it is mutually consented and agreed as followeth :

I. That all treaties made between Great Britain and Portugal since 1641, until this very time, shall be ratified and confirmed in all points and to all intents, and shall receive as full force and ratification by this treaty, as if they were herein particularly mentioned and inserted word by word.

II. The King of Portugal, by and with the advice of his council, doth give, transfer, grant, and by these presents confirm unto the King of Great Britain, his heirs and successors forever, the city and castle of Tangier, with all its rights, territories, profits, and appurtenances whatsoever, and also as well the profits and revenue, as the direct, full, and absolute dominion and sovereignty of the same city and castle and territories aforesaid, with their royalties, freely, fully, entirely, and absolutely. He doth also covenant and grant, that the full and peaceable possession of the aforesaid city and castle, and other the premises, be freely and effectually delivered unto the King of Great Britain, and for his use, with as much speed as the same can be dispatched in: and it is agreed, that as soon as this treaty shall be signed by the King of Great Britain, and the matrimonial contract between his Majesty and the Lady Infanta *per verba de presold facta,* [presold before the actual marriage] the said King of Great Britain shall send five frigates (or as many as he shall think fit) to Lisbon, there to receive orders to go and lie before Tangier, as well for the transportation of the garrison as the security of the place. And as soon as notice is given by the governor of that place, that he hath put in execution the King of Portugal's orders concerning the delivery of the said places, the treaty being confirmed and ratified by his Majesty of Portugal, notice thereof shall with all speed be given to his Majesty of Great Britain, who shall thereupon, immediately send away his fleet of twelve men of war for the port of Lisbon, which, within four or five days after their arrival there, shall have orders to go and take possession of the city and castle of Tangier, with other the premises, for the use of the King of Great Britain, and effectually to receive the same. Which city with the castle and territories, and other premises (as well for the dominion and absolute sovereignty, as for the possession thereof) shall be and remain to the King of Great Britain, his heirs and successors, forever, annexed unto the Imperial crown.

III. That all soldiers and other inhabitants whatsoever of the said city and castle of Tangier, who shall desire to continue and reside there, shall be very kindly treated, and have the free exercise of the Roman Catholic religion, and in all civil affairs shall be governed under the King of Great Britain, and as his subjects, by the same laws and customs which have been hither to used and approved in the said city and castle; and all such of the soldiers and inhabitants thereof, who shall desire to return into Portugal, shall have free liberty to sell and dispose of all that belongs to them, and shall be transported into Portugal whensoever they desire it (so also shall the ordnance, as much as can be spared from the fortifications of Tangier) by the fleet or ships of the King of Great Britain.

IV. As soon as the city of Tangier, with the castle and territories thereof (in performance of this treaty and grant concerning the transferring of the sovereignty and absolute dominion thereof to the King of Great Britain) shall be effectually delivered to the use and possession of his said Majesty of Great Britain, the fleet shall return to Lisbon, and the Lady Infanta shall be received on board with such signs of joy, and such other ceremonies, as may befit the excellency and quality of her person.

V. The King of Portugal doth promise and oblige himself, by these presents, to give unto the King of Great Britain, for a portion or dowry with the said Lady Infanta his sister, two millions, i.e. 2,000,000 of crowns Portuguese; and that one moiety thereof shall be really put on board the said fleet before the Infanta herself embarks; and the said money, or so much thereof as consists of money, shall be immediately delivered upon account to such persons as his Majesty of Great Britain shall appoint to receive the same, for his proper use: but so much of the said moiety as shall be put on board in jewels, sugar, or merchandise, shall not be taken upon the account of his Majesty of Great Britain, but shall be transported into the river of Thames, for the use of such persons who shall be authorised by the King of Portugal to receive the same; and those persons shall be bound (the King of Portugal obliging himself also for such payment to be really made by such persons) within two months after the delivery of the same to them, effectually to satisfy and pay the full and clear value thereof in English money (as hath been agreed) unto the King of Great Britain: and for the other moiety of the said portion, amounting to one million, i.e. 1,000,000 of crowns Portuguese, the King of Portugal doth oblige himself to pay the same within the space of one year after the arrival of the Infanta in England, by two payments, the one within six months next following, the other within the year, both to be made in the City of London, transporting as abovesaid the jewels and merchandise in the King of Great Britain's ships, and so much of this latter moiety as consists of jewels or merchandise, shall be transported into England for the use of such persons as the King of Portugal shall appoint to receive the same, and those persons shall be bound (as abovesaid) effectually to satisfy and pay the full and Clear value thereof, in English money, to the King of Great Britain, within the said terms.

VI. From the time that the Lady Infanta is embarked on his Majesty's fleet, she and her whole train shall be transported upon the account and at the charge of his Majesty of Great Britain; who will, as soon as he shall receive the longed-for news of her Majesty's arrival, make all possible haste to receive her, which he will do with all those expressions and demonstrations of affection as shall be agreeable to her dignity, and answerable to her Majesty's expectation; when the instrument of matrimony shall be publicly read, whereunto as well the King of Great Britain, as the Lady Infanta, shall personally give their consents, and all other acts for the further solemnisation thereof shall be performed, which shall be desired on the behalf of the King of Portugal.

VII. It is also agreed, that her Majesty and whole family shall enjoy the free exercise of the Roman Catholic religion, and to that purpose shall have a chapel, or some other place set apart for the exercise thereof, in all the royal palaces where she shall at any time reside, in as full a manner, to all intents and purposes, as the Queen mother now living enjoyed the same, and shall have such chaplains and ecclesiastical persons in number and quality about her, as the said Queen mother hath had, with the same privileges and immunities. And the King of Great Britain promiseth not to disquiet or disturb, nor permit that any others should disquiet or disturb, the said Lady Infanta his wife, in anything appertaining to religion and conscience.

VIII. That the King of Great Britain shall, within one year after the arrival of her Majesty in England, settle upon her a jointure of thirty thousand pounds of English money by the year, together with at least one such palace or house as her Majesty may make her ordinary residence in, which shall be so furnished as may befit her dignity; all which her Majesty shall enjoy during her life if she survive his Majesty.

IX. That her Majesty's household, from the time of her arrival in England, shall be formed and composed of such a number of officers and servants as are agreeable to her dignity, and in the same manner as the Queen mother enjoyed the same.

X. If her Majesty shall survive the King of Great Britain, and shall then desire to return to Portugal, or any other country, she shall have the liberty so to do, and to carry with her all her jewels, goods, and moveables; and the King of Great Britain doth here by oblige his heirs and successors to take care for the safe and honourable transportation of her Majesty, in such a manner as is agreeable to the greatness of her person, and at his and their proper costs and charges: moreover, he obligeth his said heirs and successors to pay the aforesaid sum of thirty thousand pounds yearly unto her said Majesty, no otherwise than as if she had still continued and remained in England.

XI. That for the better improvement of the English interest and trade in the East Indies, and that the King of Great Britain may be better enabled to assist, defend, and protect the subjects of the King of Portugal, in those parts, from the power and invasion of the States of the United Provinces, the King of Portugal, with the advice and consent of his council, doth give, transfer, and by these presents grant and confirm unto the King of Great Britain, his heirs and successors, forever, the port and island of Bombay in the East Indies, with all the rights, profits, territories, and appurtenances whatsoever thereunto belonging, and as well the profits and revenue, as the direct, full, and absolute dominion and sovereignty of the said port, island, and premises, with all the royalties thereof, freely, fully, entirely, and absolutely. He doth also covenant and grant, that the quiet and peaceable possession thereof shall, with all possible speed, be freely and effectually delivered to the King of Great Britain, or such person as his Majesty shall thereunto appoint, for his use, in performance of this grant: the inhabitants of the said island (as the King of Great Britain's subjects, and under his sovereignty, crown, jurisdiction, and government) being suffered still to live there, and enjoy the free exercise of the Roman Catholic religion, in the same manner as now they do; it being understood, and declared once for all, that the same order shall be observed for the exercise and preservation of the Roman Catholic religion in Tangier, and all other places which shall be delivered by the King of Portugal into the possession of the King of Great Britain, as was provided for and agreed, upon the delivery of Dunkirk into the hands of the English. And when the King of Great Britain shall send his fleet to take possession of the said port and island of Bombay, they shall have instructions to give all manner of encouragement, help, and assistance, to the subjects of the King of Portugal in the East Indies, and to protect them in their trade and navigation there.

XII. That the subjects of the King of Great Britain may enjoy the more full benefit of trade and commerce, in all the dominions of the King of Portugal, it is agreed, that their merchants or factors (above what hath been granted by former treaties) may, by virtue of this treaty, reside in all places they shall choose, and particularly that they shall live, and enjoy all privileges and immunities, in order to trade, which the Portuguese themselves enjoy, in the cities and towns of Goa, Cochim, and Dio, provided that the subjects of his Majesty of Great Britain, who are to reside in any of the said places, shall not exceed the number of four families in any one place.

XIII. The like privileges, liberties, and immunities the King of Great Britain's subjects shall enjoy in the towns of Bahia de todos os santos, Pernambuco, and Rio de Janeiro, in the territory of Brazil, and in all other of the King of Portugal's dominions in the West Indies.

XIV. But if the King of Great Britain, or his subjects, shall at any time hereafter take out of the hands of the Hollanders, or others, any towns, castles, or territories, formerly belonging to the crown of Portugal, the King of Portugal, with the advice and consent of his council, doth grant the sovereignty, and full, entire, and absolute dominion of them and every of them, unto the King of Great Britain, his heirs and successors, forever, freely, entirely, and absolutely, except Mascata, which is at present inhabited by the Arabians: and if at any time the island of Zeilon [Ceylon], by what means soever, come into the hands of the King of Portugal, he is by this treaty obliged to deliver unto the King of Great Britain the town and port of Galle, and to grant and transfer the full and absolute dominion and sovereignty of the said town and port, with the possession, thereof, and all the appurtenances thereunto belonging, unto the said King of Great Britain, effectually, yet reserving unto him the said King of Portugal the town and port of Columbo; but the cinnamon trade to be equally divided between the English and the Portuguese. As also, if at any time the said island shall fall into the hands of the King of Great Britain, he is obliged, and with the consent and advice of his council doth promise, effectually to restore and deliver the dominion and possession of the town and port of Columbo unto the King of Portugal, the cinnamon trade being, in such manner as aforesaid, divided and to be divided between the English and the Portuguese.

XV. In consideration of all which grants and privileges, so much to the benefit of the King of Great Britain and his subjects in general, and of the delivery of those important places to his said Majesty and his heirs so ever, whereby the greatness of his empire is so far extended; and even in consideration of the portion itself, which far exceeds the proportion that hath ever yet been given to any daughter of Portugal; the King of Great Britain doth profess and declare, with the consent and advice of his council, that he will take the interest of Portugal and all its dominions to heart defending the same with his utmost power by sea and land, even as England itself, and that he will transport thither at his proper costs and charges two regiments of horse, each regiment consisting of five hundred, and two regiments of foot, each consisting of one thousand, all which shall be armed at the charge of the King of Great Britain, but after they are landed in Portugal, shall be paid by the King of Portugal; and in case the said regiments come to be diminished, by fight or otherwise, the King of Great Britain shall be obliged to fill up the number at his own charge; and that he shall cause the said regiments to be transported as soon as the Lady Infanta shall arrive in England, if it be so desired by the King of Portugal.

XVI. The King of Great Britain doth also promise, with the advice and consent of his council, that when and as often as Portugal shall be invaded, he will send thither (being thereunto desired by the King of Portugal) ten good ships of war; but when and as often as it shall be infested by pirates, three or four ships, all sufficiently manned and victualled for eight months, from the time of their setting sail from England, to obey the orders of the King of Portugal. And if it shall be required that they stay above six months there, the King of Portugal shall be obliged to victual them for so long time as they are to stay, and to put in one month's victuals at the time they are to set sail for England: but if the King of Portugal shall be pressed in any extraordinary manner by the power of the enemies, all the King of Great Britain's ships, which shall at any time be in the Mediterranean Sea, or at Tangier, shall have instructions in such cases to obey any orders they shall receive from the King of Portugal, and shall betake themselves to his succour and relief. And in regard of the above-mentioned concessions and grants of the King of Portugal, his Majesty of Great Britain, his heirs and successors, shall not at any time require any thing for these succours.

XVII. Besides the levies the King of Portugal hath liberty to make by virtue of past treaties, the King of Great Britain doth oblige himself by this present treaty, that in case Lisbon, Porto, or any other sea town, shall be besieged or blocked up by the power of Castile, or any other enemy, he will afford timely assistance of men and shipping, according to the exigence of the circumstances, and proportionable to the necessity of the King of Portugal.

XVIII. The King of Great Britain doth profess and promise, with the advice and consent of his council, that he will never make a peace with Castile, which may be the least impediment to him, directly or indirectly, in his giving full and entire assistance to Portugal, in order to its necessary defence; and that he will never deliver Dunkirk or Jamaica unto the King of Castile, nor ever forbear to do any act that is necessary for the relief of Portugal, though by so doing he shall be engaged in a war with the King of Castile.

XIX. Lastly, it is agreed and covenanted by the King of Great Britain, that the said Infanta, in consideration of the portion given with her by the King of Portugal, shall renounce all her right and inheritances, by either father or mother, or any other descendency, as well for lands and houses, as moveables, jewels, or monies, by what right or way soever belonging unto her, as also what else shall belong unto her for the future (except hereafter excepted) as derived unto her by the late King her father, or by his death descending to her by the laws of Portugal as her portion, or that is to descend unto her upon the decease of the Queen her mother by the said laws; always provided, that the said Lady Infanta shall in no wise renounce, nor willeth nor intendeth to renounce, any right, inheritance, title, claim, or interest, that doth or shall anywise belong or appertain unto her, or any of her heirs or descendants, to or in the crown or kingdom of Portugal, or any the dominions thereof; but doth totally and expressly reserve unto herself, her heirs and descendants, all those rights whatsoever to the said crown and kingdom, which may any way belong or appertain unto her for the future, and doth and will retain the same entirely and effectually now and forever.

A Secret Article

Over and above all and singular agreed and concluded in the treaty of marriage between the most Serene and most powerful Charles, the second of that name, King of Great Britain, and the most virtuous and Serene Lady Catherine, Infanta of Portugal. It is by this secret article concluded and accorded, that his Majesty of Great Britain, in regard of the great advantages and increase of dominion be hath purchased by the above-mentioned treaty of marriage, shall promise and oblige himself, as by this present article he doth, to defend and protect all conquests or colonies belonging to the crown of Portugal, against all his enemies, as well future as present: moreover, his Majesty of Great Britain doth oblige himself to mediate a good peace between the King of Portugal and the States of the United Provinces, and all companies or societies of merchants subject unto them, upon conditions convenient and becoming the mutual interest of England and Portugal; and in case such a peace ensue not, then his Majesty of Great Britain shall be obliged to defend, with men and ships, the said dominions and conquests of the King of Portugal. In case also that any towns, forts, castles, or any other places, shall be taken by the Dutch, after the first of May this present year 1661, then his Majesty of Great Britain doth promise and engage to oblige the Dutch to a full and perfect restitution thereof. His Majesty of Great Britain doth moreover oblige himself to send, the next monsoon ensuing after the ratification of the treaty of marriage, and this article, a convenient succour to the East Indies, proportionable to the necessity of Portugal and strength of our enemies. It being declared that his Majesty nor his successors shall not at any time require any pay or satisfaction for the same.[1]

Appendix Two

Catherine's Health

From the historical record, it appears Catherine had some serious illnesses and she clearly suffered from infertility. Conversely, she seems to have been quite resilient, managing to bounce back from several near fatal sicknesses. We can glean from the record the causes of her inability to get pregnant and carry a child to full term.

Later in life, she wrote of her bout of quinsy when she was 3 years old. Today we would call this illness tonsillitis. She notes her treatment included holy oil from a lamp from the chapel in the town of Viçosa; more of a mystical cure than an actual medical one. She must have been relatively healthy up until she left for England as there is no other record of any illnesses.

During her rough sea journey, she became seasick. Once she arrived in Portsmouth, we are told she had a cold, compelling her to meet her new husband in her bed. Fortunately, she recovered from this and was well enough to go through with her wedding as planned, although they did not sleep together the night after their marriage due to her menses.

Once at court, the stress of her new surroundings and culture shock caused Catherine to become ill. The Venetian ambassador mentions she did not like English food and only drank water, which could be considered a dangerous thing to do in seventeenth-century England. Catherine did not drink alcohol. It is mentioned as unusual for her to drink to the king's health shortly after her ordeal related to the Popish Plot. 'One afternoon, after she had watched the king's greyhounds hunt hare for a short time on the estate of her husband's faithful servant, Chaffinch, she who never drank raised her glass to drink a toast to Charles' health, with the fervent tenderness that love transforms into a gesture of adoration'.[1]

When Catherine did not become pregnant within the first year of her marriage, it was a serious business. Once she resolved to end the early crisis regarding her servants, and Charles became more motivated to do his duty, Catherine embarked on a series of many attempts to enhance her fertility, notably visiting Tunbridge Wells and Bath. Of course, these treatments had little effect as we now know.

Daphna Oren-Magidor has some pertinent information about water treatments for fertility in her book *Infertility in Early Modern England*. She states infertility was a social as well as a medical issue and the treatment of fertility problems had a direct link to religion. Women at the time believed and understood the efficacy of medical treatment was a God-given gift and patients were advised to practise specific forms of prayer before taking treatments.[2]

For devout women, infertility was meant to test their faith and to teach them to accept their lot in life. Relying on prayer to give them hope they might bear children, they kept their faith even if they did not have a child, because they believed it was part of a providential plan.[3] Catherine, with her deeply religious devotion, would have believed this.

During the seventeenth century, baths gained popularity as medical sites for the upper echelons of society and were associated in particular with the treatment of fertility problems. At the same time, they also became sites of social interaction, and writers often characterised this as informal and even immoral. The French ambassador, the Count de Grammont, described a visit by Catherine to Tunbridge Wells to treat her infertility, noting that there was 'dancing every day at the queen's apartments'.[4] The Queen tried to create a more relaxed atmosphere by surpassing 'even herself in originating or sustaining new amusements. She tried to increase the natural ease of Tunbridge by dispensing with such ceremonies as were due to her'.[5]

Water treatments for infertility were an elite practice, usually requiring a lengthy visit to a spa town such as Bath or Tunbridge Wells. These visits would often include a social element such as entertainment or travelling with companions. The growth of English spas as elite medical locations grew in the seventeenth and eighteenth century and this was directly related to their use by royal women, such as Catherine and her sister-in-law, Mary Beatrice of Modena, to promote conception or to frequently treat reproductive disorders. As a result, water cures gained a reputation for treating these concerns that extended into popular culture as well as to medicine.[6]

The best advertisement for water cures as a treatment for infertility was the use of the spas by England's queens. Henrietta Maria took the waters in 1627, 1628 and 1629 and would give birth to seven children. Catherine and her sister-in-law Mary Beatrice, Duchess of York, pursued water treatments at Tunbridge Wells and Bath. Catherine failed to sustain a pregnancy but Mary Beatrice gave birth to Prince Charles Edward, the purported 'Warming Pan baby' shortly after one such treatment.[7]

When queens took water treatments, they were usually accompanied by their ladies and other courtiers. These visits served to further the fame of the baths as medical locations and to increase their status as popular social venues. For aristocratic women, baths were the treatment of choice from the middle of the seventeenth century and it seems likely the attraction of the baths for them was not simply their potential for cure but also for their fashionable social advantages.[8]

Taking the waters allowed royal and aristocratic women to remove themselves from certain requisite duties while at the same time experience the company of their friends and courtiers. As bathing became more popular, spa towns began developing housing and amenities for entertaining upper-class guests. In this way, taking the waters increased as a source of pleasure as well as medicinal aid. The relaxed atmosphere of the spas would have been pleasant for royal women, on whom the pressures of reproduction were particularly high.[9]

Sir Arthur Bryant has a description of the treatment a woman would receive at Bath. It is worth quoting here as Catherine would have gone through a similar experience:

> In the Cross Bath, the gentlemen sat on a circular seat surrounding the stone cross in the centre, while the ladies faced them from arches along the side, each sitting up to her neck in water with a laced toilet curtain hanging down from the arch top to hide the rest of her, and, as though this were not protection enough, swathed in stiff yellow canvas garments with episcopal sleeves. These the water modestly blew out like balloons, 'so that your shape is not seen'. Some added to this precautionary attire cork shoes. And beside each nymph floated a little dish keeping inviolate from the waters her handkerchief and nosegay.
>
> Above, in the gallery, spectators gazed and promenaded while the music played and the Sergeant of the Bath walked to and fro, complimenting persons of fashion and showering on them obliging attentions, for all the world like the chief steward of a modern cruising liner, and for the same reason. To add to the decorum of the proceedings, a number of guides of both sexes stood about in the water, and, whenever a lady bather wished to move, a female guide would lend her arm, while two male guides at a suitable distance walked before to clear the way.
>
> The departure from the bath was hidden from spectators, but we are more privileged. For we know that as the lady bather ascended the steps that led out of the bath her costume dropped from her, slipping back into the sulphurous waters, while, as she still ascended, a flannel night-gown was smartly dropped over her head by her maid, the guides behind twitching down the tail of it. Thus clad, she entered a small chamber called the 'Slips', where a fire and a sedan chair awaited her, in which last, completely enclosed in red baize and sweating profusely, she was carried, chair and all, to the bedroom of her lodgings by two chairmen, and put to bed.
>
> This was for the morning; in the afternoon, the company took its diversion in the pleasant walks of the King's Mead, and the cloisters, or visited the little cake-houses for gossip and the consumption of fruit lulibubs [lollipops]. And in the evening, while the hot, bubbling springs refilled the baths, there were balls.[10]

After the first of several trips to the baths, Catherine returned to London and some sources say she was pregnant during this time. However, there is no concrete historical evidence from her doctors to confirm this. She then became extremely ill with a spotted fever which nearly killed her, and at one point she received the Catholic last rites. This potentially could be measles or chickenpox. The high fever caused her to be disoriented, talk nonsense, temporarily lose her hearing and the ability to stand on her feet and walk. Charles did stay by her bedside and perhaps his tender concern helped her recover.

The pregnancy at Oxford is the surest confirmation we have that she was with child at least once with the doctors confirming a miscarriage in February 1666. The pregnancies mentioned by Charles in letters to his sister in 1668 and 1669 are suspect. In one of the cases, he wrote a month later she had miscarried. In another case, Castlemaine did her best to convince Charles that Catherine made up the pregnancy. The miscarriage of 1669 is said to be attributed to the king's pet fox running across the bed, terrorising Catherine. Medicine was not an exact science in the seventeenth century, especially when it came to women and their menstrual cycles and the timing of pregnancies and estimating birth dates. The bottom line is, she was definitely with child once and may have had as many as a total of four pregnancies and four miscarriages.

We have ample historical evidence that Catherine apparently suffered from abnormal uterine bleeding[11] as it is mentioned she had heavy periods in two historical sources. Sir John Reresby wrote in his memoirs that Catherine 'had a constant flux upon her'.[12] The other reference is from Lorenzo Magaliotti. 'The Queen, her mother, out of revenge for an old enmity to the mother of the Duke, would not have it; the Duke, offended at this, as soon as he heard of the first negotiations for a treaty with England, thinking to spoil them completely, gave the chancellor to understand that the Princess, because of her slender figure, the dry temper of her constitution, and the extraordinary frequency and abundance of her menses, was firmly judged incapable of bearing children.'[13]

We have already seen Charles and Catherine did not sleep together on their wedding night. Abnormal uterine bleeding can result in frequent, heavy periods with a tendency toward miscarriage. Some causes include problems with ovulation, fibroids and polyps, a condition in which the endometrium grows into the wall of the uterus, bleeding disorders, miscarriage and ectopic pregnancy. The condition can cause discomfort and would have been a disruption of normal sexual relations for Catherine and the king. It is unfortunate for Catherine the whole court knew about her condition, most likely causing her embarrassment and stress.[14]

Following the long summer progress of 1671, during which Kéroualle surrendered and had sex with Charles, Dr Frazier diagnosed Catherine with a 'consumption' and predicted her condition was fatal, but she recovered. During this time, the rapid elevation of Kéroualle to official *maîtresse-en-titre* and the increasingly visible hatred of Catholics created extreme stress and caused Catherine to suffer from nervous headaches. The mistress was now de facto queen but Catherine would not surrender. The situation motivated her to make an independent life for herself from this point forward.

After the House of Lords cleared Catherine of any involvement in the Popish Plot in the fall of 1679, the nervous headaches recurred, which is understandable due to the extraordinary stress she had been under. She sought treatment at the baths but the benefits would have been negligible. In a letter to her brother, she explained her illness, saying she was sick for four months and describing repeated chills and fevers for eighteen or sixteen hours, which left her weak. The medicines administered to her were 'troublesome' and she feared the rigors of the weather would never allow her to recover her health. Charles stayed by her side during her illness.[15]

In 1681, as Edward Fitzharris went to trial, Catherine was depressed during her trip to Newmarket. The depression would return after the death of Charles and last for a year. Following her return to Somerset House as a widow, she suffered another painful illness which she described to her brother:

> I was in bed having been there for twelve days, so ill with pain that was so strong and continuous that after groaning and perspiring for three or four hours without its diminishing, by increasing, I sent for one of the priests, being persuaded my hour was come. While he was at my bedside, God be praised! At that time, the pain began to lessen, which I impute to a little oil which I have from the lamp of the Immaculate Conception of the Blessed Virgin of the town of Viçosa, which on the occasion of my quinsy at three years of age, had the same effect. I continue somewhat better, though far from being well, since I am so devoted to my bed that I cannot stay all day out of it, which is never my custom, without great necessity.[16]

In 1688, just as she was expecting to return to Portugal, the doctors diagnosed her with a suppurating lump on her breast. Her physicians forbid her to travel and the recuperation took some time. Her troubles increased when James II fled to France and William and Mary became sovereigns. Persecution of Catholics forced her to flee to her little retreat in Islington and her health suffered greatly, most likely due to stress. The turmoil in England solidified Catherine's faith in her decision to return to Portugal.

We first hear of Catherine being treated for erysipelas at Newcastle in 1669 by her Portuguese *converso* physician, Fernando Mendes.[17] Her brother Pedro also suffered from this condition. It is an acute, sometimes recurrent disease caused by a bacterial infection, characterised by large, raised red patches on the skin, especially around the face and on the legs, but it can occur anywhere on the skin. Erysipelas has been around for centuries, affecting the upper dermis of the skin and sometimes extending into the superficial lymphatic vessels within the skin. Caused by the bacteria *Streptococcus pyogenes*, it enters the body through a break in the skin such as from a scratch or an insect bite.

Aside from the raised rash, the patient may develop a fever, shivering, chills, fatigue, headaches, vomiting and general illness. The affected area may appear swollen, feel firm, warm and tender to the touch with the worst symptom being extreme pain. If the infection migrates, it can cause the lymph nodes to become swollen and lymphedema may occur.[18]

In modern times, we have antibiotics to treat erysipelas but in the seventeenth century, these were unknown and Catherine would have relied on her physicians to treat her until the infection disappeared. It was common for the condition to recur. She experienced an outbreak in 1669, on her arduous journey to Portugal in 1692, and when the Archduke Charles visited Lisbon in 1704.

Like many of the Braganza dynasty, Catherine inherited a tendency towards obesity. In portraits of her later in life, it is clear she gained some weight. This may explain her habit of taking long walks for exercise and her tampering of her diet. She mentions in a letter to her brother from her retreat at Islington that she experimented with a milk diet for a few months.

Catherine's final, fatal illness came on her suddenly and is labelled a 'collique'. This is a pathology of the abdominal cavity with severe abdominal pain resulting from violent and intense contractions. Most often, it is a benign disease concerning the stomach, usually accompanied by diarrhoea. In Catherine's case it was fatal and we have no historical record for the cause of the inflammation of the gut.

Appendix Three

Last Will and Testament of Catherine of Braganza

In the Name of the Most Holy Trinity Father, Son, and Holy Ghost, three distinct persons, and one only true God, and of the glorious Virgin Mary our Lady, and of all the Saints of the Celestial Court.

I, Catherine Queen of Great Britain, by the grace of God, believing as I do firmly believe in all that is commanded in the Holy Roman Church and being desirous to dispose and adjust the affairs of my Conscience and Estate with the understanding which God our Lord hath been pleased to give me, do make my testament and last Will in manner following.

First, I recommend my soul to God the Lord who created it, trusting in His infinite mercy and goodness that He will pardon all my Faults and Sins, and carry me to the enjoyment of His happiness, where I may praise Him to all Eternity.

When God our Lord shall be pleased to take me to Him, I order that my Body shall be buried in the Convent of Belem, near to that of the Prince Dom Theodozio, my Brother (now with God), and in case his Bones shall be carried to the Convent of St Vincent without this city (as King Dom Joao the Fourth, my Lord and Father, ordered by his will), it is my will that mine shall likewise be carried and buried in the Great Chapel of the same Convent, and the Manner of my Burial and Funeral shall be according to the Will and Disposition of my Executors.

Together with this my Will, and as part thereof, I leave a paper signed with my hand, in which I declare the Bequests, pious legacies, and other Dispositions which I order may be performed after my Decease. I institute for my universal Heir the King Dom Pedro the Second of Portugal, my much beloved and dear Brother, and do desire him likewise to be my Executor and to cause my Dispositions to be executed, which in this or any other Kingdoms can be performed in the Kingdom of England, and in the Dominions thereof, I constitute for that purpose for my Executor Philip, Earl of Chesterfield, of my Council, Lewis, Earl of Feversham, my Chief Chamberlain, Sir Stephen Fox, Knight, Sir Richard Bellings, Knight, my secretary, and Manoel Dias, my Almoner, and charge them with the care and diligence which I confide in them in the recovery of the debts which shall be due to me in the said Kingdom, and the Dominions thereof at the time of my Decease, and hope that they will perform all the same according to the Trust which I repose in them.

So, I conclude this my Will, which I desire may be valid as such, or as a codicil, in the best manner that may have place in Law, and thereby revoke any Testament and Codicils by me made, although there may be any Cause derogatory, general or special, for that I hold them all for revoked, and by reason I do not remember them I do not make particular mention thereof.

And for the Confirmation of all that is before, and the Contents of this Testament, which I ordered to be made by Rog Montiero Paym, of the Council of the King my Brother and Lord, and his Secretary, I have signed the same at the end thereof with my own hand, conforming myself to the style and practice of this Kingdom, and notwithstanding that by the Custom of the English I should have signed at the beginning thereof, if I had made it in England.

And I, the said Rog Monto Paym, of the Council of His Majesty, and his Secretary, wrote this by command of the said Catherina, Queen of Great Britain, in the Court and City of Lisbon, in her Palace situate at Moinho de Vento, on the Fourteenth day of the Month of February, One Thousand Six Hundred and Ninety-Nine.

Catherina R.

The will was translated into English and proved in London on April 1, 1706.

I, Catherine, by the grace of God, Queen of Great Britain, do declare that this is the paper signed with my hand, to which I refer myself in my will, and which I desire may take place as part thereof, and that due and full execution may be given as to the requests and pious legacies to be performed after my decease in the order and manner following.

I order that on the three days immediately following after my decease there shall be caused to be said for my soul as many masses as can be celebrated in the convents and parishes of this Court, and shall continue the following days for the alms whereof I give the sum of ten thousand cruzados.

I order that there shall be once given for alms to the Convent of the Sacrament of the Dominican Nuns, three thousand cruzados. To the Professed House of St Roque of the Society of Jesus three thousand cruzados, to the convent of the Me de Deos of the Franciscan nuns of the first rule, two thousand cruzados, to the Convent of the Crucifix of the French Nuns of the Order of St Francis, one thousand cruzados. To the Convent of St Anthony of Capuchins, of this city, one thousand cruzados. To the Fryers of the Province of Arabida for the help of their wardrove, three thousand cruzados; to the Convent of Chagas of the Franciscan Nuns of Villa Viçosa, one thousand cruzados; to the Professed House of the Society of Jesus of the same town, one thousand cruzados. To the Convent of St Francis Capuchins of Piedade of the same town, one thousand cruzados. To the Convent of Bosque, also Capuchins of the Province of Piedade, one thousand cruzados.

Whereas there is in this Court five communities of two nations, English and Irish, viz the Convent of Corpo, St of the Dominican Irish Fryers, the Convent of Bon Suecco of the Dominican Irish Nuns, the Convent of Sta Brigada of English Nuns, the College or Seminary of St Peter and St Paul of English, the College or Seminary of St Patrick of Irish, and by reason they are all my subjects I ought to consider them. I therefore order that to each of the said three convents there shall be given three thousand cruzados, and to each of the two colleges or seminaries there shall be given one thousand cruzados one time only, and I order that the one thousand cruzados left to each of the said two colleges or seminaries shall be delivered to the order of the President or Prelate thereof, that they may freely employ the same in what they shall judge most necessary and useful in their communities.

For that hath been represented to me that the expenses on account of the Nurses of Children which are exposed in this city do much exceed the revenues and alms applied for them. I being desirous to remedy in part this defect, I do therefore order that there shall be given for that purpose ten thousand cruzados, which shall be put out at interest, to the end that with the annual income of the said Nurses the number of the said Nurses may be always kept entire without diminishing or lessening any part thereof. The same shall be delivered to the Commissioners appointed for this work of charity, with the assents, changes and conditions necessary for that purpose.

I order that election shall be made of six honest and virtuous young Virgins who desire to be nuns and to each of them shall be applied two thousand cruzados for her portion, that she may take the state of a nun in such Convent as she shall think fit, which portion as to the part which relates to Convents shall be delivered with due security that they may keep the same in case the said Virgins shall come to profess themselves therein, and in case any of them shall die in the year of the trial, or shall not be minded to continue there to make profession, all that shall belong to her for the alms determined for her shall be applied for another to be chosen for the same purpose, and shall actually be a Nun. The election of the said six Virgins (if my Executor shall approve thereof) may be committed to the Father Prior of S Deos of this city, and to the Father Preposito of St Roque of the Society of Jesus.

I order that there shall be given six hundred milreis for the Redemption of slaves, as is customary to do by the religion of the Holy Trinity, which I will shall be employed in the first Redemption which the Fryers shall make, on condition nevertheless that if there shall be amongst the said slaves any little boys or girls they shall be the first which shall be redeemed, and if there be none, the women shall have the preference of the men, for that in this manner the remedy may be applied where there is the most danger, and that those shall be redeemed shall be of the Portuguese nation.

To the father of the professed house of St Roque of the Society of Jesus appointed to assist the prisons in the name of the Solicitor of the prisoners, I order there shall be delivered six hundred milreis, that he may lay out the same in setting at liberty such prisoners as are for debts not exceeding twenty milreis, as well in Limoeyro as in Tronco, and if after satisfaction of those debts there shall be anything remaining of the said sum the same shall be employed in the help of such prisoners as are most necessitated. Especially of those whose claims are neglected for want of money, for the forwarding of their papers, and it shall be sufficient to give account to the Father Preposito when and how he disposes of the same. My family who serve me in this kingdom have been exactly paid all their salaries, expect what shall grow due to them from the time of payment of the last quarter to the day of my decease, and this shall likewise be paid with the same exactness, and mourning shall be given to all the servants to whom liveries used to be given, and besides that I will and order that for one time only there shall be given over and above to every one of my men and women servants the amount of one year's salary, according to the following list:

To Thomas Sandis there shall be given seven hundred and fifty milreis.
To Thomas Keri six hundred milreis.
To John Carneiro Brim three hundred milreis.
To Francis da Motta Guilherme three hundred milreis.
To Andrea Mendes de Almeida three hundred milreis.
To Anthony Keri three hundred milreis.
To Joseph Sandis three hundred milreis.
To Manoel Dyas X. Campos three hundred milreis.
To Francis Nicholson three hundred milreis.
To Natael Bois three hundred milreis.
To Dom Juan Bernardez six hundred milreis.
To Dr Jame Mendes six hundred milreis.
To Dr Robert Layful seven hundred milreis.
To Sangrado Antonio Monteiro two hundred and forty milreis.
To Thadeo Kenedini two hundred milreis.
To John Martin two hundred forty milreis.
To Manoel Cazado two hundred and forty milreis.
To John de Aquar two hundred and forty milreis.
To Manoel Pra Berges a hundred and fifty milreis.
To the Architector John Autumez a hundred milreis.
To Dos Mig. A hundred twenty milreis.
To Francis Monteira ninety milreis.

To Francis Ferra seventy-two milreis.
To Edward Keri Copiero a hundred and fifty milreis.
To Anthony Francesco two hundred and forty milreis.
To Michal Lureiro two hundred and forty milreis.
To Peter Fry a hundred and twenty milreis.
To Francis Gil a hundred and twenty milreis.
To Daniel Nich a hundred and twenty milreis.
To Anthony João ninety milreis.
To Michal João ninety milreis.
To Anthony Mig. sixty milreis.
To John Gill sixty milreis.
To Anthony Fernandez sixty milreis.
To Sangrado Francis Antimes two hundred and forty milreis.
To Wm Bremen a hundred and fifty milreis.
To George Hilliard a hundred and fifty milreis.
To Walter Gre a hundred and fifty milreis.
To Feliciano Pinto a hundred and fifty milreis.
To Gonzalo Glž a hundred and fifty milreis.
To Agostino da Cunha a hundred and fifty milreis.
To Anthony de la Borde a hundred and fifty milreis.
To Charles Gueron a hundred and fifty milreis.
To Manoel dos Keys a hundred and fifty milreis.
To Anthony Fernandez a hundred and fifty milreis.
To John Gomez a hundred and fifty milreis.
To Anthony Gomez a hundred and fifty milreis.
To Henry Simon a hundred and fifty milreis.
To Paul Ferreira a hundred and fifty milreis.
To Anthony Roiz a hundred and thirty-five milreis.
To Thomas Meron a hundred and twenty milreis.
To David Mouch a hundred and twenty milreis.
To John Ribeiro a hundred and twenty milreis.
To Domingo Pinto a hundred and twenty milreis.
To Manoel Lopes a hundred and twenty milreis.
To Joseph Franco a hundred and twenty milreis.
To Consalo Pinheiro a hundred and twenty milreis.
To Francesco da Costa a hundred and twenty milreis.
To Antonio de Oliveira a hundred and twenty milreis.
To Dominges da Silva Liteirero the Father Confessor seventy-two milreis.
To Jacincto Cardozo his comp seventy-two milreis.
To Stephen Galhardo Farrier a hundred and ten milreis.
To Domingo Niera seventy-two milreis.

To Joseph Reiz Azamel seventy-two milreis.
To Consalo da Rocha seventy-two milreis.
To Lewis Gonvales seventy-two milreis.
To Francis Cazado seventy-two milreis.
To Joseph Roiz Cazeiro eighty milreis.
To Manoel João the gardener sixty milreis.
To M Glž Pidgeon keeper ninety milreis.
To Richard Cotham a hundred and eighty milreis.
To Ignatio Cayeiro seventy-two milreis.
To Matthew Cayeiro seventy-two milreis.
To Domingos Antonio fifty-eight milreis.
To Matthew João fifty-eight milreis.
To Lewis das Newes Monro eighty milreis.

WOMEN SERVANTS

To Donna Maria de Quinta there shall be given seven hundred and fifty milreis.
To Donna Luisa Francesca X Vasconselos seven hundred and fifty milreis.
To Donna Francesca Ignacia de Vaslos seven hundred and fifty milreis.
To Donna Anna Keri seven hundred and fifty milreis.
Do Donna Izabel Toache six hundred milreis.
To Donna Luisa Catherina de Sa. three hundred milreis.
To Donna Benta Maria three hundred milreis.
To Donna Mariana Jacintha three hundred milreis.
To Donna M. Catherina de Sandis three hundred milreis.
To Anna Ma. Three hundred milreis.
To Mrs McBrain a hundred and fifty milreis.
To Grace Lopes a hundred and eighty milreis.
To M Cothan a hundred and twenty milreis.
To Margarida Thediman a hundred and twenty milreis.
To M Guvnel sixty milreis.
To Luisa de Spirito Sancto forty-five milreis.
To Isabell da Encarcão forty-five milreis.
To Catherina da Conseicão forty-five milreis.

THE CHAPPELL

To Father McPra there shall be given seven hundred and fifty milreis.
To Father Manoel Dias seven hundred and fifty milreis.
To Father Michal Ferreira four hundred and fifty milreis.
To Father Domingos de Miranda Three hundred milreis.

To Father Richard Brani three hundred milreis.
The Father Andrew Brani three hundred milreis.
To Father Manoel Mostarda two hundred milreis.
To Father John Roiz Coelho two hundred milreis.
To Father Antonio Soarez Rua two hundred milreis.
To Father Manoel Lewis Ribeiro two hundred milreis.
To Father Joseph Lewis Ribeiro two hundred milreis.
To Father Balthazar Gomez two hundred milreis.
To Father Antonio de Olivera two hundred milreis.
To Father Joseph Ferra two hundred milreis.
To Father Ant. Mustarda two hundred milreis.
To Father Franco da Costa two hundred milreis.
To Father John de Azenedo two hundred milreis.
To Father Manuel de Magathais a hundred and fifty milreis.
To Timothy de Faria four hundred and fifty milreis.
To James Martin a hundred and twenty milreis.
To Ceriaco Petit a hundred and fifty milreis.
To Joseph de Azenedo eighty milreis.
To Felix da Costa eighty milreis.
To John Pinto de Miranda eighty milreis.
To Francesco Voras Bitherme eighty milreis.
To Francesco Azuedo eighty milreis.
To Dionisio Mostarda eighty milreis.
To Jacintho Panares eighty milreis.
To Father Antonio de S. Bernardo Fryer of Loyo sixty milreis.
To Father Fra John Ribeiro Fryer of Carmo sixty milreis.
To Father Fra Simão de Sancta Catherina Fryer da Graca sixty milreis.
To Joseph da Costa the harpist sixty milreis.
To Lewis de Brillo player on the violin sixty milreis.
To Hilario Gomes player on the Guittar sixty milreis.
To Antonio de Spirito Sancto organist a hundred milreis.
To Michael de Oliveira seventy milreis.

If there shall be any new men or women servants taken in besides these above mentioned, I will that they have the benefit as I have ordered as to the rest of my family, in such manner that they shall not only be paid what shall be due to them from the time of the payment of the last quarter, but also there shall be paid to them for one time only, the amount of one year's salary.

I declare nevertheless that if at the time of the exemption of this my disposition there shall be any of the Chaplains or Men or Women servants therein married deceased or gone from my service I will that the same sums which I have left to them shall be given to the persons who shall succeed in their places, and if I shall not have caused the same places to be filled up, but they shall be totally vacant then the same sums shall be distributed in the same manner as I have ordered as to the remainder of the twenty thousand crowns for my Funeral if there be any. Some of my men and women servants for just reasons that I have do move me to consider them with special attention. I therefore order that besides what I have already ordered to be given them amongst the rest of my Family there shall be given for one time only to Father Domingos de Miranda a thousand cruzados. To Ju Carneiro Brum a thousand cruzados. To Francesco da Mota Guilheme a thousand cruzados. To Andrea Mendez de Aloncida a thousand cruzados. To Donna Luisa Catherina de Sa three thousand cruzados. To Luisa de Spirito Sancta two hundred milreis. To Isabel da Encarnacão two hundred milreis. To Catherina da Concicas two hundred milreis.

To Donna Berta Ma three thousand cruzados. To Donna Maria Jacintha three thousand cruzados.

LASTLY

By reason of the Love and Civility with which these and other of my men and women servants have served me there is due to them all the demonstrations of esteem and thanks which I could not be wanting to them in, and that there only remains for me to desire the King my Brother and Lord favorably to consider and support them with such particular attention as I have always had for those who I have had an affection for.

Before I came from England I caused to be declared to my family which I had in that Kingdom that I had ordered the ministers of my Council and Treasury to remit me to Portugal every year Thirty Thousand Pounds sterling, and that out of the remainder of my yearly revenues, which at that time amounted to forty-six thousand pounds, they should make payment of their salaries, and in case by any accident my said yearly revenues should not amount to more than the thirty thousand pounds which I ordered to be sent to me, in Portugal, I should not be obliged to make good the same by any other means, for that the thirty thousand pounds which by my order was to be sent me every year to this Kingdom was for the expense of my house, and for the payment of my servants who should serve me here. In pursuance of this my resolution and declaration I order that the same be accordingly performed, and that in the manner aforesaid their salaries which are due may be paid as far as the rest of my yearly revenues amounted to, beside the thirty thousand pounds which comes to me in Portugal.

The manner in which I will disposal to be made as well of all that is actually applied for the ornament of my Chappel, and of the jewels which I have a present will appear by a paper signed by my hand, which with the said Jewels and Toylett will be found in a trunk, and I order that what is thereby ordered shall be justly performed.

I order that as well as all the Images as Pictures, Relicks, ornaments and other vestments belonging to the Holy Worship which shall be found in the private oratory, wardrobe and other places of this Palace, which shall not be for the Confessor and to Father Manuel Pra, my Almoner, that both of them jointly, or either of them, if one be dead, may dispose of all the same in such manner as I have charged them, and for that I have also declared my will to them how I would have my papers disposed of, and how they should apply my books, I order that in like manner all the same may be delivered to them of what sord soever, that they may perform this my disposition with all exactness, and they shall not be obliged to give account how they perform the same.

I have committed to the care of Donna Luisa Fraca de Vasconcelos and Donna Francesca Ignatia de Vasconcelos the management of my clothes, apparel and other particular things of my use, and by reason of the great trust and satisfaction which I have of their fidelity and zeal with which they always served me, I am certain that they will execute in this part all that I have declared to them to be my will. And I will and order that to them only, or to such as I order them to substitute in this case, and no other person, shall belong the disposal of the things which shall be in their charge, and which are under their keys, and that no person shall take or demand account of them of what or how they have disposed of this particular.

CATHERINE R.[1]

List of Illustrations/Photo credits

15. The *Aqua Triumphalis* celebration on the River Thames, 1662. (Photo credit: Rijksmuseum; public domain image from the Look and Learn website.)
16. Portrait of Queen Catherine and King Charles II of England. (Photo credit: Public domain from Wikimedia Commons.)
17. Portrait of Queen Catherine of Braganza by Peter Lely. (Photo credit: Ian Dagnall Computing/Alamy Stock Photo.)
18. The Catherine of Braganza Shield which is very generously on permanent loan to the Victoria and Albert Museum by the Royal Toxophilite Society. (Photo credit: Image © Victoria and Albert Museum, London.)
19. Portrait of Barbara Villers, Duchess of Cleveland. (Photo credit: BTEU/RKMLGE/Alamy Stock Photo.)
20. Portrait of Louise de Kéroualle, Duchess of Portsmouth. (Photo credit: Rijksmuseum; public domain image from the Look and Learn website.)
21. Drawing of Old Somerset House. (Photo credit: Public domain from Wikimedia Commons.)
22. Engraving of Catherine of Braganza, queen of England. (Photo credit: Rijksmuseum; public domain image from the Look and Learn website.)
23. Titus Oates in the stocks. (Photo credit: Wellcome Collection; public domain image from the Look and Learn website.)
24. King Pedro II of Portugal. (Photo credit: Grafik aus dem Klebeband Nr 1 der Fürstlich Waldeckschen Hofbibliothek Arolsen, Motiv: König Peter II von Portugal, from the University of Heidelberg Library; public domain.)
25. Façade of the chapel of the Bemposta Palace, Lisbon. (Photo credit: Attributed to Rick Morais; public domain image from Wikimedia Commons.)
26. Engraving of Catherine of Braganza. (Photo credit: Classic Image/Alamy Stock Photo.)
27. View of the Jerónimos Monastery, Lisbon, 1662. (Photo credit: Rijksmuseum; public domain image from the Look and Learn website.)
28. Monastery of St Vincent de Fora, Lisbon. (Photo credit: Attributed to Brian Snelson; public domain image from Wikimedia Commons.)
29. Prospect of the inner part of Tangier. (Photo credit: Folger Shakespeare Library; public domain image from the Look and Learn website.)
30. Map of Bombay or Mumbai, India, 1764. (Photo credit: Public domain from Wikimedia Commons.)
31. Red Chinese lacquer cabinet. (Photo credit: Public domain image from the Metropolitan Museum of Art, New York open access program.)
32. Fine china teapot. (Photo credit: Public domain image from The Graphics Fairy website.)
33. Cane and walnut chair. (Photo credit: © Victoria and Albert Museum, London.)

Bibliography

Primary Sources

Bedloe, Captain William, *A Narrative and Discovery of the Horrid Popish Plot*, (William Bedloe, London, UK, 1679).

Braganza, Catherine, *Letters of Queen Catherine of Braganza*, (Egerton MS, I. 534, British Library).

Burnet, Gilbert, *Bishop Burnet's History of His Own Time: With the Suppressed Passages of the First Volume, and Notes by the Earls of Dartmouth and Hardwicke, and Speaker Onslow, Hitherto Unpublished, to which are added the Cursory Remarks of Swift and Other Observations*, (Clarendon Press, 1823).

Chamberlayne, Edward, *Angliae Notitia: or the Present State of England, 15th Edition*, (J. Playford, London, UK, 1684).

Charles II, *The Letters, Speeches and Declarations of King Charles II*, (edited by Sir Arthur Bryant, Cassell & Company LTD, London, UK, 1968).

Charles II: April 1683, in *Calendar of State Papers Domestic: Charles II, 1683 January–June*, (F H Blackburne Daniell (ed.), London: His Majesty's Stationery Office, 1933), pp.150–222. British History Online, http://www.british-history.ac.uk/cal-state-papers/domestic/chas2/1683-jan-jun/pp150-222.

Colbatch, John, *An Account of the Court of Portugal, Under the Reign of the Present King Dom Pedro II, With Some Discourses on the Interests of Portugal, with Regard to Other Sovereigns; Containing a Relation of the Most Considerable Transactions that Have Pass'd of Late Between that Court, and Those of Rome, Spain, France, Vienna, England, &c*, (Thomas Bennet, at the Half Moon in St Paul's Churchyard, London, UK, 1700).

De Sousa, Antonio Caetano, *Historia genealogica da Casa Real Portugueza: desde a sua orgem até o p presente, com as familias illustres, que procedem dos Reys, e dos Serenissimos Duques de Bragança..., Tomo VII*, (na Regia Officina Sylviana e da Academia Real, Lisbon, Portugal, 1735).

Evelyn, John, *The Diary of John Evelyn in Two Volumes*, (M. Walter Dunne, Publishers, London, UK, 1910).

Guilford, Francis North, Baron, 1637–1685; Jenkins, Secretary; Williams, William, Sir, 1634–1700; *et al.*, 2005, *The examination of Captain William Bedlow, deceased, relating to the Popish Plot taken in his last sickness, by Sir Francis North, Chief Justice of the Court of Common Pleas; together with the narrative of Sir Francis North at the council board, and the letter of Sir Francis North to Mr. Secretary Jenkins relating to this examination*, (Oxford Text Archive, http://hdl.handle.net/20.500.12024/A70153).

Hamilton, Anthony, *Memoirs of Count Grammont Volume 1*, (James Carpenter, Old Bond St & William Miller, Albemarle St, London, UK, 1811).

Hyde, Edward, *The Life of Edward Earl of Clarendon, Lord High Chancellor of England, and Chancellor of the University of Oxford in which is included a continuation of his 'History of the Grand Rebellion'*, (carefully reprinted from the original MS preserved in the Bodleian Library in three volumes).

Lopes, Fernão, *The English in Portugal 1367–87: Extracts from the Chronicles of Dom Fernando and Dom João with an introduction, translation and notes by Derek W. Lomax and R.J. Oakley*, (Aris & Phillips Ltd., Warminster, UK, 1988).

Magaliotti, Lorenzo, *Lorenzo Magaliotti at the Court of Charles II: his Relazione d'Inghilterra of 1668*, (edited and translated by W.E. Knowles Middleton, Wilfrid Laurier University Press, 1980).

Monconys, Balthasar de, *Iovrnal des voyages de Monsievr de Monconys, Second Partie. Voyage d'Angleterre, Pais-Bas, Allemagne, & Italie*, (Chez Horace Boissaat, & George Remevs, Lyon, France, 1666).

Oates, Titus, *A True Narrative of the Horrid Plot and Conspiracy of the Popish Party Against the Life of His Majesty...*, (Titus Oates, London, UK, 1679).

Pepys, Samuel, *The Globe Edition: The Diary of Samuel Pepys with an introduction and notes by G. Gregory Smith*, (Macmillan and Co., Limited, London, UK, 1905).

Reresby, Sir John, *The Memoirs of the Honorable Sir John Reresby, Baronet*, (London, UK, 1734).

Sainte-Marthe, Scévole de, and Sainte-Marthe, Louis de, *A Genealogical History of the Kings of Portugal, And of All Those Illustrious Houses that in Masculine Line are Branched from that Royal Family. Containing a Discourse of Their Several Lives ... With Their Armes and Emblazons ... as Also Their Symboles and Mottoes ...*, (rendered into English by Francis Sandford, Rouge-Dragon, Pursuivant of Arms, 1662).

Schellinks, William, *The journal of William Schellinks' travels in England, 1661–1663*, (M. Exwood and H.L. Lehmann, S.C. (eds.) fifth series, 1 [1993]).

Stanhope, Philip, *Letters of Philip, second Earl of Chesterfield*, (William Clowes, London, UK 1835).

Swift, Jonathan, *On the Conduct of the Allies and of the Late Ministry, in bringing and carrying on the War*, (Adelaide, South Australia, The University of South Adelaide Library, 1711).

'Venice: June 1662' in *Calendar of State Papers Relating To English Affairs in the Archives of Venice, Volume 33, 1661–1664*, (Allen B Hinds (ed.), London: His Majesty's Stationery Office, 1932), pp.146–158. British History Online, http://www.british-history.ac.uk/cal-state-papers/venice/vol33/pp146-158.

Vertot, L'Abbe de, *The History of the Revolutions of Portugal*, (Knapton, D., Midwinter, E., Durll, W., Innys, R., Robinson *et al.*, London, UK, 1735).

Waller, Edmond, *Poems, etc., written upon several occasions, and to several persons by Edmond Waller, Esq., Ninth Edition*, (printed for Jacob Tonson, at Shakespeare's Head over against Catherine Street in the Strand, London, UK, 1712).

Colonial Office Papers, Tangier (C.O. 279, 1-49). 1–33 Correspondence and Misc. Papers. 34-49, Entry Books

A Description of Tangier, The Country and People adjoining, with an Account of the Person and Government OF GAYLAND, the present Usurper of the Kingdome of FEZ; and a short Narrative of the Proceedings of the English in those Parts. Whereunto is added, the Copy of a Letter from the King of FEZ to the King of ENGLAND, for Assistance against his Rebellious Subjects; and another from GAYLAND to his Sacred Majesty CHARLES the Second. With divers Letters and Passages worthy of Note, translated from the Spanish into English, and Published by Authority. (London, printed for Samuel Speed, at the Rainbow in Fleet-street, near the Inner Temple-Gate, 1664.)

A History of the Revolutions of Portugal from the foundation of that Kingdom to the year MDCLXVII with Letters of Sir Robert Southwell, during his embassy there to the Duke of Ormond; giving a particular account of the deposing Alfonso and placing Don Pedro on the throne. (Printed for John Osborn at the Golden Ball in Paternoster Row, London, UK, MDCCXL [1740].)

The Tryals of Sir George Wakeman, Barronet, William Marshall, William Lumley, James Corker and Benedictine Monks for High Treason and Conspiring the Death of the King, Subversion of the Government and Protestant Religion. (Published by Authority, Printed for H. Hills, T. Parkhurst, J. Starkey, D. Newman, T. Cockeril, and T. Simmons, London, UK, 1679.)

Secondary Sources

Adams, Tracy, Adams, Christine, *The Creation of the French Royal Mistress: From Agnès Sorel to Madame Du Barry*, (The Pennsylvania State University Press, University Park, Pennsylvania, 2020).

Beauclerk, Charles, *Nell Gwyn: Mistress to a King*, (Grove Press, New York, NY, 2005).

Beirão, Caetano, *As negociações para o casamento da Infanta D. Catarina com Carlos II da Inglaterra*, (Academia Portuguese da História, Lisbon, 1942).

Bevan, Bryan, *Charles the Second's French Mistress: A Biography of Louise de Kéroualle, Duchess of Portsmouth*, (Robert Hale and Company, London, UK, 1972).

Boswell, Eleanore, *The Restoration Court Stage (1660–1702) with a particular account of the production of 'Calisto'*, (Harvard University Press, Cambridge, Massachusetts, 1932).

Boxer, Charles R., *The Portuguese Seaborne Empire: 1415–1825*, (Alfred A. Knopf, Inc., New York, NY, USA, 1969).

Brazão, Eduardo, *A Restauracão, relaões diplomáticas de Portugal de 1640 a 1668*, (Bertrand, Lisbon Portugal, 1938).

Bryant, Sir Arthur, *The England of Charles II*, (Longmans, Green and Co., London, UK, 1935).

Burnet, Ian, *East Indies: The 200-year struggle between the Portuguese Crown, the Dutch East India Company and the English East India Company for supremacy in the Eastern Seas*, (Rosenberg Publishing Pty Ltd, New South Wales, Australia, 2013).

Cartwright, Julia (Mrs Henry Ady), *Madame: A Life of Henrietta, Daughter of Charles I, and Duchess of Orleans*, (Seeley and Co. Limited, London, UK, 1903).

Chalmers, George, *A Collection of Treaties Between Great Britain and Other Powers, Volume Two*, (John Stockdale, London, UK, 1790).

Chambers, Mary Catherine Elizabeth, *Life of Mary Ward, Foundress of the Institute of the B.V.M.; compiled from various sources*, (Burns & Oates, Limited, London, UK, 1909).

Chapman, Hester W., *Great Villiers: A Study of George Villiers, Second Duke of Buckingham 1628–1687*, (Secker & Warburg, London, UK, 1949).

Cousin, Victor, *Secret History of the French Court Under Richelieu and Mazarin; or, Life and Times of Madame de Chevreuse, translated by Mary L. Booth*, (Delisser & Proctor, New York, NY, 1859).

Crowley, Roger, *Conquerors: How Portugal Forged the First Global Empire*, (Random House, New York, NY, 2015).

Dalrymple, William, *The Anarchy: The East India Company, Corporate Violence, and the Pillage of an Empire*, (Bloomsbury Publishing, New York, NY, 2019).

Davenport, Frances G. (ed.), *European Treaties Bearing on the History of the United States and its Dependencies, Volume II, 1650–1697*, (Carnegie Institute of Washington, Washington, DC, 1929).

Davidson, Lillias Campbell, *Catherine of Bragança: Infanta of Portugal & Queen-Consort of England*, (John Murray, Albemarle Street, W., London, UK, 1908).

Day, Ivan and Brown, Peter B., *The Pleasures of the Table: Ritual and Display in the European Dining Room, 1600–1900*, (York Civic Trust, York, UK, 1997).

Day, Samuel, *Tea, its mystery and history*, (Simpkins, Marshall & Co., London, 1878).

Disney, A.R., *A History of Portugal and the Portuguese Empire: From Beginnings to 1807, Volume 1: Portugal*, (Cambridge University Press, New York, NY, 2009).

Disney, A.R., *A History of Portugal and the Portuguese Empire: From the Beginnings to 1807, Volume 2: The Portuguese Empire*, (Cambridge University Press, New York, NY, 2009).

D'Oyley, Elizabeth, *James Duke of Monmouth*, (Geoffrey Bles, London, UK, 1938).

Downey, Kirstin, *Isabella: The Warrior Queen*, (Nan A Talese/Doubleday, a division of Random House LLC, New York, New York, 2014).

Edwardes, Stephen Meredyth, *The Rise of Bombay: A Retrospect, Reprinted from Volume X of The Census of India Series 1901 by the Government of Bombay*, (Times of India Press, Bombay, India, 1902).

Ellis, Henry (ed.), *Original Letters Illustrative of English History; including numerous royal letters: from autographs in the British Museum, and one or two other collections*, (Harding and Lepard, London, UK, 1827).

Ellis, Markman, Coulton, Richard, Mauger, Matthew, *Empire of Tea: The Asian Leaf that Conquered the World*, (Reaktion Books, London, UK, 2015).

Falkner, James, *The War of the Spanish Succession 1701–1714*, (Pen and Sword Military, Yorkshire, UK, 2018).

Faulkner, Thomas, *The History and Antiquities of the Parish of Hammersmith*, (Nicols & Son, J. Weale, E. Page, T.S. Rayner, and Simkin, Marshall, & Co., London, UK, 1839).

Fea, Allan, *James II and his Wives*, (Methuen and Co., London, UK, 1908).

Forrest, Denys, *Tea for the British: The Social and Economic History of a Famous Trade*, (Chatto and Windus, London, UK, 1973).

Foster, William, C.I.E., *The English Factories in India 1661–64, Volume 11*, (published under the Patronage of His Majesties Secretary of State for India in Council, Clarendon Press, Oxford, UK, 1923).

Fraser, Antonia, *Cromwell*, (Grove Press, New York, NY, 1973).

Fraser, Antonia, *Royal Charles: Charles II and the Restoration*, (Alfred A. Knopf, New York, NY, 1979).

Furdell, Elizabeth Lane, *The Royal Doctors 1485–1714: Medical Personnel at the Tudor and Stuart Courts*, (University of Rochester Press, Rochester, NY, 2001).

Gardner, Brian, *The East India Company – A History*, (Rupert Hart-Davis, London, UK, 1971).

Gerard, John, *The Popish Plot and Its Newest Historian*, (Longmans, Green and Co., London, UK, 1903).

Gerli, E. Michael and Armistead, Samuel G., *Medieval Iberia: An Encyclopedia*, (Taylor and Francis, New York, NY, 2003).

Gribble, Francis, *The Royal House of Portugal*, (Kenikat Press, Port Washington, NY, 1970).

Hallé, Marie as Martin Haile, *Mary of Modena: Her Life and Letters*, (J.M. Dent, London, UK, 1905).

Harris, Tim, *Restoration: Charles II and His Kingdoms 1660–1685*, (Penguin Books, London, UK, 2006).

Harris, F.R., *The Life of Edward Montagu, K.G., first Earl of Sandwich, 1625–1672 in Two Volumes*, (John Murray, London, UK, 1912).

Hartmann, Cyril Hughes, *Charles II and Madame*, (William Heinemann Ltd, London, UK, 1934).

Herman, Eleanor, *Sex with Kings: 500 Years of Adultery, Power, Rivalry, and Revenge*, (HarperCollins Publishers Inc., New York, NY, 2004).

Hibbard, Caroline, *Charles I and the Popish Plot*, (The University of North Carolina Press, Chapel Hill, NC, USA, 1983).

Hopkirk, Mary, *The Queen Over the Water: Mary Beatrice of Modena, Queen of James II*, (John Murray, London, UK, 1953).

Howe, Elizabeth, *The first English actresses: Women and drama 1660–1700*, (Cambridge University Press, Cambridge, UK, 1994).

Howe, Malcolm, *The Braganza Story: A visit to the Royal Pantheon of Portugal*, (The British Historical Society, Carcavelos, Portugal, 1999).

Hutton, Ronald, *Charles II: King of England, Scotland, and Ireland*, (Clarendon Press, Oxford, UK, 1989).

Hyde, J.A. Lloyd, Espirito Santo Silva, Ricardo, and Malta, Eduardo, *Chinese Porcelain for the European Market*, (Editions R.E.S., Lisbon, Portugal, 1957).

Jordan, Dan and Walsh, Michael, *The King's Bed: Sex and Power in the Court of Charles II*, (Pegasus Books, New York, NY, 2015).

Kamen, Henry, *Philip of Spain*, (Yale University Press, London, UK, 1997).

Kamen, Henry, *The War of the Spanish Succession in Spain 1700–15*, (Indiana University Press, London, UK, 1969).

Keay, Anna, *The Last Royal Rebel: The Life and Death of James, Duke of Monmouth*, (Bloomsbury, New York, NY, 2016).

Keay, Anna, *Magnificent Monarch: Charles II and the Ceremonies of Power*, (Continuum, London, UK, 2008).

Keay, John, *The Honourable Company: A History of the English East India Company*, (HarperCollins Publishers, London, UK, 1993).

Kenyon, John, *The Popish Plot*, (Penguin Books, Middlesex, UK, 1974).

Khan, Shafaat Ahmad, *Anglo-Portuguese Negotiations Relating to Bombay, 1660–1677*, (Humphrey Milford, Oxford University Press, London, UK, 1922 [reprint edition 2019]).

The Killigrew and Davenant Patents, in *Survey of London: Volume 35, the theatre Royal, Drury Lane, and the Royal Opera House, Covent Garden*, (F.H.W.

Sheppard (ed.), London: London County Council, 1970), pp.1–8. British History Online, http://www.british-history.ac.uk/survey-london/vol35/pp1-8.

Levin, Carole, Bucholz, Robert (eds.), *Queens and Power in Medieval and Early Modern England*, (University of Nebraska Press, Lincoln, NB, 2009).

Longman, Charles James and Walrond, Henry, *Archery, volume from The Badminton Library of Sports and Pastimes*, (Longmans, Green and Co., London, UK, 1901).

Liss, Peggy K., *Isabel the Queen: Life and Times*, (University of Pennsylvania Press, Philadelphia, PA, revised edition published 2004).

Livermore, H.V., *Portugal: A Short History*, (Edinburgh University Press, Chicago, IL, 1973).

Lynn, John, A., *The Wars of Louis XIV 1667–1714*, (Routledge, UK, 2013).

Mac Curtain, Margaret, *Ambassador Extraordinaire: Daniel O'Daly 1595–1662*, (Arlen House, Dublin, Ireland, 2017).

MacKay, Janet, *Catherine of Braganza*, (John Long Limited, London, UK, 1937).

Mainwaring, Arthur Edward, *Crown and Company: The Historical Records of the 2nd Battalion Royal Dublin Fusiliers, Formerly the 1st Bombay European Regiment, 1662–1911*, (Arthur L. Humphreys, London, UK, 1911).

Malabari, Phiroze B.M., *Bombay in the Making 1661–1726*, (T. Fisher Unwin, London, UK, 1910).

Masters, Brian, *The Mistresses of Charles II*, (Constable and Company Ltd., London, UK, 1997).

Merriman, Roger Bigelow, *The Rise of the Spanish Empire in the Old World and the New, Volume IV, Philip the Prudent*, (The Macmillan Company, New York, NY, 1934).

Mignet, François Auguste M.A., *Négotiations relatives à la succession d'Espagne sous Louis XIV, ou correspondances, mémoires, et actes diplomatiques concernant les pretentions et l'avénement de la maison de Bourbon au trône d'Espagne, accompagnées d'un texte historique et précédées d'une intr. par m. Miguet; Volume 3*, (Imprimerie Royale, Paris, France, 1842).

Miller, John, *Popery and Politics in England 1660–1688*, (Syndics of the Cambridge University Press, London, UK, 1973).

Miller, John, *The Stuarts*, (Hambledon Continuum, London, UK, 2006).

Mortimer, Ian, *The Time Traveller's Guide to Restoration Britain: A Handbook for Visitors to the Seventeenth Century: 1660–1700*, (Pegasus Books Ltd., New York, NY, 2017).

Needham, Raymond and Webster. Alexander, *Somerset House: Past and Present*, (E.P. Dutton and Company, New York, NY, 1905).

Newitt, Malyn, *The Braganzas: The Rise and Fall of the Ruling Dynasties of Portugal and Brazil, 1640–1910*, (Reaktion Books Ltd., London, UK, 2019).

Newitt, Malyn, *A History of Portuguese Overseas Expansion, 1400–1668*, (Routledge, London, UK, 2005).

Newitt, Malyn, *Portugal in European and World History*, (Reaktion Books, London, UK, 2009).

Nicoll, Allardyce, *A History of English Drama 1660–1900, Volume I, Restoration Drama 1660–1700, Fourth Edition*, (Cambridge at the University Press, London, UK, 1952).

Norrington, Ruth (ed.), *My Dearest Minette: The Letters between Charles II and his Sister, the Duchesse d'Orleans*, (Peter Owen Limited, London, UK, 1999).

Oliveira Marques, A.H. de, *History of Portugal Volume 1: From Lusitania to Empire*, (Columbia University Press, New York, NY, 1972).

Oman, Carola, *Mary of Modena*, (Hodder and Stoughton, Bungay, Suffolk, UK, 1962).

Oren-Magidor, Daphna, *Infertility in Early Modern England*, (Palgrave Macmillan, London, UK, 2017).

Parker, Geoffrey, *Imprudent King: A New Life of Philip II*, (Yale University Press, New Haven, CT, 2014).

Payne, Stanley G., *A History of Spain and Portugal in Two Volumes*, (The University of Wisconsin Press, Madison, WI, 1973).

Picard, Liza, *Restoration London: From Poverty to Pets, From Medicine to Magic, From Slang to Sex, From Wallpaper to Women's Rights*, (St Martin's Press, New York, NY, 1998).

Pollock, Sir John, *Popish Plot: A Study in the History of the Reign of Charles II*, (Cambridge University Press, Cambridge, UK, 2014).

Porter, Linda, *Mistresses: Sex and Scandal at the Court of Charles II*, (Picador, London, UK, 2020).

Powell, Roger, *Royal Sex: Mistresses & Lovers of the British Royal Family*, (MJF Books, Fine Communications, New York, NY, 2010).

Prestage, Edgar, *Portugal and the War of the Spanish Succession*, (Cambridge University Press, Cambridge, UK, 2015).

Pritchard, R. E., *Scandalous Liaisons: Charles II and His Court*, (Amberley Publishing, Gloucestershire, UK, 2015).

Rau, Virginia, D., *Catarina de Bragança, Rainha de Inglaterra*, (Coimbra Editora, Limited, Coimbra, Portugal, 1941).

Rivercourt House and the site of the Queen Dowager's House, in *Survey of London: Volume 6, Hammersmith*, (James Bird and Philip Norman (eds.), London: London County Council, 1915), pp.74–80. British History Online, http://www.british-history.ac.uk/survey-london/vol6/pp74-80.

Robins, Nick, *The Corporation That Changed the World: How the East India Company Shaped the Modern Multinational, second edition*, (Pluto Press, London, UK, 2012).

Roche, T.W.E., *Philippa: Dona Filipa of Portugal*, (Phillimore & Co., Ltd., Shopwyke Hall, Chichester, Sussex, UK, 1971).

Rogers, Clifford J. (ed.), *The Oxford Encyclopedia of Medieval Warfare and Military Technology, Volumes 1–3*, (Oxford University Press, New York, NY, 2010).

Routh, E.M.G., *Tangier: England's Lost Atlantic Outpost, 1661–1684*, (John Murray, London, UK, 1912).

Russell, P.E., *The English Intervention in Spain and Portugal in the time of Edward III and Richard II*, (Oxford, Oxford, UK, 1955).

Russell, Peter, *Prince Henry 'the Navigator': A Life*, (Yale University Press, USA, 2001).

Sanceau, Elaine, *The Perfect Prince: A Biography of the King Dom João II who continued the work of Henry the Navigator*, (Livraria Civilização – Editora, Porto, Portugal, 1959).

Santarem, Viscount of, *Quadro Elementar das Relaçõ Politicas e Diplomáticas de Portugal com as Diversas Potências do Mundo, Desde o Princípio da Monarchia Portuguesa até aos Nossos Dias, Volume IV, Part I*, (Paris: J.P. Aillaud; Lisbon: Tip. Academia Real das Sciências, 1843).

Saraiva, José Hermano, *Portugal: A Companion History*, (Carcanet Press Limited, Manchester, UK, 1997).

Scott, Lord George, *Lucy Walter: Wife or Mistress*, (George G. Harrap & Co. Ltd., London, UK, 1947).

Sabugosa, António Maria José de Melo César e Meneses (conde de), *Donas de Tempos Idos., 4th edition.*, (Livraria Bertrand, Lisbon, Portugal, 1922).

Shaw, Leslie M.E., *The Anglo-Portuguese Alliance and The English Merchants in Portugal 1654–1810,* (Ashgate Publishing Limited, Aldershot, UK, 1998).

Shaw, Leslie M.E., *Trade, Inquisition and the English Nation in Portugal, 1650–1690*, (Carcenet Press Limited, Manchester, UK, 1989).

Somerset, Anne, *Queen Anne: The Politics of Passion*, (Vintage Books, New York, NY, 2014).

Sousa, Manuel Andrade E, *Catherine of Braganza: Princess of Portugal, Wife to Charles II*, (Edições Inapa, Lisbon, Portugal, 1994).

Sport, ancient and modern: Pastimes, in *A History of the County of Middlesex: Volume 2, General; Ashford, East Bedfont With Hatton, Feltham, Hampton With Hampton Wick, Hanworth, Laleham, Littleton*, (William Page (ed.), London: Victoria County History, 1911), pp.283–292. British History Online, http://www.british-history.ac.uk/vch/middx/vol2/pp283-292.

Stephens, Henry Morse, *The Story of Portugal*, (G.P. Putnam's Sons, New York, NY, 1903).

Stratton Holloway, Edward, *American Furniture and Decoration Colonial and Federal*, (J.B. Lippincott Company, Philadelphia & London, 1928).

Strickland, Agnes, *Lives of the Queens of England from the Norman Conquest compiled from Official Records and Authentic Documents, Private as Well as Public, in Eight Volumes, Volume V*, (George Bell and Sons, London, UK, 1885).

Strickland, Agnes, *Lives of the Queens of England from the Norman Conquest, Volume 6, Mary of Modena*, (George Bell and Sons, London, UK, 1885).

Sturdy, David, *Richelieu and Mazarin: A Study in Statesmanship*, (Palgrave Macmillan, Basingstoke, UK, 2004).

Thomas, Gertrude Z., *Richer Than Spices: How a royal bride's dowry introduced cane, lacquer, cottons, tea, and porcelain to England and so revolutionized taste, manners, craftsmanship, and history in both England and America*, (Alfred A. Knopf, New York, NY, 1965).

Thurley, Simon, *Somerset House: The Palace of England's Queens 1551–1692*, (London Topographical Society, London, UK, 2009).

Tinniswood, Adrian, *By Permission of Heaven: The True Story of the Great Fire of London*, (Penguin Group, USA, New York, NY, 2003).

Torgal, Luis Reis, *Ideologia política e teoria do estado na Restauração, Volume 1*, (General Library of the University, Coimbra, Portugal, 1981).

Torres, João Romano Torres (ed.), *Portugal – Dicionário Histórico, Corográfico, Heráldico, Biográfico, Bibliográfico, Numismático e Artístico, 1904–1915, Volume II*, (https://www.arqnet.pt/dicionario/).

Treasure, Geoffrey, *Mazarin: The Crisis of Absolutism in France*, (Routledge, New York, NY, 1997).

Treasure, Geoffrey, *Richelieu & Mazarin*, (Lancaster Pamphlet, Routledge, London, UK, 1998).

Turner, Dawson, *Narrative of the Visit of His Majesty King Charles II to Norwich in the September of the Year 1671*, (Charles Sloman, King-Street, Yarmouth, UK, 1847).

Ukers, William Harrison, *All About Tea, Volume 1*, (Kingsport Press, The Tea and Trade Journal Company, New York, NY, 1935).

Vale, Malcolm M.G., *Charles VII*, (University of California Press, Los Angeles, CA, 1974).

Verney, Frances Parthenope and Verney, Margaret, M. (eds.), *Memoirs of the Verney Family during the Seventeenth Century, Volume II, 3rd edition*, (Longmans, Green, and Co., London and Bombay, 1925).

Vertot, The Abbe, *The History of the Revolutions of Portugal, edited and translated by Louis de Boisgelin, Chevalier de Malthe, R. Juigné*, (London, UK, 1809).

Walford, Edward, 'St James's Palace', in *Old and New London: Volume 4* (London, 1878), pp. 100–122. British History Online, http://www.british-history.ac.uk/old-new-london/vol4/pp100-122.

Waller, Maureen, *Ungrateful Daughters: The Stuart Princesses Who Stole Their Father's Crown*, (St Martin's Griffin, New York, NY, 2002).

Waterhouse, Ellis, *Painting in Britain 1530 to 1790*, (Penguin Books LTD., Harmondsworth, Middlesex, UK, 1986).

Waterson, Nellie M., *Mary II, Queen of England 1689–1694*, (The Seeman Press, Durham, NC, 1928).

Watkins, Sarah-Beth, *Catherine of Braganza: Charles II's Restoration Queen*, (Chronos Books, Winchester, UK, 2007).

Weale, J. Cyril M. (ed.), *Registers of the Catholic Chapels Royal and of the Portuguese Embassy Chapel 1662–1829, Volume 1, Marriages*, (Catholic Record Society, privately printed for the Society by John Whitehead & Son, Ltd., London, UK, 1941).

Wellman, Kathleen, *Queens and Mistresses of Renaissance France*, (Yale University Press, New Haven, CT, USA, 2013).

Wewitzer, Ralph, *A Brief Dramatic Chronology of Actors, Etc. on the London Stage from the Introduction of Theatrical Entertainments Into England to Present Time*, (John Miller, London, UK, 1817).

Whitaker, Katie, *A Royal Passion: The Turbulent Marriage of King Charles I of England and Henrietta Maria of France*, (W.W. Norton & Co., Inc., New York, NY, 2010).

Wilkinson, Josephine, *Louis XIV: The Power and the Glory*, (Pegasus Publishers, Cambridge, UK, 2019).

Wilson, C. Anne, *The Book of Marmalade: Its Antecedents, Its History and Its Role in the World Today Together with a Collection of Recipes for Marmalades and Marmalade Cookery*, (Prospect Books, Totnes, Devon, UK, 2010).

Wilson, Derek, *All the King's Women: Love, sex and politics in the life of Charles II*, (Pimlico, London, UK, 2004).

Wilson, James Grant, *Love in Letters*, (G.W. Carleton & Company, Publishers, New York, NY, 1867).

Wolf, John B., *Louis XIV*, (W.W. Norton & Company, INC., New York, NY, 1968).

Wright, H.P., M.A., *The Story of the 'Domus Dei' of Portsmouth, commonly called the Royal Garrison Church*, (James Parker & Co., London, UK, 1873).

Articles

Almond, Joseph Cuthbert, 'Oates's Plot' in *The Catholic Encyclopedia*, Volume 11, (New York: Robert Appleton Company, 1911; http://www.newadvent.org/cathen/11173c.htm).

Barclay, Andrew, 'Edward Colman' [Coleman] in *Oxford Dictionary of National Biography*, (September 2004).

Bassett, D.K., 'Early English trade and settlement in Asia, 1602–1690' in *The East India Company: 1600–1858, Volume IV, Trade Finance and Power*, (Patrick Tuck (ed.), Routledge, London, UK, 2001).

Belcher, Gerald L., 'Spain and the Anglo-Portuguese Alliance of 1661: A Reassessment of Charles II's Foreign Policy at the Restoration' in *Journal of British Studies*, Volume 15, No. 1 (Autumn, 1975), pp.67–88.

Bowden, C., 'Convent Schooling for English Girls in the "Exile" Period, 1600–1800' in *Studies in Church History, 55*, pp.177–204, (2019; doi:10.1017/stc.2018.27).

Boxer, C.R., 'The Dutch East India Company and the China Trade' in *History Today*, Volume 29, Issue 1, (November 1979).

Boxer, C.R., 'Second Thoughts on the Anglo-Portuguese Alliance 1661–1808' in *History Today*, Volume 36, Issue 6, (June 1986).

Brown, Mark N., 'Savile, George, first Marquess of Halifax' in *Oxford Dictionary of National Biography*, (September 2004).

Corp, Edward, *Catherine of Braganza and cultural politics* in *Queenship in Britain 1660–1837: Royal patronage court culture and dynastic politics*, edited by Clarissa Campbell Orr (Manchester University Press, Manchester, UK, 2002).

Crowne, J. Vincent, 'Frances Bedingfeld' in *The Catholic Encyclopedia*, Volume 2, (New York: Robert Appleton Company, 1907; http://www.newadvent.org/cathen/02386c.htm).

Dalemain.com, *The History of Marmalade*, (https://www.dalemain.com/the-history-of-marmalade/).

Davies, J.D., 'Legge, George, first Baron Dartmouth' in *Oxford Dictionary of National Biography*, (September 2006).

Davies, J.D., 'Montagu [Mountagu], Edward, first Earl of Sandwich' in *Oxford Dictionary of National Biography*, (September 2004).

Day, Ivan, *The Art of Confectionery*, (https://www.historicfood.com/The%20Art%20of%20Confectionery.pdf).

Dethloff, Diana, 'Sir Peter Lely' in *Oxford Dictionary of National Biography*, (May 2009).

Farrington, Anthony, 'Trading Places: The East India Company and Asia' in *History Today*, Volume 52, Issue 5, (May 2002).

Flor, Susana Varela, *D. Francisco De Melo Manuel Da Câmara (1626–1678): Biografia, Património, Estatuto Social e Fidelidades. Análise Social*, Volume 50, No. 215, (2015; *JSTOR*, www.jstor.org/stable/43596808), pp. 356–381.

Forster, Anne M.C., 'The Chronicles of the English Poor Clares of Rouen I' in *Recusant History*, 18: 1 (May 1986), pp.59–102

Giles, Elizabeth, 'Mary Ward' in *The Catholic Encyclopedia*, Volume 15, (New York: Robert Appleton Company, 1912; http://www.newadvent.org/cathen/15551c.htm).

Glickman, G. (2015), 'Empire, 'Popery', and the Fall of English Tangier, 1662–1684' in *The Journal of Modern History, 87*(2), pp.247-280. doi:10.1086/681305.

Goff, Moira, *Catherine of Braganza: A Dancing Queen*, (https://danceinhistory.com/2019/09/03/catherine-of-braganza-a-dancing-queen/).

Goff, Moira, *England's Royal Dancing Masters, 1660–1714*, (https://danceinhistory.com/2019/09/09/englands-royal-dancing-masters-1660-1714/).

Graves, Robert Edmund, 'Jacob Huysmans' in *Dictionary of National Biography, 1885–1900*, Volume 28.

Gregory, Eilish, 'Catherine of Braganza's Relationship with her Catholic Household' in *Forgotten Queens in Medieval and Early Modern Europe: Political Agency, Myth-Making, and Patronage*, (Valerie Schutte and Estelle Paranque (eds.), Routledge, Abingdon, UK, 2019).

Grose, Clyde L, 'The Anglo-Portuguese Marriage of 1662' in *The Hispanic American Historical Review* 10, No. 3 (1930): pp.313–52. (https://doi.org/10.2307/2506378.)

Handley, Stuart, 'Duras, Louis, second earl of Feversham' in *Oxford Dictionary of National Biography*, (May 2016)

Hutchinson, Amélia P, 'Leonor Teles: Representations of a Portuguese Queen' in *Historical Reflections / Réflexions Historiques*, Volume 30, No. 1, (2004; JSTOR, www.jstor.org/stable/41299297), pp.73–87.

Hutton, R, 'The Making of the Secret Treaty of Dover, 1668–1670' in *The Historical Journal, 29*(2), (1986. doi:10.1017/S0018246X00018756), pp.297–318.

Hutton, Ronald, 'Monck [Monk], George, first duke of Albemarle' in *Oxford Dictionary of National Biography*, (September 2004).

Jones, Guernsey, *Beginnings of the Oldest European Alliance: England and Portugal, 1640–1661*, reprinted from the *Annual Report of the American Historical Association for 1916*, Volume I, pp.405–418.

Karst, Sander, 'Off to a new Cockaigne: Dutch migrant artists in London, 1660–1715' in *Simiolus* 37 (2013–2014), pp.25–60.

Kenyon, J. P., 'The Acquittal of Sir George Wakeman: 18 July 1679' in *The Historical Journal* 14, No. 4, (1971; http://www.jstor.org/stable/2638101) pp.693–708.

Leech, Peter, 'Musicians in the Catholic Chapel of Catherine of Braganza, 1662–92' in *Early Music* 29, No. 4 (2001; http://www.jstor.org/stable/3519117) pp.571–87.

Linnell, Anna-Marie, 'Becoming a Stuart queen consort: Nuptial texts for Henrietta Maria of France and Catherine of Braganza, Queen of Britain' in *Queens Consort, Cultural Transfer and European Politics, c. 1500–1800*, (Helen Watanabe-O'Kelly and Adam Morton (eds.), Routledge, Abingdon, UK, 2017).

Marshall, Alan, 'William Bedloe' in *Oxford Dictionary of National Biography*, (January 2008).

Marshall, Alan, 'Israel Tonge' in *Oxford Dictionary of National Biography*, (January 2008).

Marshall, Alan, 'Titus Oates' in *Oxford Dictionary of National Biography*, (September 2004).

Maus, Katharine Eisaman, 'Playhouse Flesh and Blood': Sexual Ideology and the Restoration Actress' in *English Literary History* 46, No. 4 (1979; doi:10.2307/2872481) pp.595–617.

McManaway, James G., 'Philip Massinger and the Restoration Drama' in *English Literary History* 1, No. 3 (1934; doi:10.2307/2871758) pp.276–304.

Madway, Lorraine, 'Rites of Deliverance and Disenchantment: The Marriage Celebrations for Charles II and Catherine of Braganza, 1661–2' in *The Seventeenth Century*, 27:1, pp.79–103.

Marques, Paulo, 'Catherine of Braganza: A Widow' in *The British Historical Society of Portugal, Annual Report 8,* (1981) pp.14–25.

Milne, Doreen J, 'The Results of the Rye House Plot and Their Influence upon the Revolution of 1688: The Alexander Prize Essay' in *Transactions of the Royal Historical Society* 1 (1951; doi:10.2307/3678564) pp.91–108.

Morton, Adam, 'Sanctity and suspicion: Catholicism, conspiracy and the representation of Henrietta Maria of France and Catherine of Braganza, Queens of Britain' in *Queens Consort, Cultural Transfer and European Politics, c.1500–1800*, (Helen Watanabe-O'Kelly and Adam Morton (eds.), Routledge, Abingdon, UK, 2017).

National Center for Biotechnology Information, *Erysipelas and cellulitis: Overview*, https://www.ncbi.nlm.nih.gov/books/NBK303996/.

Ó hAnnracháin, Tadhg, 'Sir Richard Bellings' in *Oxford Dictionary of National Biography*, (September 2004).

O'Brien, Susan, 'Mary Ward' in *Oxford Dictionary of National Biography*, (September 2004).

O'Connor, Thomas, 'Daniel Dominic O'Daly' in *Oxford Dictionary of National Biograp*hy, (September 2004).

Rau, V., (ed.), 'Letters from Catherine of Bragança, queen-consort of Charles II to her brother; Dom Pedro II, king of Portugal (1679–1691)' in *The Historical Association; Lisbon branch. Annual Report and Review,* 9 (1945) pp.559–572.

Rau, V., (ed.), 'King Charles and Queen Catherine: two letters' in *The Historical Association: Lisbon Branch. Annual Report and Review,* 8 (1944) pp.514–21.

Rosenthal, E., 'Notes on Catherine of Bragança, queen consort of King Charles II of England' in *The Historical Association: Lisbon branch. Annual Report and Review,* 1 (1937) pp.14–17.

Rosenthal, E., 'Notes on Catherine of Bragança, queen of Charles II of England and her life in Portugal' in *The Historical Association: Lisbon branch. Annual Report and Review,* 2 (1938) pp.68–75.

Sainty, J.C., Wassmann, Lydia, and R.O. Bucholz, *Household of Queen (from 1685 Queen Dowager) Catherine 1660–1705*, Household of Queen Catherine. (https://courtofficers.ctsdh.luc.edu/indices/Index%2002%20Household%20of%20Queen%20Catherine%201662b.pdf.)

Scammell, G. V., 'England, Portugal and the Estado Da India C. 1500–1635' in *Modern Asian Studies* 16, No. 2 (1982; www.jstor.org/stable/312198) pp.177–92.

Seccombe, Thomas, revised by Michael Bevan, 'Sir George Wakeman, baronet' in *Oxford Dictionary of National Biography* (September 2004).

Sheils, William Joseph, 'Bedingfield [Bedingfeld] family' in *Oxford Dictionary of National Biography* (May 2009).

Shillington, Violet, 'The Beginnings of the Anglo-Portuguese Alliance Transactions of the Royal Historical Society' in *New Series*, 20, (1906; doi:10.2307/3678093) pp.109–32.

Shimp, Robert E,. 'A Catholic Marriage for an Anglican Prince' in *Historical Magazine of the Protestant Episcopal Church*, Volume 50, No. 1, (1981; www.jstor.org/stable/42973815) pp.3–18.

Society of Finsbury Archers (https://www.longbow-archers.com/finsburyarchers.html).

Sousa, M. Leonor Machado de Sousa, 'Richard Russell' in *Oxford Dictionary of National Biography* (September 2004).

Tindall, Gillian, 'Bombay: City of Gold' in *History Today*, Volume 32, Issue 5, (May 1982).

Tout, Thomas Frederick, 'Catherine of Braganza' in *Oxford Dictionary of National Biography*, 1855–1900, Volume 9.

Trowbridge, Ben, *History's Unparalleled Alliance: The Anglo-Portuguese Treaty of Windsor, 9 May 1386*, (https://history.blog.gov.uk/2016/05/09/historys-unparalleled-alliance-the-anglo-portuguese-treaty-of-windsor-9th-may-1386/).

Vale, Malcolm, *The Treaty of Windsor (1386) in a European Context*, (https://www.mod-langs.ox.ac.uk/files/windsor/1_vale.pdfz).

Villas-Boas, Manuel, *II – In the Wake of the Treaty of Windsor: A Tale of Two Ladies*, (https://www.mod-langs.ox.ac.uk/files/windsor/2_villas_boas.pdf).

Wynne, S.M., 'Catherine' [Catherine of Braganza, Catarina Henriqueta de Bragança] in *Oxford Dictionary of National Biography*, (January 2008).

Wynne, S.M., 'Louise Renée de Penancoët de Kéroualle, suo jure duchess of Portsmouth and suo jure duchess of Aubigny in the French nobility' in *Oxford Dictionary of National Biography* (September 2004).

Endnotes

Chapter One – Sunny Portugal

1. Newitt, Malyn, *Portugal in European and World History*, p.23.
2. Trowbridge, Ben, *History's Unparalleled Alliance: The Anglo-Portuguese Treaty of Windsor*, 9 May 1386.
3. Vale, Malcom, *The Treaty of Windsor (1386) in Context*, p.4, https://www.mod-langs.ox.ac.uk/files/windsor/1_vale.pdfz.
4. De Oliveira Marques, A.H., *History of Portugal: Volume 1: From Lusitania to Empire*, p.126.
5. Ibid.
6. Disney, A.R., *A History of Portugal and the Portuguese Empire: Volume 1: Portugal*, p.119.
7. Trowbridge, Ben, op. cit.
8. Disney, A.R., op. cit., p.120.
9. Ibid., p.121.
10. Vale, Malcolm, op. cit., p.8.
11. Newitt, Malyn, *A History of Portuguese Expansion, 1400–1668*, p.13.
12. Saraiva, José Hermano, *Portugal: A Companion History*, p.30.
13. Trowbridge, Ben, op. cit.
14. Newitt, Malyn, op. cit., p.5
15. Disney, A.R., op. cit., p.110
16. Newitt, Malyn, op. cit., p.10
17. Russell, Peter, *Prince Henry 'the Navigator': A Life*, p.210.
18. Newitt, Malyn, op. cit., p.10.
19. Boxer, Charles, *The Portuguese Seaborne Empire, 1415–1825*, p.xxii.
20. Saraiva, José Hermano, op. cit., p.35.
21. Boxer, Charles, op. cit., p.17.
22. Ibid., p.18.
23. Ibid., p.19.
24. Ibid., p.23.
25. Disney, A.R., op. cit., p.142.
26. Russell, Peter, op. cit., pp.30–1.
27. Ibid., p.39.
28. Ibid., p.64.
29. Ibid., p.155.
30. Ibid., p.210.
31. Newitt, Malyn, op. cit., p.27.

32. Russell, Peter, op. cit., p.342.
33. De Oliveira Marques, A.H., op. cit., p.257.
34. Ibid., p.218.
35. Russell, Peter, op. cit., p.334.
36. Ibid., p.340.
37. De Oliveira Marques, A.H., op. cit., p.208.
38. De Oliveira Marques, A.H., op. cit., p.209.
39. Disney, A.R., op. cit., p.7.
40. Sanceau, Elaine, *The Perfect Prince: A Biography of the King Dom João II*, p.23.
41. De Oliveira Marques, A.H., op. cit., p.218.
42. Newitt, Malyn, op. cit., p.27.
43. Ibid., p.37.
44. De Oliveira Marques, A. H., op. cit., p.219.
45. Ibid., p.220.
46. Newitt, Malyn, op. cit., p.46.
47. Ibid., p.47.
48. De Oliveira Marques, A.H., op. cit., p.220.
49. Newitt, Malyn, op. cit., pp.53–4.
50. De Oliveira Marques, A.H., op. cit., p.211.
51. Disney, A.R., op. cit., p.10.
52. Newitt, Malyn, op. cit., p.57.
53. Ibid., p.58.
54. De Oliveira Marques, A.H., op. cit., p.226
55. Ibid.
56. Ibid., p.233.
57. Ibid., p.249.
58. Ibid., p.258.
59. Newitt, Malyn, op. cit., p.258.
60. Ibid., p.72.
61. Ibid., p.73.
62. Ibid., p.258.
63. Ibid., p.117.
64. Ibid., p.143.
65. Disney, A.R., op. cit., pp.10–11.
66. Ibid., p.15.
67. Ibid., p.17.
68. Ibid.
69. Ibid., pp.18–19.
70. Ibid., p.23.
71. Ibid., p.25.
72. Ibid., p.26.
73. Saraiva, José Hermano, op. cit., p.63.
74. De Oliveira Marques, A.H., op. cit., p.312.
75. St Marthe, Scévole de and Louis de, *A Genealogical History of the Kings of Portugal*, And of All Those Illustrious Houses that in Masculine Line are Branched from that Royal Family, pp.89–92.
76. De Oliveira Marques, A.H., op. cit., p.313.
77. Saraiva, José Hermano, op. cit., p.63.
78. De Oliveira Marques, A.H., op. cit., p.313.

79. Saraiva, José Hermano, op. cit., p.63.
80. Ibid.
81. De Oliveira Marques, A.H., op. cit., p.314.
82. Ibid.
83. Saraiva, José Hermano, op. cit., pp.63–4.
84. Newitt, Malyn, op. cit., p.194.
85. De Oliveira Marques, op. cit., p.259.
86. Ibid., p.260.
87. Boxer, Charles, op. cit., p.51.
88. Ibid., p.52.
89. De Oliveira Marques, op. cit., p.259.
90. Ibid., p.163.
91. Newitt, Malyn, op. cit., p.193.
92. Ibid., p.212.
93. Ibid., pp.203–4.
94. Burnet, Ian, *East Indies: The 200-year struggle between the Portuguese Crown, the Dutch East India Company and the English East India Company for supremacy in the Eastern Seas*, p.72.
95. Boxer, Charles, op. cit., p.110.
96. Ibid., p.113.
97. Ibid., p.110.
98. Shaw, Leslie M.E., *Trade, Inquisition and the English Nation in Portugal, 1650–1690*, pp.10–11.
99. Newitt, Malyn, op. cit., p.218.
100. Ibid., p.222.
101. Ibid., p.219.
102. Boxer, Charles, op. cit., p.110.
103. Shaw, Leslie, op. cit., p.11.
104. Ibid., pp.10–11.
105. Robins, Nick, *The Corporation That Changed the World: How the East India Company Shaped the Modern Multinational*, p.47.
106. Burnet, Ian, op. cit., p.65.
107. Newitt, Malyn, op. cit., p.217.
108. Ibid., p.223.
109. Ibid., p.219.
110. Boxer, Charles, op. cit., p.113.
111. Newitt, Malyn, op. cit., p.236.
112. Russell, Peter, op. cit., p.141.
113. Roche, T.W.E., *Philippa: Dona Filipa of Portugal*, p.77.
114. Gerli, E. Michael and Armistead, Samuel G., *Medieval Iberia: An Encyclopedia*, p.182.
115. Saraiva, José Hermano, op. cit., p.173.
116. Roche, T.W.E., op. cit., p.77.
117. St Marthe, Scévole de and Louis de, op. cit., p.150.
118. Disney, A.R., op. cit., p.129.
119. Ibid.
120. Sanceau, Elaine, op. cit., p.43.
121. Disney, A.R., op. cit., p.130.
122. Saraiva, José Hermano, op. cit., p.31.

123. Newitt, Malyn, op. cit., p.27.
124. Gerli, E. Michael and Armistead, Samuel G., op. cit., p.182.
125. Disney, A.R., op. cit., p.132.
126. Newitt, Malyn, op. cit., p.47.
127. Ibid.
128. Disney, A.R., op. cit., p.132.
129. Newitt, Malyn, op. cit., p.47.
130. Disney, A.R., op. cit., p.134.
131. De Oliveira Marques, op. cit., p.210.
132. Sanceau, Elaine, op. cit., p.138.
133. Disney, A.R., op. cit., p.134.
134. Newitt, Malyn, op. cit., p.47.
135. Disney, A.R., op. cit., p.135.
136. De Oliveira Marques, op. cit., p.210.
137. Disney, A.R., op. cit., p.135.
138. De Oliveira Marques, op. cit., p.210.
139. Ibid.
140. Saraiva, José Hermano, op. cit., p.45.
141. Disney, A.R., op. cit., p.155.
142. Newitt, Malyn, *History of Portuguese Expansion*, p.47.
143. St Marthe, Scévole de and Louis de, op. cit., p.153.
144. Ibid., p.154
145. Parker, Geoffrey, *Imprudent King: A New Life of Philip II*, p.267.
146. Merriman, Roger Bigelow, *The Rise of the Spanish Empire in the Old World and the New, Volume IV, Philip the Prudent*, p.347.
147. Merriman, Roger Bigelow, op. cit., p.349.
148. Ibid., p.361.
149. Ibid., p.346.
150. Ibid., p.370.
151. St Marthe, Scévole de and Louis de, op. cit., p.156.
152. Vertot, The Abbe, *The History of the Revolutions of Portugal*, p.39.
153. Payne, Stanley G., *A History of Spain and Portugal in Two Volumes*, p.393.
154. Disney, A.R., op. cit., p.216.
155. Payne, Stanley G., op. cit., p.393.
156. Ibid., p.392.
157. Ibid., p.394.
158. Disney, A.R., op. cit., pp.214–5.
159. Newitt, Malyn, *The Braganza Story: The Rise and Fall of the Ruling Dynasties of Portugal and Brazil, 1640–1910*, p.69.
160. Disney, A.R., op. cit., p.215.
161. Ibid., p.216.
162. Ibid., p.217.
163. Disney, A.R., op. cit., p.218.
164. Ibid., p.219.
165. Payne, Stanley G., op. cit., p.395.
166. Saraiva, José Hermano, op. cit., p.67.
167. Payne, Stanley G., op. cit., p.395
168. Livermore, H.V., *Portugal: A Short History*, p.104.
169. Disney, A.R., op. cit., p.220.

170. Payne, Stanley G., op. cit., p.394.
171. Howe, Malcolm, *The Braganza Story: A visit to the Royal Pantheon of Portugal*, p.13.
172. Newitt, Malyn, op. cit., p.44.
173. Payne, Stanley G., op. cit., p.395.
174. Vertot, The Abbe, op. cit., p.56.

Chapter Two – Early Years and Marriage

1. Rau, Virginia, D. *Catarina de Bragança, Rainha de Inglaterra*, footnote on p.7.
2. Ibid., p.10
3. Ibid., p.7
4. Vertot, The Abbe, *The History of the Revolutions of Portugal*, p.39.
5. Newitt, Malyn, *The Braganzas: The Rise and Fall of the Ruling Dynasties of Portugal and Brazil, 1640–1910*, p.55.
6. Boxer, Charles R., *The Portuguese Seaborne Empire: 1415–1825*, p.359.
7. Vertot, The Abbe, op. cit., p.49.
8. Davidson, Lillias Campbell, *Catherine of Bragança: Infanta of Portugal & Queen-Consort of England*, p.5.
9. Rau, Virginia, op. cit., p.12.
10. Letter 51, Egerton, I.534.
11. Rau, Virginia, op. cit., p.8.
12. Shaw, Leslie M.E., *The Anglo-Portuguese Alliance and The English Merchants in Portugal 1654–1810*, p.170.
13. Davidson, Lillias Campbell, op. cit., pp.16–17.
14. Rau, Virginia, op. cit., p.8.
15. Davidson, Lillias Campbell, op. cit., p.11.
16. Rosenthal, E., 'Notes on Catherine of Bragança, queen of Charles II of England and her life in Portugal' in *The Historical Association: Lisbon branch. Annual Report and Review,* 2 (1938), p.70.
17. Sabugosa, António Maria José de Melo César e Meneses (conde de), *Donas de Tempos Idos., 4th edition*, p.232.
18. Davidson, Lillias Campbell, op. cit., p.11.
19. Rau, Virginia, op. cit., p.8.
20. MacKay, Janet, *Catherine of Braganza*, p.17.
21. Magaliotti, Lorenzo, *Lorenzo Magaliotti at the Court of Charles II: his Relazione d'Inghilterra of 1668*, p.14.
22. Davidson, Lillias Campbell, op. cit., p.12.
23. Rau, Virginia, op. cit., p.10.
24. Davidson, Lillias Campbell, op. cit., p.11.
25. Rau, Virginia, op. cit., p.10.
26. Davidson, Lillias Campbell, op. cit., p.17.
27. Ibid., p.16.
28. Newitt, Malyn, op. cit., p.81.
29. Sousa, Manuel Andrade E, *Catherine of Braganza: Princess of Portugal, Wife to Charles II*, p.1.
30. Rau, Virginia, op. cit., p.10.
31. Brazão, Eduardo, *A Restauracão, relaões diplomáticas de Portugal de 1640 a 1668*, p.9.
32. Mac Curtain, Margaret, *Ambassador Extraordinaire: Daniel O'Daly, 1595–1662*, p.114.

33. MacKay, Janet, op. cit., p.15.
34. Newitt, Malyn, op. cit., p.86.
35. Newitt, Malyn, op. cit., p.83.
36. Newitt, Malyn, *A History of Portuguese Overseas Expansion, 1400–1668*, pp.242–3.
37. Newitt, Malyn, op. cit., p.243.
38. Davenport, Frances G. (editor), *European Treaties Bearing on the History of the United States and its Dependencies, Volume II, 1650–1697*, p.31.
39. Newitt, Malyn, *The Braganzas: The Rise and Fall of the Ruling Dynasties of Portugal and Brazil, 1640–1910*, p.84.
40. Newitt, Malyn, *A History of Portuguese Overseas Expansion, 1400–1668*, p.243.
41. Payne, Stanley G., *A History of Spain and Portugal in Two Volumes, Volume 2*, p.396.
42. Newitt, Malyn, op. cit., p.79.
43. Gribble, Francis, *The Royal House of Portugal*, p.44.
44. Rau, Virginia, op. cit., p.10.
45. Newitt, Malyn, op. cit., p.84.
46. Rau, Virginia, op. cit., p.10.
47. Davidson, Lillias Campbell, op. cit., p.9.
48. Ibid., p.13.
49. Newitt, Malyn, op. cit., p.98.
50. Rau, Virginia, op. cit., p.26. Francisco de Melo e Torres, ambassador to England was the first Marquis of Sande, governor of Olivença, and artillery general of Alentejo during the Restoration Wars. He resigned this post for health reasons. He was a member of the Council of State and War and would be assassinated on the night of December 7, 1667.
51. Newitt, Malyn, *A History of Portuguese Overseas Expansion, 1400–1668*, p.244.
52. Newitt, Malyn, op. cit., pp.244–5.
53. Davidson, Lillias Campbell, op. cit., p.14.
54. Gribble, Francis, op. cit., p.56.
55. Rau, Virginia, op. cit., p.8.
56. Newitt, Malyn, *The Braganzas: The Rise and Fall of the Ruling Dynasties of Portugal and Brazil, 1640–1910*, pp. 47–8.
57. Vertot, The Abbe, op. cit., p.34.
58. Torgal, Luis Reis, *Ideologia política e teoria do estado na Restauracão, Volume 1*, pp.231–233.
59. Newitt, Malyn, op. cit., p.87.
60. Rau, Virginia, op. cit., p.10.
61. Sousa, Manuel Andrade E, op. cit., p.9.
62. Ibid., p.10.
63. Rau, Virginia, op. cit., p.26.
64. Sousa, Manuel Andrade E, op. cit., p.10.
65. Santarem, Viscount of, *Quadro Elementar das Relaçõ Politicas e Diplomáticas de Portugal com as Diversas Potências do Mundo, Desde o Princípio da Monarchia Portuguesa até aos Nossos Dias, Volume IV, Part I*, p.227.
66. Rau, Virginia, op. cit., p.15.
67. Sturdy, David, *Richelieu and Mazarin: A Study in Statesmanship*, p.62.
68. Sturdy, David, op. cit., p. 98.
69. Rau, Virginia, op. cit., p.15.
70. This is the alias as given by O'Daly's biographer, Margaret Mac Curtain.
71. Rau, Virginia, op. cit., p.1.

72. Santarem, Viscount of, op. cit., pp.382–3.
73. Sousa, Manuel Andrade E, op. cit., p.6.
74. Ibid., p.7.
75. Ibid., p.8.
76. Beirão, Caetano, *As negociações para o casamento da Infanta D. Catarina com Carlos II da Inglaterra*, p.8.
77. Newitt, Malyn, *A History of Portuguese Overseas Expansion, 1400–1668*, p.245.
78. Shaw, Leslie M.E., *Trade, Inquisition and the English Nation in Portugal, 1650–1690*, p.69.
79. Hutton, Ronald, *Charles II: King of England, Scotland, and Ireland*, p.126.
80. Hutton, Ronald., op. cit., p.160.
81. Davidson, Lillias Campbell, op. cit., p.38.
82. Rau, Virginia, op. cit., pp.28–9.
83. Ibid., p.88.
84. Mac Curtain, Margaret, op. cit., p.141.
85. Davidson, Lillias Campbell, op. cit., p.44.
86. Rau, Virginia, op. cit., p.38.
87. *The Life of Edward Earl of Clarendon, Lord High Chancellor of England, and Chancellor of the University of Oxford in which is included a continuation of his History of the Grand Rebellion*, Volume I, p.416.
88. Davidson, Lillias Campbell, op. cit., p.44.
89. Ibid., p.46.
90. Routh, E.M.G., *Tangier: England's Lost Atlantic Outpost 1661–1684*, p.6.
91. Shaw, Leslie M.E., op. cit., p.88.
92. Ibid., p.144.
93. Rau, Virginia, op. cit., p.33.
94. Shaw, Leslie M.E., op. cit., p.88.
95. Rau, Virginia, op. cit., p.36.
96. Belcher, Gerald L., 'Spain and the Anglo-Portuguese Alliance of 1661: A Reassessment of Charles II's Foreign Policy at the Restoration' in *Journal of British Studies*, Volume 15, No. 1, p.80.
97. Watkins, Sarah-Beth, *Catherine of Braganza: Charles II's Restoration Queen*, p.9.
98. Belcher, Gerald L., op. cit., p.80.
99. Ibid., p.82.
100. Rau, Virginia, op. cit., p.60.
101. Boxer, Charles, op. cit., p.114.
102. Newitt, Malyn, *The Braganzas: The Rise and Fall of the Ruling Dynasties of Portugal and Brazil, 1640–1910*, p.87.
103. Boxer, Charles, op. cit., p.147.
104. Newitt, Malyn, *A History of Portuguese Overseas Expansion, 1400–1668*, p.245.
105. Hutton, Ronald, op. cit., pp.158–9.
106. Belcher, Gerald L., op. cit., p.83.
107. Ibid.
108. Sousa, Manuel Andrade E, op. cit., p.22.
109. MacKay, Janet, op. cit., p.9.
110. Hutton, Ronald, op. cit., p.160.
111. Belcher, Gerald L., op. cit., p.85.
112. Newitt, Malyn, op. cit., pp.245–6.
113. Newitt, Malyn, op. cit., p.246.

114. Newitt, Malyn, *Portugal in European and World History*, p.1340.
115. Watkins, Sarah-Beth, op. cit., p.11.
116. Payne, Stanley G., *A History of Spain and Portugal in Two Volumes*, p.398.
117. Charles II, *The Letters, Speeches and Declarations of King Charles II*, edited by Sir Arthur Bryant, p.115.
118. MacKay, Janet, op. cit., p.47.
119. Rau, Virginia, op. cit., p.9.
120. Davidson, Lillias Campbell, op. cit., p.59.
121. Ibid., p.64.
122. Rau, Virginia, op. cit., p.61.
123. Harris, F.R., *The Life of Edward Montagu, K.G., first Earl of Sandwich, 1625–1672 in Two Volumes*, p.210.
124. Rau, Virginia, op. cit., p.62.
125. Grose, Clyde L. 'The Anglo-Portuguese Marriage of 1662' in *The Hispanic American Historical Review* 10, No. 3 (1930), p.333.
126. *The Life of Edward Earl of Clarendon, Lord High Chancellor of England, and Chancellor of the University of Oxford in which is included a continuation of his History of the Grand Rebellion*, p.160.
127. Davies, J.D., 'Montagu [Mountagu], Edward, first Earl of Sandwich' in *Oxford Dictionary of National Biography*, p.5.
128. Grose, Clyde L., op. cit., p.345.
129. Ibid., p.349.
130. Rau, Virginia, op. cit., p.70.
131. Jones, Guernsey, *Beginnings of the Oldest European Alliance: England and Portugal, 1640–1661*, reprinted from the *Annual Report of the American Historical Association for 1916,* Volume I, p.415.
132. Rosenthal, E., 'Notes on Catherine of Bragança, queen of Charles II of England and her life in Portugal' in *The Historical Association: Lisbon branch. Annual Report and Review,* 1 (1937), p.71.
133. Rau, Virginia, op. cit., p.71.
134. Davidson, Lillias Campbell, op. cit., p.74.
135. Rau, Virginia, op. cit., p.72.
136. Ibid., p.72.
137. Davidson, Lillias Campbell, op. cit., p.76.
138. Rau, Virginia, op. cit., p.73.
139. Ibid., p.74.
140. MacKay, Janet, op. cit., p.60.
141. Rau, Virginia, op. cit., p.75.
142. Davidson, Lillias Campbell, op. cit., p.80.
143. Rau, Virginia, op. cit., p.78.
144. Davidson, Lillias Campbell, op. cit., p.85.
145. Barbara Villiers, daughter of William Villiers, Viscount of Grandison, who was a fervent supporter of King Charles I. After several sexual intrigues, she married Roger Palmer in April 1659. Her connection with Charles probably began around 1660. In 1661, her husband was made Count of Castlemaine.
146. Rau, Virginia, op. cit., p.79.
147. Rau, Virginia, op. cit., p.83.
148. Ibid.
149. Davidson, Lillias Campbell, op. cit., p.99.

150. Tout, Thomas Frederick, 'Catherine of Braganza', in *Dictionary of National Biography*, 1855–1900. Volume 9, p.2.
151. Davidson, Lillias Campbell, op. cit., p.100.
152. Wright, H.P., M.A., *The Story of the 'Domus Dei' of Portsmouth, commonly called the Royal Garrison Church*, p.21.
153. Davidson, Lillias Campbell, op. cit., p.102.
154. Ibid., p.104. The date of the marriage register is incorrect. It should read 21.
155. Charles II, *The Letters, Speeches and Declarations of King Charles II*, edited by Sir Arthur Bryant, p.127.

Chapter Three – Married Life, Pregnancies and Troubles

1. Wellman, Kathleen, *Queens and Mistresses of Renaissance France*, p.7.
2. Norrington, Ruth (ed.), *My Dearest Minette: The Letters Between Charles II and His Sister, the Duchesse d'Orleans*, letter dated from Portsmouth, May 23, 1662, p.55.
3. Sousa, Manuel Andrade E, *Catherine of Braganza: Princess of Portugal, Wife to Charles II*, p.44.
4. Stanhope, Philip, *Letters of Philip, second Earl of Chesterfield*, pp.122–3.
5. Watkins, Sarah-Beth, *Catherine of Braganza: Charles II's Restoration Queen*, p.23.
6. Schellinks, William, *The journal of William Schellinks' travels in England, 1661–1663*, p.90.
7. Evelyn, John, *The Diary of John Evelyn in Two Volumes, Vol 1*, p.371.
8. Davidson, Lillias Campbell, *Catherine of Bragança: Infanta of Portugal & Queen Consort of England*, p.211.
9. Newitt, Malyn, *The Braganzas: The Rise and Fall of the Ruling Dynasties of Portugal and Brazil, 1640–1910*, pp.89–90; Sousa, Manuel Andrade E., op. cit., p.50.
10. Hamilton, Anthony, *Memoirs of Count Grammont Volume 1*, pp.136–7.
11. Pepys, Samuel, *The Diary of Samuel Pepys: The Globe Edition*, entry for September 7, 1662, p.149.
12. Verney, Frances Parthenope and Verney, Margaret, M. (eds.), *Memoirs of the Verney Family during the Seventeenth Century, Volume II, third edition*, p.173.
13. Newitt, Malyn, op. cit., p.89.
14. Pepys, Samuel, op. cit., p.238.
15. Ibid., entry on October 24, 1662, p.155–6.
16. Hamilton, Anthony, op. cit., p.163.
17. Newitt, Malyn, op. cit., p.90.
18. Sousa, Manuel Andrade E, op. cit., p.50.
19. 'Venice: June 1662' in *Calendar of State Papers Relating To English Affairs in the Archives of Venice, Volume 33, 1661–1664*, (Allen B Hinds (ed.), London: His Majesty's Stationery Office, 1932), p.157.
20. Harrington, Ruth, op. cit., letter dated from Paris July 22, 1662, p.56.
21. Madway, Lorraine, 'Rites of Deliverance and Disenchantment: The Marriage Celebrations for Charles II and Catherine of Braganza, 1661–2' in *The Seventeenth Century*, 27:1, p.101, note 40.
22. Sousa, Manuel Andrade E, op. cit., p.57.
23. Madway, Lorraine, op. cit., p.79.
24. Ibid., p.102, note 66.
25. Ibid., p.93.
26. Ibid, op. cit., p.95.

27. These engravings can be found in the British Museum, the London Metropolitan Archives, the National Library of Portugal, Rijksmuseum and the City Museum of Lisbon.
28. Madway, Lorraine, op. cit., p.95.
29. Davidson, Lillias Campbell, op. cit., p.147.
30. Evelyn, John, op. cit., pp.374–5. Evelyn is referring to the bucintoro, the state barge of Venice; used in the sposalizio ceremony, the ritual wedding of Venice with the sea in which a ring is dropped into the water by a Doge from a bucintoro.
31. Pepys, Samuel, op. cit., entry for August 23, 1662, p.146.
32. Madway, Lorraine, op. cit., p.97.
33. Weale, J. Cyril M. (ed.), *Registers of the Catholic Chapels Royal and of the Portuguese Embassy Chapel 1662–1829, Volume I, Marriages*, p.vii.
34. Pepys, Samuel, op. cit., entry on September 21, 1662, p.150.
35. Sousa, Manuel Andrade E, op. cit., p.58.
36. Porter, Linda, *Mistresses: Sex and Scandal at the Court of Charles II*, p.108.
37. Norrington, Ruth, op. cit., letter dated February 9, 1663, p.63.
38. Howe, Elizabeth, *The first English actresses: Women and drama 1660–1700*, p.21.
39. Keay, Anna, *The Magnificent Monarch: Charles II and the Ceremonies of Power*, p.126.
40. Pepys, Samuel, op. cit., p.149.
41. Keay, Anna, op. cit., p.126.
42. Ibid., p.127.
43. Keay, Anna, op. cit., p.127.
44. Ibid., p.128.
45. Ibid., p.129.
46. Ibid., p.132.
47. Nicoll, Allardyce, *A History of English Drama 1660–1900, Volume I, Restoration Drama 1660–1700, Fourth Edition*, p.364.
48. McManaway, James G., 'Philip Massinger and the Restoration Drama' in *English Literary History* 1, No. 3 (1934), p.286, note 18. McManaway speculates there were several actors from the Red Bull Theatre troupe who were the cast members of the Queenes Comoedians.
49. Boswell. Eleanore, *The Restoration Court Stage (1660–1702) with a particular account of the production of 'Calisto'*, p.56.
50. Ibid., p.57.
51. Pepys, Samuel, op. cit., p.152.
52. Sainty, J.C., Wassmann, Lydia, and R.O. Bucholz, *Household of Queen (from 1685 Queen Dowager) Catherine 1660–1705*, p.31. (https://courtofficers.ctsdh.luc.edu/indices/Index%2002%20Household%20of%20Queen%20Catherine%201662b.pdf).
53. Evelyn, John, op. cit., p.381.
54. Monconys, Balthasar de, Iovrnal des voyages de Monsievr de Monconys, Second Partie. Voyage d'Angleterre, Pais-Bas, Allemagne, & Italie, p.24.
55. Goff, Moira, *Catherine of Braganza: A Dancing Queen*, (https:/danceinhistory.com/2019/09/03/catherine-of-braganza-a-dancing-queen/).
56. Norrington, Ruth, op. cit., letter dated February 9, 1663, p.63.
57. Davidson, Lillias Campbell, op. cit., pp.154–5.
58. Wynne, S.M., 'Catherine' [Catherine of Braganza, Catarina Henriqueta de Bragança] in *Oxford Dictionary of National Biography*, p.5.
59. Nicoll, Allardyce, op. cit., p.8.
60. Ibid., p.293.
61. Ibid., p.71.

62. Howe, Elizabeth, op. cit., p.19.
63. Nicoll, Allardyce, op. cit., pp.8–9.
64. Wewitzer, Ralph, A Brief Dramatic Chronology of Actors, Etc. on the London Stage from the Introduction of Theatrical Entertainments Into England to Present Time, p.42.
65. Howe, Elizabeth, op. cit., p.23.
66. Nicoll, Allardyce, op. cit., p.71.
67. Ibid., p.296.
68. Pepys, Samuel, op. cit., entry dated July 13, 1663, p.209.
69. Ibid., entry dated August 11, 1663, p.214.
70. Furdell, Elizabeth Lane, *The Royal Doctors 1485–1714: Medical Personnel at the Tudor and Stuart Courts*, p.191, note 27.
71. Pepys, Samuel, op. cit., entry dated October 17, 1663, p.220.
72. Ibid., entry dated October 20, 1663, pp.221–2.
73. Sousa, Manuel Andrade E, op. cit., p.71.
74. Davidson, Lillias Campbell, op. cit., p.198.
75. Sousa, Manuel Andrade E, op. cit., p.71.
76. Norrington, Ruth, op. cit., letter from Whitehall dated November 2, 1663, p.71.
77. Charles II, *The Letters, Speeches and Declarations of King Charles II*, edited by Sir Arthur Bryant, letter to Minette dated November 20, 1663, p.148.
78. Norrington, Ruth, op. cit., letter from Whitehall dated December 10, 1663, p.72.
79. Pepys, Samuel, op. cit., entry dated February 28, 1664, p.26.3
80. Waterhouse, Ellis, *Painting in Britain 1530 to 1790*, p.92.
81. Corp, Edward, *Catherine of Braganza and cultural politics* in *Queenship in Britain 1660–1837: Royal patronage court culture and dynastic politics*, edited by Clarissa Campbell Orr, p.60.
82. Pepys, Samuel, op. cit., p.277.
83. Corp, Edward, op. cit., p.61.
84. Leech, Peter, 'Musicians in the Catholic Chapel of Catherine of Braganza, 1662–92' in *Early Music* 29, No. 4 (2001), p.572.
85. Walford, Edward, 'St James Palace' in *Old and New London, Volume 4*, London, 1878, pp. 100–122. (*British History Online* http://www.british-history.ac.uk/old-new-london/vol4/pp100-122.)
86. Weale, J. Cyril M. (ed.), *Registers of the Catholic Chapels Royal and the Portuguese Embassy Chapel 1662–1829, Volume 1, Marriages*, p.xiii.
87. Leech, Peter, op. cit., p.572.
88. Wynne, S.M., op. cit., p.5.
89. Pepys, Samuel, op. cit., entry dated January 23, 1667, p.457.
90. Corp, Edward, op. cit., p.6.5
91. Watkins, Sarah-Beth, op. cit., p.50.
92. Norrington, Ruth, op. cit., letter from Salisbury dated September 9, 1665, p.126.
93. Pepys, Samuel, op. cit., entry dated September 6, 1666, p.389.
94. MacKay, Janet, *Catherine of Braganza*, p.161.
95. Tinniswood, Adrian, *By Permission of Heaven: The True Story of the Great Fire of London*, p.94.
96. Ibid., p.96
97. Evelyn, John, *The Diary of John Evelyn in Two Volumes, Volume 2*, entry dated September 13, 1666, p.17.
98. Boswell, Eleanor, op. cit., p.57.
99. Thomas, Gertrude, op. cit., p.93.

Chapter Four – Catherine's Independent Life

1. Sousa, Manuel Andrade E, *Catherine of Braganza: Princess of Portugal, Wife to Charles II*, p.78.
2. Pepys, Samuel, *The Globe Edition: The Diary of Samuel Pepys*, entry for May 31, 1668, p.656.
3. Corp, Edward, *Catherine of Braganza and cultural politics* in *Queenship in Britain 1660–1837: Royal patronage court culture and dynastic politics*, edited by Clarissa Campbell Orr, p.58.
4. Porter, Linda, *Mistresses: Sex and Scandal at the Court of Charles II*, p.117.
5. Chapman, Hester W., *Great Villiers: A Study of George Villiers, Second Duke of Buckingham 1628–1687*, p.152.
6. Sousa, Manuel Andrade E., op. cit., p.80.
7. Watkins, Sara-Beth, *Catherine of Braganza: Charles II's Restoration Queen*, p.67.
8. Thomas, Gertrude Z., *Richer Than Spices: How a royal bride's dowry introduced cane, lacquer, cottons, tea, and porcelain to England and so revolutionized taste, manners, craftsmanship, and history in both England and America*, p.93.
9. Norrington, Ruth (ed.), *My Dearest Minette: The Letters between Charles II and his Sister, the Duchesse d'Orleans*, letter from Whitehall, May 7, 1668, p.151.
10. Newitt, Malyn, *The Braganzas: The Rise and Fall of the Ruling Dynasties of Portugal and Brazil, 1640–1910*, p.102.
11. Newitt, Malyn, op. cit., p.103.
12. Ibid., p.111.
13. Corp, Edward, op. cit., p.59.
14. Ibid., p.60.
15. Ibid.
16. Leech, Peter, 'Musicians in the Catholic Chapel of Catherine of Braganza, 1662–92' in *Early Music* 29, No. 4 (2001), p.581.
17. Pepys, Samuel, op. cit., entry dated September 28, 1668, p.683.
18. Bowden, C., 'Convent Schooling for English Girls in the "Exile" Period, 1600–1800' in *Studies in Church History, 55* (2019), p.177.
19. Bowden, C., op. cit., p.177.
20. O'Brien, Susan, 'Mary Ward' in *Oxford Dictionary of National Biography*, p.2.
21. Ibid., p.3.
22. Bowden, C., op. cit., p.179.
23. Ibid., p.181.
24. O'Brien, Susan, op. cit., p.4.
25. Sheils, William Joseph, 'Bedingfield [Bedingfeld] family' in *Oxford Dictionary of National Biography*, p.3.
26. Crowne, J. Vincent, 'Frances Bedingfeld' in *The Catholic Encyclopedia*, Volume 2 (New York: Robert Appleton Company, 1907; http://www.newadvent.org/cath/02386c.htm).
27. Bowden, C., op. cit., p.195.
28. Ibid., pp.178–9.
29. Faulkner, Thomas, *The History and Antiquities of the Parish of Hammersmith*, p.243.
30. Norrington, Ruth, op. cit., letter from Whitehall dated May 6, 1669, p.177.
31. Ibid., letter from Whitehall dated June 7, 1669, p.182.
32. Newitt, Malyn, *The Braganzas: The Rise and Fall of the Ruling Dynasties of Portugal and Brazil, 1640–1910*, p.94.

33. Boswell, Eleanore, *The Restoration Court Stage (1660–1702) with a particular account of the production of 'Calisto'*, p.130.
34. Hutton, Ronald, *Charles II: King of England, Scotland, and Ireland*, p.270.
35. Porter, Linda, op. cit., p.112.
36. Hutton, Ronald, op. cit., p.270.
37. Ibid., p.263.
38. Mignet, François Auguste M.A., *Négotiations relatives à la succession d'Espagne sous Louis XIV, ou correspondances, mémoires, et actes diplomatiques concernant les pretentions et l'avénement de la maison de Bourbon au trône d'Espagne, accompagnées d'un texte historique et précédées d'une intr,par m. Miguet; Volume Three*, pp.184–200.
39. Sainty, J.C., Wassmann, Lydia, and R.O. Bucholz, *Household of Queen (from 1685 Queen Dowager) Catherine 1660–1705*, p.6. (https://courtofficers.ctsdh.luc.edu/indices/Index%2002%20Household%20of%20Queen%20Catherine%201662b.pdf)
40. Hutton, R. (1986), 'The Making of the Secret Treaty of Dover, 1668–1670' in *The Historical Journal, 29*(2), p.297, note 2.
41. Hartmann, Cyril Hughes, *Charles II and Madame*, p.333.
42. Porter, Linda, op. cit., p.175.
43. Boswell, Eleanore, op. cit., p.47.
44. Ibid., p.48.
45. Definition of a retiring room in English from the Oxford Lexico: retiring room, noun, A room set aside for seclusion, rest or quiet; (in later use also) a public toilet. Origin seventeenth century.
46. Boswell, Eleanore, op. cit., p.93.
47. Ibid., p.138.
48. Wynne, S.M., 'Catherine' [Catherine of Braganza, Catarina Henriqueta de Bragança] in *Oxford Dictionary of National Biography*, p.6.
49. Needham, Raymond and Webster, Alexander, *Somerset House: Past and Present*, p.83.
50. Ibid., p.104.
51. Ibid., p.106.
52. Ibid., pp.111–2.
53. Ibid., p.115.
54. Ibid., p.140.
55. Pepys, Samuel, op. cit., p.246.
56. Ibid., p.298.
57. Needham, Raymond and Webster, Alexander, op. cit., p.140.
58. Ibid., p.157.
59. Corp, Edward, op. cit., p.57.
60. Ibid., pp.57–8.
61. Verney, Frances Parthenope and Verney, Margaret, M. (eds.), *Memoirs of the Verney Family during the Seventeenth Century, Volume II, third edition*, pp.316–7.
62. Turner, Dawson, *Narrative of the Visit of His Majesty King Charles II to Norwich in the September of the Year 1671*, pp.16–7.
63. Page, William (ed.), 'Sport, ancient and modern: Pastimes' in *A History of the County of Middlesex: Volume 2, General; Ashford, East Bedfont With Hatton, Feltham, Hampton With Hampton Wick, Hanworth, Laleham, Littleton*, (London: Victoria County History, 1911), p.171.
64. Society of Finsbury Archers on the Longbow Archers website.
65. Fraser, Antonia, *Royal Charles: Charles II and the Restoration*, p.208.
66. Sousa, Manuel Andrade E, op. cit., p.85.

67. Longman, Charles James and Walrond, Henry, *Archery*, volume from The Badminton Library of Sports and Pastimes, pp.170–2.
68. Page, William (ed.), op. cit., p.171.
69. Society of Finsbury Archers on the Longbow Archers website.
70. Fraser, Antonia, op. cit., p.323.
71. Oman, Carola, *Mary of Modena*, p.37.
72. Fea, Allan, *James II and his wives*, p.83.
73. Watkins, Sarah-Beth, *Catherine of Braganza: Chares II's Restoration Queen*, p.85.
74. Oman, Carola, op. cit., p.35.
75. Ibid., p.37.
76. Corp, Edward, op. cit., p.63.
77. Evelyn, John, *The Diary of John Evelyn in Two Volumes*, Volume II, p.93.
78. Sousa, Manuel Andrade E, op. cit., p.89.
79. Oman, Carola, op. cit., p.48.
80. Waller, Maureen, *Ungrateful Daughters: The Stuart Princesses Who Stole Their Father's Crown*, p.21.
81. Strickland, Agnes, *Lives of the Queens of England from the Norman Conquest, Volume 6, Mary of Modena*, p.73. She notes these are Mary Beatrice's own words from MS Memorials of Mary Beatrice in the Archives of France.
82. Porter, Linda, op. cit., p.77.
83. Newitt, Malyn, op. cit., p.102.
84. Evelyn, John, op. cit., Volume II, entry dated February 28, 1678, p.123.
85. Torres, João Romano Torres (ed.), *Portugal - Dicionário Histórico, Corográfico, Heráldico, Biográfico, Bibliográfico, Numismático e Artístico, 1904–1915, Volume II*, pp.890–1.
86. Charles II, *The Letters, Speeches and Declarations of King Charles II*, edited by Sir Arthur Bryant, p.312.
87. Waller, Maureen, op. cit., p.96.

Chapter Five – The Popish Plot

1. Miller, John, *Popery and Politics in England 1660–1688*, p.11.
2. Morton, Adam, *Sanctity and suspicion: Catholicism, conspiracy and the representation of Henrietta Maria of France and Catherine of Braganza, Queens of Britain* in *Queens Consort, Cultural Transfer and European Politics, c.1500–1800*, p.187.
3. Kenyon, John, *The Popish Plot*, p.56.
4. Pollock, Sir John, *Popish Plot: A Study in the History of the Reign of Charles II*, p.7.
5. Ibid., p.54.
6. Marshall, Alan, 'Titus Oates', in *Oxford Dictionary of National Biography*, p.2.
7. Almond, Joseph Cuthbert, 'Oates' Plot' in *The Catholic Encyclopedia*, Volume 11 (New York: Robert Appleton Company, 1911; http://www.newadvent.org/cathen/11173c.htm).
8. Kenyon, John, op. cit., p.54.
9. Marshall, Alan, 'Israel Tonge' in *Oxford Dictionary of National Biography*, p.2.
10. Marshall, Alan, 'Titus Oates' in Oxford Dictionary of National Biography, p.4.
11. Weale, J. Cyril M. (ed.), *Registers of the Catholic Chapels Royal and of the Portuguese Embassy Chapel 1662–1829, Volume 1, Marriages*, p.xxxi.
12. MacKay, Janet, *Catherine of Braganza*, p.205.
13. Kenyon, John, op. cit., p.41.
14. Barclay, Andrew, 'Edward Colman' [Coleman] in *Oxford Dictionary of National Biography*, p.1.

15. Pollock, Sir John, op. cit., p.75.
16. Porter, Linda, *Mistresses: Sex and Scandal at the Court of Charles II*, p.164.
17. Kenyon, John, op. cit., pp.302–309. Kenyon speculates Godfrey's murder had nothing to do with the plot and was committed by ordinary persons.
18. Davidson, Lillias Campbell, *Catherine of Bragança: Infanta of Portugal & Queen-Consort of England*, p.306.
19. Ibid., p.315.
20. Pollock, Sir John, op. cit., p.160.
21. Kenyon, John, op. cit., p.125.
22. Morton, Adam, op. cit., p.185.
23. Tout, Thomas Frederick, 'Catherine of Braganza' in *Dictionary of National Biography*, 1855–1900, Volume 9, p.6.
24. Kenyon, John, op. cit., p.126.
25. Morton, Adam, op. cit., p.189.
26. Furdell, Elizabeth Lane, *The Royal Doctors 1485–1714: Medical Personnel at the Tudor and Stuart Courts*, p.164.
27. Seccombe, Thomas, revised by Michael Bevan, 'Sir George Wakeman, baronet' in *Oxford Dictionary of National Biography*, p.1.
28. Ibid., pp.1–2.
29. Evelyn, John, *The Diary of John Evelyn in Two Volumes*, entry dated November 15, 1678, Volume 2, p.124.
30. Newitt, Malyn, *The Braganzas: The Rise and Fall of the Ruling Dynasties of Portugal and Brazil, 1640–1910*, p.95.
31. Fraser, Antonia, *Royal Charles: Charles II and the Restoration*, p.358.
32. Morton, Adam, op. cit., p.189.
33. Barclay, Andrews, op. cit., p.2.
34. MacKay, Janet, op. cit., p.214.
35. Gregory, Eilish, *Catherine of Braganza's Relationship with Her Catholic Household* in *Forgotten Queens in Medieval and Early Modern Europe: Political Agency, Myth-Making, and Patronage,* Valerie Schutte and Estelle Paranque (eds.), p.140.
36. Davidson, Lillias Campbell, p.318.
37. Sousa, Manuel Andrade E, *Catherine of Braganza: Princess of Portugal, Wife to Charles II*, p.99.
38. Charles II, *The Letters, Speeches and Declarations of King Charles II*, edited by Sir Arthur Bryant, pp.303–4.
39. Rau, V. (ed.), 'Letters from Catherine of Bragança, Queen-Consort of Charles II to her brother, Dom Pedro II, King of Portugal (1679–1691)' in *The Historical Association: Lisbon branch. Annual Report and Review,* 9 (1945), pp.564–5.
40. Davidson, Lillias Campbell, op. cit., p.329.
41. Sousa, Manuel Andrade E, op. cit., p.99.
42. Rau, V. (ed.), op. cit., pp.565–7.
43. Kenyon, John, op. cit., p.150.
44. Morton, Adam, op. cit., p.190.
45. Kenyon, John, op. cit., p.83.
46. Seccombe, Thomas, op. cit., p.2.
47. Morton, Adam, op. cit., p.190.
48. Kenyon, J.P., 'The Acquittal of Sir George Wakeman: 18 July 1679' in *The Historical Journal* 14, No. 4 (1971), p.706.
49. Kenyon, J.P., op. cit., p.699.
50. Hutton, Ronald, *Charles II: King of England, Scotland, and Ireland*, p.378.

51. Kenyon, J.P., op. cit., p.703.
52. Pollock, Sir John, op. cit., p.352.
53. Hutton, Ronald, op. cit., p.378.
54. Barclay, Andrew, op. cit., p.4.
55. Hutton, Ronald, op. cit., p.403.

Chapter Six – Last Years of Her Marriage, Charles' Death and Widowhood in England

1. Miller, John, *Popery and Politics in England 1660–1688*, p.22.
2. Davidson, Lillias Campbell, *Catherine of Bragança: Infanta of Portugal & Queen-Consort of England*, p.459.
3. Faulkner, Thomas, *The History and Antiquities of the Parish of Hammersmith*, p.244.
4. Ibid., p.245.
5. MacKay, Janet, *Catherine of Braganza*, p.227.
6. Guilford, Francis North, Baron, 1637–1685; Jenkins, Secretary; Williams, William, Sir, 1634–1700; *et al.*, *The examination of Captain William Bedlow, deceased, relating to the Popish Plot taken in his last sickness, by Sir Francis North, Chief Justice of the Court of Common Pleas, etc*., (2005) p.7.
7. Tout, Thomas Frederick, 'Catherine of Braganza' in *Dictionary of National Biography*, 1855–1900, Volume 9, p.7.
8. Reresby, Sir John, *The Memoirs of the Honorable Sir John Reresby*, Baronet, p.196.
9. Flor, Susan Varela, *D. Francisco De Melo Manuel Da Câmara (1626–1678): Biografia, Património, Estatuto Social e Fedelidades* in *Análise Social*, Volume 50, No. 215, p.356. Da Câmara was a cousin of the Portuguese ambassador Francisco de Melo, Marquis de Sande, who brokered Catherine's marriage treaty.
10. Tout, Thomas Frederick, op. cit., p.7.
11. Wynne, S.M., 'Catherine' [Catherine of Braganza, Catarina Henriqueta de Bragança], p.8.
12. Waller, Maureen, *Ungrateful Daughters: The Stuart Princesses Who Stole Their Father's Crown*, p.140.
13. Somerset, Anne, *Queen Anne: The Politics of Passion*, p.36.
14. Keay, Anna, *The Magnificent Monarch: Charles II and the Ceremonies of Power*, p.107.
15. Braganza, Catherine, *Letters of Queen Catherine of Braganza*, Egerton MS, I. 534, Letter 1.
16. Gregory, Eilish, *Catherine of Braganza's Relationship with her Catholic Household* in *Forgotten Queens in Medieval and Early Modern Europe: Political Agency, Myth-Making, and Patronage*, p.140.
17. Keay, Anna, op. cit., p.203.
18. Charles II: April 1683, in *Calendar of State Papers Domestic: Charles II, 1683 January June*, (F H Blackburne Daniell (ed.), London: His Majesty's Stationery Office, 1933), p.202.
19. Davidson, Lillias Campbell, op. cit., p.365.
20. Somerset, Anne, op. cit., p.45.
21. Corp, Edward, *Catherine of Braganza and cultural politics* in *Queenship in Britain 1660–1837: Royal patronage court culture and dynastic politics*, edited by Clarissa Campbell Orr, p.57.
22. Thomas, Gertrude Z., *Richer Than Spices: How a royal bride's dowry introduced cane, lacquer, cottons, tea, and porcelain to England and so revolutionized taste, manners, craftsmanship, and history in both England and America*, p.95.

23. Somerset, Anne, op. cit., p.57.
24. Fraser, Antonia, *Royal Charles: Charles II and the Restoration*, p.456.
25. Hutton, Ronald, *Charles II: King of England, Scotland, and Ireland*, pp.443–4.
26. Sousa, Manuel Andrade E, *Catherine of Braganza: Princess of Portugal, Wife to Charles II*, p.110.
27. Hutton, Ronald, op. cit., p.445.
28. Rau, V. (ed.), 'King Charles and Queen Catherine: two letters' in *The Historical Association: Lisbon Branch. Annual Report and Review,* 8 (1944), p.517.
29. Sousa, Manuel Andrade E, op. cit., p.110.
30. Oman, Carola, *Mary of Modena*, p.82.
31. Rau, V. (ed.), 'King Charles and Queen Catherine: two letters' in *The Historical Association: Lisbon Branch. Annual Report and Review,* 8 (1944), p.518.
32. Watkins, Sarah-Beth, *Catherine of Braganza: Charles II's Restoration Queen*, p.124.
33. Oman, Carola, op. cit., p.84.
34. Rau, V. (ed.), op. cit., p.520. The original bust is now lost.
35. MacKay, Janet, op. cit., p.258.
36. Wynne, S.M., op. cit., p.9.
37. Davidson, Lilias Campbell, op. cit., p.458.
38. 'Rivercourt House and the site of the Queen Dowager's House' in *Survey of London: Volume 6, Hammersmith*, (James Bird and Philip Norman (eds.), London: London County Council, 1915), p.80.
39. Ibid., p.74.
40. Ibid., p.79.
41. Ibid., p.74.
42. Sousa, Manuel Andrade E, op. cit., p.111.
43. Braganza, Catherine, *Letters of Queen Catherine of Braganza*, Egerton MS, I. 534, Letter 62.
44. Davidson, Lilias Campbell, op. cit., p.395.
45. MacKay, Janet, op. cit., p.263.
46. Ibid., p.265.
47. Ibid., p.266.
48. Corp, Edward, op. cit., p.66.
49. Waller, Maureen, op. cit., p.192.
50. Ibid., p.210.
51. Davidson, Lilias Campbell, op. cit., p.424.
52. Corp, Edward, op. cit., note 73, p.72.
53. Davidson, Lilias Campbell, op. cit., p.450.
54. Hopkirk, Mary, *The Queen Over the Water: Mary Beatrice of Modena, Queen of James II*, p.195. Hopkirk cites the Dalrymple Index, 1773 with no page number.
55. Davidson, Lilias Campbell, op. cit., p.450.
56. Braganza, Catherine, *Letters of Queen Catherine of Braganza*, Egerton MS, I. 534, Letter 56.
57. Ibid., Letter 43.
58. Davidson, Lilias Campbell, op. cit., pp.451–2.
59. Handley, Stuart, 'Louis Duras, second earl of Feversham' in *Oxford Dictionary of National Biography*, p.3.
60. Watkins, Sarah-Beth, op. cit., pp.136–7.
61. Ibid., p.137.
62. Davidson, Lilias Campbell, op. cit., p.458.
63. Ibid., p.464.

Chapter Seven – Return to Sunny Portugal

1. Rau, Virginia, D., *Catarina de Bragança, Rainha de Inglaterra*, pp.310–11.
2. Davidson, Lillias Campbell, *Catherine of Bragança: Infanta of Portugal & Queen Consort of England*, p.472.
3. MacKay, Janet, *Catherine of Braganza*, p.295.
4. Ibid., p.295.
5. Davidson, Lillias Campbell, op. cit., p.473.
6. Forster, Anne M.C., 'Chronicles of the English The Poor Clares of Rouen: I' in *Recusant History*, 18:1 (May 1986), p.59; see also Bowden, Caroline, 'Convent Schooling for English Girls in the "Exile" Period, 1600–1800' in *Studies in Church History*, *55* (2019), p.203.
7. Forster, Anne M.C., op. cit., p.97.
8. Rau, Virginia, op. cit., p.313.
9. Corp, Edward, *Catherine of Braganza and cultural politics* in *Queenship in Britain 1660–1837: Royal patronage court culture and dynastic politics*, edited by Clarissa Campbell Orr, p.66.
10. Rau, Virginia, op. cit., p.314.
11. Ibid., p.315.
12. Ibid., pp.315–6.
13. Ibid., p.316.
14. Ibid., p.318.
15. Ibid., pp.319–20.
16. Rau, Virginia, op. cit., p.320.
17. Ibid., pp.321–2.
18. Rosenthal, E., 'Notes on Catherine of Bragança, queen consort of King Charles II of England' in *The Historical Association: Lisbon branch. Annual Report and Review,* 1 (1937), p.15.
19. Rau, Virginia, op. cit., p.322.
20. Rosenthal, E., op. cit., p.15.
21. Rau, Virginia, op. cit., p.325.
22. Ibid., p.326.
23. Rosenthal, E., op. cit., p.15.
24. Rau, Virginia, op. cit., pp.327–8.
25. Colbatch, John, *An Account of the Court of Portugal, Under the Reign of the Present King Dom Pedro II…*, p.126.
26. Saraiva, José Hermano, *Portugal: A Companion History*, p.74.
27. Rau, Virginia, op. cit., p.327.
28. MacKay, Janet, op. cit., p.300.
29. Falkner, James, *The War of the Spanish Succession 1701–1714*, p.36.
30. Ibid., p.42.
31. Swift, Jonathan, *On the Conduct of the Allies and of the Late Ministry, in bringing and carrying on the War.*
32. Falkner, James, op. cit., p.43.
33. Marques, Paulo, *Catherine of Braganza: A Widow, The British Historical Society of Portugal, Annual Report 8,* (1981), p.23.
34. Rau, Virginia, p.328.
35. Kamen, Henry, *The War of the Spanish Succession in Spain 1700–1715*, p.10.
36. Disney, A.R., *A History of Portugal and the Portuguese Empire: From Beginnings to 1807, Volume 1: Portugal*, p.248.

37. Saraiva, José Hermano, op. cit., p.74.
38. Disney, A.R., op. cit., p.234.
39. Falkner, James, op. cit., p.43.
40. Rau, Virginia, op. cit., p.328.
41. Rau, Virginia, op. cit., pp.329–30.
42. Ibid., p.331.
43. MacKay, Janet, op. cit., p.306.
44. Rau, Virginia, op. cit., p.331.
45. MacKay, Janet., op. cit., p.307.
46. Rau, Virginia, op. cit., p.331.
47. De Sousa, Antonio Caetano, *Historia Genealogica da Casa Real Portugueza: desde a sua orgem até o p presente, com as familias illuestres, que precede dos Reys, e dos Serenissimos Duques de Bragança..., Tomo VII*, p.577.
48. Kamen, Henry, op. cit., p.14.
49. Rau, Virginia, op. cit., p.330.
50. Kamen, Henry, op. cit., p.14.
51. Ibid., p.17.
52. Rau, Virginia, op. cit., p.332.
53. Ibid., pp.332–3.
54. MacKay, Janet, op. cit., p.309.
55. Ibid., p.308.
56. Rau, Virginia, op. cit., p.335.
57. Kamen, Henry, op. cit., p.17.
58. Rau, Virginia, op. cit., p.335.
59. De Sousa, Antonio Caetano, op. cit., p.133.
60. MacKay, Janet, op. cit., p.305.
61. Rau, Virginia, op. cit., pp.345–6.
62. De Sousa, Antonio Caetano, op. cit., p.133.
63. Oman, Carola, *Mary of Modena*, p.213.
64. Rau, Virginia, op. cit., p.346.
65. Rosenthal, E., op. cit., p.16.
66. Davidson, Lillias Campbell, op. cit., p.501.
67. Rau, Virginia, op. cit., p.347.
68. Davidson, Lillias Campbell, op. cit., p.501.
69. Rau, Virginia, op. cit., p.347.
70. De Sousa, Antonio Caetano, op. cit., pp.334–6.
71. Rau, Virginia, op. cit., p.349.

Chapter Eight – The Legacy of Catherine's Marriage

1. https://www.moedanumismatica.com/coins/portugal.html.
2. Madway, Lorraine, 'Rites of Deliverance and Disenchantment: The Marriage Celebrations for Charles II and Catherine of Braganza, 1661–2' in *The Seventeenth Century,* 27:1, Note 7, p.99.
3. https://www.nationalarchives.gov.uk/currency-converter/.
4. Madway, Lorraine, op. cit., p.99.
5. Shaw, Leslie M.E., *Trade, Inquisition and the English Nation in Portugal, 1650–1690*, p.90.
6. Ibid., p.90.

7. Shaw, Leslie M.E., *The Anglo-Portuguese Alliance and the English Merchants in Portugal, 1654–1810*, p.79.
8. Ibid., p.80.
9. Ibid., p.91.
10. Routh, E.M.G., *Tangier: England's Lost Atlantic Outpost 1661–1684*, p.10.
11. Routh, E.M.G., op. cit., p.14.
12. Davies, J.D., 'Montagu [Mountagu], Edward, 1st Earl of Sandwich' in *Oxford Dictionary of National Biography*, p.5.
13. 'Venice: June 1662' in *Calendar of State Papers Relating To English Affairs in the Archives of Venice, Volume 33, 1661–1664*, (Allen B Hinds (ed.), London: His Majesty's Stationery Office, 1932), pp.146–158. *British History Online*, http://www.british-history.ac.uk/cal-state-papers/venice/vol33/pp146-158.
14. Grose, Clyde L., 'The Anglo-Portuguese Marriage of 1662' in *The Hispanic American Historical Review* 10, No. 3 (1930) p.320.
15. Colonial Office Papers, Tangier (C.O. 279, p.32, f. 274).
16. Routh, E.M.G., op. cit., p.245.
17. Hutton, Ronald, *Charles II: King of England, Scotland and Ireland*, pp.426–7.
18. Disney, A.R., *A History of Portugal and the Portuguese Empire: From the Beginnings to 1807, Volume 2: The Portuguese Empire*, p.300.
19. Tindall, Gillian, 'Bombay: City of Gold' in *History Today*, p.1.
20. Disney, A.R., op. cit., pp.299–300.
21. Tindall, Gillian, op. cit., p.1.
22. Keay, John, *The Honourable Company: A History of the East India Company*, p.132.
23. Khan, Shafaat Ahmad, *Anglo Portuguese Negotiations Relating to Bombay, 1660–1677*, p.486.
24. Thomas, Gertrude Z., *Richer Than Spices: How a royal bride's dowry introduced cane, lacquer, cottons, tea, and porcelain to England and so revolutionized taste, manners, craftsmanship, and history in both England and America*, p.23.
25. Keay, John, op, cit., p.76.
26. Ibid., p.86.
27. Ibid., p.98.
28. Ibid., p.99.
29. Ibid., p.108.
30. Robins, Nick, *The Corporation That Ruled the World: How the East India Company Shaped the Modern Multinational*, p.48.
31. Bassett, D.K., *Early English Settlement and Trade in Asia, 1602–1690, The East India Company: 1600–1858, Volume IV, Trade, Finance and Power*, p.9.
32. Keay, John, op. cit., p.125.
33. Bassett, D.K., op. cit., p.9.
34. Keay, John, op. cit., p.127.
35. Ibid., p.128.
36. Khan, Shafaat Ahmad, op. cit., p.439.
37. Keay, John, op. cit., p.131.
38. Khan, Shafaat Ahmad, op. cit., p.439.
39. Keay, John, op. cit., pp.131–2.
40. Khan, Shafaat Ahmad, op. cit., p.440.
41. Malabari, Phiroze B.M., *The Making of Bombay 1661–1726*, p.83.
42. Tindall, Gillian, op. cit., p.1.
43. Khan, Shafaat Ahmad, op. cit., p.486.

44. Ibid., p.497.
45. Edwardes, Stephen Meredyth, *The Rise of Bombay*, p.102.
46. Khan, Shafaat Ahmad, op. cit., p.514.
47. Gardner, Brian, *The East India Company – A History*, p.42.
48. Keay, John, op. cit., p.130.
49. Ibid., p.131.
50. Tindall, Gillian, op. cit., p.2.
51. Ibid.
52. Keay, John, op. cit., p.134.
53. Tindall, Gillian, op. cit., p.2.
54. Malabari, Phiroze B.M., op. cit., p.88.
55. Ibid., p.122.
56. Tindall, Gillian, op. cit., p.2.
57. Keay, John, op. cit., p.141.
58. Gardner, Brian, op. cit., p.44.
59. Disney, A. R., op. cit., p.313.
60. Keay, John, op. cit., p.193.
61. Newitt, Malyn, op. cit., p.12.
62. Newitt, Malyn, *Portugal in European and World History*, p.129.
63. Boxer, Charles, *The Portuguese Seaborne Empire: 1415–1825*, p.168.
64. Farrington, Anthony, 'Trading Places: The East India Company and Asia' in *History Today,* Volume 52, Issue 5, (May 2002), p.1.
65. Keay, John, op. cit., pp.98–9.
66. Thomas, Gertrude Z., *Richer Than Spices….*, p.48.
67. Chamberlayne, Edward, *Angliae Notitia: or the Present State of England*, pp.179 and 226.
68. Thomas, Gertrude Z., op. cit., p.31.
69. Ibid., p.60.
70. Ibid., p.63.
71. Victorian and Albert Museum website entry on cane chairs.
72. Thomas, Gertrude Z., op. cit., p.48.
73. Stratton Holloway, Edward, *American Furniture and Decoration Colonial and Federal*, p.14.
74. Thomas, Gertrude Z, op. cit., p.80.
75. Ibid., p.67.
76. Wilson, C. Anne, *The Book of Marmalade*, p.11.
77. Ibid., p.20.
78. Ibid., p.22.
79. Ibid., p.15.
80. Day, Ivan, *The Art of Confectionery*, p.15.
81. Pepys, Samuel, *The Diary of Samuel Pepys*, p.33.
82. Day, Ivan, op. cit., p.17.
83. Hyde, J.A. Lloyd, Espirito Santo Silva, Ricardo, and Malta, Eduardo, *Chinese Porcelain for the European Market*, p.13.
84. Ellis, Markham, Coulton, Richard, Mauger, Matthew, *Empire of Tea*, p.20.
85. Ibid., p.23.
86. Forrest, Denys, *Tea for the British: The Social and Economic History of a Famous Trade*, p.23.
87. Pepys, Samuel, op. cit., p.49.

88. Forrest, Denys, op. cit., p.33.
89. Ellis, Markham…, op cit., p.57.
90. Forrest, Denys, op. cit., p.30.
91. Ellis, Markham…, op. cit., p.49.
92. Ibid., p.51.
93. Disney, A.R., op. cit., p.335.
94. Ellis, Markham…, op. cit., p.58.
95. Robins, Nick., op. cit., p.147.
96. Forest, Denys, op. cit., pp.31–2.
97. Ellis, Markham…op. cit., p.39.
98. Ibid., p.31.
99. Ibid., p.38.
100. Ibid.
101. Ibid., p.37.
102. Boxer, Charles, 'The Dutch East India Company and the China Trade' in *History Today*, Volume 29, Issue 1, (November 1979), p.2.
103. Ellis, Markham…op. cit., p.114.
104. Ibid., p.151.
105. Hyde, J.A.…op. cit., p.48.
106. Ibid., p.34.
107. Ibid., p.18.
108. Ibid., p.48.
109. Hyde, J.A……op. cit., p.13.
110. Boxer, Charles, op. cit., p.1.
111. Hyde, J.A.…op. cit., p.49.
112. Ibid., p.51.
113. Ibid., p.47.
114. Ellis, Markham…op. cit., p.153.
115. Forrest, Denys, op. cit., p.28.
116. Waller, Edmond, *Poems, etc., written upon several occasions, and to several persons by Edmond Waller, Esp., Ninth Edition*, p.228.
117. Ellis, Markham…op. cit., p.39.
118. Ibid., p.221.
119. Corp, Edward, *Catherine of Braganza and Cultural Politics*, in *Queenship in Britain 1660–1837: Royal Patronage, Court Culture and Dynastic Politics* edited by Clarissa Campbell Orr, p.67.

Appendix One – Complete Text of the Articles of Marriage between his Majesty and the Lady Infanta of Portugal, 1661

1. *Collection of treaties between Great Britain and Other Powers, Volume II*, pp.286–296. The text is printed from the copy in the Board of Trade-Entries relating to Portugal, p. 144.

Appendix Two – Catherine's Health

1. Sousa, Manuel Andrade E, *Catherine of Braganza: Princess of Portugal, Wife to Charles II*, p.101. He quotes from Virginia Rau's Portuguese biography of Catherine. Lilias Campbell Davidson mentions it on p.337.
2. Oren-Magidor, Daphna, *Infertility in Early Modern England*, p.2.

3. Ibid., p.16.
4. Hamilton, Anthony, *Memoirs of Count Grammont Volume 1*, p.314.
5. Ibid., p.311.
6. Oren-Magidor, Daphna, op. cit., p.147.
7. Ibid., p.150.
8. Ibid., pp.151–2.
9. Ibid., p.152.
10. Bryant, Sir Arthur, *The England of Charles II*, pp.97–99.
11. Wynne, S.M., 'Catherine' [Catherine of Braganza, Catarina Henriqueta de Bragança], p.3.
12. Reresby, Sir John, *The Memoirs of the Honorable Sir John Reresby, Baronet*, entry for May 6, 1662, p.6.
13. Magaliotti, Lorenzo, *Lorenzo Magaliotti at the Court of Charles II: his Relazione d'Inghilterra of 1668*, p.15.
14. Porter, Linda, *Mistresses: Sex and Scandal at the Court of Charles II*, p.109.
15. Davidson, Lillias Campbell, *Catherine of Bragança: Infanta of Portugal & Queen-Consort of England*, pp.349–50.
16. MacKay, Janet, *Catherine of Braganza*, pp.254–5.
17. Furdell, Elizabeth Lane, *The Royal Doctors 1485–1714: Medical Personnel at the Tudor and Stuart Courts*, p.168.
18. National Center for Biotechnology Information, *Erysipelas and cellulitis: An Overview*, https://www.ncbi.nlm.nih.gov/books/NBK303996/.

Appendix Three – Last Will and Testament of Catherine of Braganza

1. Davidson, Lillias Campbell, *Catherine of Bragança: Infanta of Portugal & Queen-Consort of England*, pp.489–99.

Index